Culture and the

Religion, Culture and Society

Series Editors:
Oliver Davies and Gavin Flood,
Department of Theology and Religious Studies,
University of Wales, Lampeter

Religion, Culture and Society is a series presented by leading scholars on a wide range of contemporary religious issues. The emphasis throughout is generally multicultural, and the approach is often interdisciplinary. The clarity and accessibility of the series, as well as its authoritative scholarship, will recommend it to students and a non-specialist readership alike.

Culture and the Nonconformist Tradition

Edited by

JANE SHAW and ALAN KREIDER

UNIVERSITY OF WALES PRESS
CARDIFF
1999

© The Contributors, 1999

British Library Cataloguing-in-Publication Data
A catalogue record for this book is available from
the British Library.

ISBN 0-7083-1532-1 (paperback)

Cover illustration: The City Temple in 1874. This view encapsulates the
outward spirit of Victorian Nonconformity. It puts St Paul's suggestively in its
place, offering a Dissenting interpretation of the Age of Wren some time before
advanced artistic circles had rediscovered Wren. Its architects (Lockwood and
Mawson, of Bradford and London) were known for their public buildings in the
Midlands and the north. On the recently opened Holborn Viaduct they rehoused
a Congregational church gathered in the City since the mid-seventeenth century.
By 1874 its people reflected every layer of middle-class life. Their weekday
activities included a Literary Society which flourished into the 1960s. On
Sundays they sat under Joseph Parker, one of Britain's best-known preachers,
whose pulpit had been given by the City's Corporation. The façade survives; the
rest has been rebuilt. (Reproduced from *The City Temple in the City of London*,
London, 1958, p. 13, by permission of the City Temple United Reformed
Church.)

Typeset at the University of Wales Press
Printed in Great Britain by Dinefwr Press, Llandybïe

For
Barrie R. White,
former Principal of Regent's Park College
and eminent Free Church historian

Contents

Preface

The papers in this volume were first given as public lectures in Regent's Park College, Oxford, in the autumn of 1996. (Jane Shaw and I are grateful to Phyllis Mack for allowing us to include her article here, even though she did not present it in lecture form at the Centre.) 'Culture and the Nonconformist Tradition' was the topic that we chose for the first lecture series of the college's new Centre for the Study of Christianity and Culture. This was in part because of the nature of Regent's Park College. Regent's originated in the mid-eighteenth century as a Dissenting academy: Christian Nonconformity and culture are at the roots of Regent's – and of its subsequent history as well. It was also in part because we sensed that Oxford, as a University and city in which the Established Church has an imposing presence, was in need of a bit of Nonconformity!

Regent's, a Baptist foundation whose Fellows are Christians of many traditions, is concerned that all its activities foster thinking about the Christian faith and its interaction with culture. The Centre for the Study of Christianity and Culture is a recent expression of this. Every term the Centre sponsors a series of public lectures; it also plans conferences and encourages the research of its Fellows. The range of the Fellows' research is wide – from Anglo-Saxon sermons to economic development as a 'human right'. Recent lecture series have been similarly wide-ranging, dealing with the novel and spirituality, the media and truth, and 'global warming and Gospel wisdom'. In all of its activities the Centre attempts to promote the development of a 'Christian mind' within the setting of Oxford University.

The Centre is eager to share its thinking with the wider public. I therefore, as the Centre's Director, find it especially gratifying that the University of Wales Press has agreed to publish this book in its Religion, Culture and Society series. For the Centre this book is an offering of 'first fruits'. I am grateful to the Press, and anticipate other fruitful collaborations in the future.

Alan Kreider, Director
Centre for the Study of Christianity and Culture
Regent's Park College
Oxford

The Contributors

David Bebbington is Reader in History, University of Stirling.

Clyde Binfield is Reader in History, University of Sheffield.

John Briggs is Principal of West Hill College, Selly Oak, Birmingham.

Jane Garnett is Fellow and Tutor in History, Wadham College, Oxford.

Alan Kreider is Director for the Centre for the Study of Christianity and Culture, Regent's Park College, Oxford.

Phyllis Mack is Professor of History, Rutgers University.

Hugh McLeod is Professor of Church History, University of Birmingham.

Marjorie Reeves was formerly Vice-Principal and Fellow and Tutor in History, St Anne's College, Oxford, and is now Honorary Fellow of St Anne's College and St Hugh's College, Oxford.

Jane Shaw is Dean, and Fellow and Tutor in Ecclesiastical History, Regent's Park College, Oxford.

1

Introduction: why 'culture and the Nonconformist tradition'?

JANE SHAW

Christianity has, from its very beginnings, had a paradoxical relationship to 'the world'. At the heart of Christianity lies the doctrine of the Incarnation. This affirms that in Christ God took human form and entered the *kosmos* that he loves, engaging with the mess of everyday human social, political and cultural life. But God's incarnation in Jesus of Nazareth was not only a divine gesture of affirmation; it also was a critique of human priorities and institutions which led to conflict, rejection and the Cross. The permutations of this affirmation and critique have had to be worked out in every subsequent generation of Christians. Their charter – and ongoing challenge – has been stated by Paul in his epistle to the Romans: 'Do not be conformed to this world but be transformed by the renewing of your minds' (Romans 12:2).

From the outset Christians were embedded in the cultures of their day. Extreme Christians might reject the world entirely, thinking of it as 'a corpse' as the author(s) of the Gnostic, non-canonical Gospel of Thomas wrote. And yet, of course, to survive as a growing religion the young churches needed the institutions of 'the world'. Thus in the early centuries they employed the household (the basic unit of Greco-Roman society) as the place to meet and evangelize; and in post-Constantinian days, when Christianity became the empire's official religion, they engaged with and used many other institutions, including the state itself. Not all Christians were happy at this development; and the ascetic movements that grew in the fourth century were in part a reaction to this increased 'worldliness' of Christianity.

It might be argued, then, that all histories of Christianity are, at least in part, about this paradoxical relationship between

Christianity and 'the world'. The present volume deals with one
of the classic ways in which this paradox has expressed itself – the
relation of Christianity and 'culture'. For Christianity has always
necessarily been affected by – and in turn has affected and
critiqued – culture. It stands within culture and is itself a cluster
of cultural expressions. Yet many individual Christians and entire
Christian communities have believed that there must be something distinctive about being Christian – a way of life, a series of
beliefs, a constellation of folkways that marks the Christian out
from other cultural options.

The Nonconformist tradition in Britain provides a particularly
interesting instance of Christianity's paradoxical response to 'the
world'. In the very act of Dissenting, these Christians made a
statement about an established church which they considered too
implicated in an 'uncritiqued' world, a state church enmeshed
with monarch and Parliament, which tried to dictate how all
Christians in Britain should worship and structure their
churches. Thus, the Nonconformists both rejected the established
church and were themselves rejected by it, for they believed that
individuals should be free to choose their forms of worship, their
church polity, and – in some cases – whether to be Christian at
all. From this the Nonconformists developed the notion of the
voluntary or 'gathered' church, groups of freely gathered believers, which in some sense stood apart from 'the world',
although this standing apart was not all of their own choosing, for
they were deliberately excluded from the heart of the establishment: politics, government and the old universities of Oxford and
Cambridge. By standing apart in this way, the Nonconformists
were free to create their own distinctive cultures and thereby
came to contribute in particular ways to British culture as a
whole. They also, of course, engaged with other aspects of British
culture, in the books they read, the designs of their churches, as
well as more mundane matters such as the food they ate and the
clothes they wore.

David Bebbington's article explores these various layers of
interaction between Victorian Nonconformity and culture. He
points to the ways in which the Nonconformists came to have an
increasing influence on British culture over the nineteenth
century, engaging with politics, especially once the restrictions
against them were removed, and developing the distinctly

'Nonconformist conscience'. He also shows that the starting-point for this engagement with the world was their own particular chapel culture, which represented 'respectability, self-improvement and getting on in the world', particularly over and against a plebeian culture rooted in the ale-house. Hugh McLeod continues this story for the later part of the nineteenth century and the early twentieth century, in some ways a 'golden age' for Nonconformity. The four cameo sketches, drawn from oral histories, with which he opens his article give a 'flavour' of the shared aspects of Nonconformist culture at the turn of the century, as well as showing the distinctions between denominations, and his comparisons with the religious 'Dissenters' of other countries in the same period illuminate the ways in which English Nonconformity was distinctly English in its cultural forms.

Marjorie Reeves's article explores these interactions of various cultures and cultural forms in the particular context of literary women of the serious and 'middling sort' in provincial (especially West Country) Nonconformity. Reeves draws a portrait of a specific subculture: the intellectual and spiritual circles which developed amongst eighteenth-century Nonconformists. Thus she shows the ways in which people who lived at quite a distance from each other saw their Nonconformist religion as an important basis for friendship and religious networks. In exploring what they read, what they learnt from their more formally educated male Nonconformist friends, and what they wrote for each other, Reeves shows how these women interacted with contemporary cultural forms and also created their own literary world, using poetry to explore theology, spirituality and even politics. Similarly, Clyde Binfield's article on twentieth-century free church architecture also examines a particular aspect of the Nonconformists' contribution to the arts, assessing the employment of certain aesthetic forms to express Nonconformist theology, spirituality and even politics.

These two articles focus on literature and the arts respectively, both easily seen as central to the provenance of 'culture'. But the volume as a whole takes a broad, anthropological understanding of 'culture' (a term for which definitions have proliferated in several disciplines, in recent years). The anthropologist Clifford Geertz's definition of culture as a web of meanings in which the human is suspended, and which he or she continues to weave, is illuminating here for it suggests that culture is everything about a particular people and how they make sense of the world.[1] (That is, culture is not just about 'high' culture in the way the term is sometimes used.) Bebbington, in his article, talks about the ways in which this broader understanding of culture has affected the field of missiology, but we must remember that it has also been deeply influential in the development of cultural history, where Geertz's work in particular has affected the work of key historians. As William J. Bouwsma puts it, this anthropological notion of culture is useful to historians because 'it is centrally concerned with the construction and symbolic expression of meaning in every dimension of human activity'.[2] This new cultural history, along with the related field of social history, has affected the methodologies of ecclesiastical history marking, in particular, a widening of interests within denominational history, and a concern to understand how the institutions and individuals of a particular denomination interacted with the larger cultural context. Hence, our decision to work on the Nonconformist tradition as a whole has been influenced not only by a wish to analyse how the shared experiences of Nonconformists (not least the experiences of persecution and marginalization) have both affected British culture as a whole and created interesting, shared subcultures, but also by a wish to explore how developments in the field of history generally might have made an impact on religious and denominational history specifically.

Phyllis Mack's article is significant here. She takes the assumptions of two fields of study – Protestant Nonconformist history and gender history – and tests them through the case of one woman of a particular denomination: a late eighteenth-century Methodist preacher, Mary Taft. She addresses the following assumptions: that with the advent of Protestantism there was a new emphasis on the masculinity of God; that women's activity within the Nonconformist churches marked the intrusion of women's 'worldly' desires for power in the churches; that women's activity within the Nonconformist churches was always an exception. In examining Taft's writing and work in light of these assumptions, Mack suggests that spiritual motherhood was a prevalent image in Nonconformist Protestantism and the source of spiritual authority for many women who, as evangelists, preachers and ministers, saw themselves as spiritual mothers, giving birth to saved souls. In this, they drew on eighteenth-century notions of motherhood and psychology, and were thus affected by the culture at large. Furthermore, Mack suggests that, far from women's activity in the churches being exceptional, or demanded only by the women themselves, several of the key male Nonconformist leaders quickly saw the importance of harnessing the spiritual authority and sheer practical energy and administrative ability of women for their churches to survive. Mack's article is therefore a model of the interaction between the insights of new fields of history and denominational history.

John Briggs's article also provides a model of 'new' denominational history, as it interacts in this case with political history, in his exploration of the nineteenth-century Baptist Robert Hall's 1820 sermon on the 'The Signs of the Times'. Hall's sermon stood in a tradition (which would continue throughout the nineteenth century) of understanding the course of history by examining the political and social conditions of the day in the light of Christian principles. In this we see what one influential Baptist preacher saw as the pressing issues of 'the world' – three decades after the French Revolution, on the eve of the Industrial Revolution, and about a decade before the Nonconformists would have many of the political disabilities against them removed. Briggs indicates the ways in which a central Nonconformist figure saw this analysis of, and engagement with, the world as a moral obligation. Thus many Nonconformists were drawn into an engagement with 'the world' – at least from their pulpits – while at the same time denouncing many of its values and 'signs'.

Jane Garnett's article explores this paradox fully in her discussion of Nonconformists who saw a conflict between their Protestant values and their economic success in the mid-nineteenth century, especially now that many of the political and other bars against them had been removed. In particular, she explores the questions the Nonconformists asked themselves about their success: was there 'a drift towards a dangerous conformity with the social mores of the establishment? In what did the essence of Nonconformity reside?' Her article analyses the ways in which the Nonconformist businessmen themselves tried to address this paradox: in their self-examination; in the church members' internal methods of examining – and potentially disciplining – each other; and in the lives of businessmen-'saints' which were published.

At the end of the twentieth century, all the churches in Britain are struggling to find an appropriate relationship to 'the world': the same questions about the possible distinctiveness of Christian cultures remain as Christians struggle to keep up with, and speak to, the varied and fast-changing cultures of our times. These articles offer historical precedents for how the Nonconformist Christians of this country have negotiated their relationship to 'the world', balancing their absorption of the cultures of their time, with the creation of their own distinctive subcultures. These articles also offer insights into the ways in which research in ecclesiastical history and denominational history is today in conversation with cultural, social, political and gender history, mirroring in methodological terms the relationship between Christianity and culture which is at the heart of this book.

Notes

[1] See Clifford Geertz, *The Interpretation of Cultures* (New York, 1973), *passim*.

[2] William J. Bouwsma, 'From history of ideas to history of meaning', in his *A Useable Past: Essays in European Cultural History* (Berkeley, CA, 1990). For the development of this sort of cultural history, see also Natalie Zemon Davis, *Society and Culture in Early Modern France* (Stanford, CA, 1965); Robert Darnton, *The Great Cat Massacre and Other Episodes in French Cultural History* (New York, 1985); and Lynn Hunt (ed.), *The New Cultural History* (Berkeley, CA, 1989).

2

Literary women in eighteenth-century Nonconformist circles

MARJORIE REEVES

I begin with an extract from a poem written in the first half of the eighteenth century:

> On the fair banks of the gentle Thames
> I Tun'd my harp nor did celestial themes
> Refuse to dance upon my strings . . .
> Sudden from Albion's western coast
> Harmonious notes came gliding by:
> The neighbouring shepherds knew the silvery sound
> 'Tis Philomena's voice' the shepherds cry . . . [1]

Philomena was a talented young woman living in Frome, Somerset, near the Wiltshire border. Her name was Elizabeth Singer Rowe. But who was the poet? I think that it may surprise you that it was Isaac Watts, the writer of hymns such as 'When I survey the wondrous cross' and 'Our God, our help in ages past'.

Elizabeth came from sturdy Nonconformist stock: her father, Walter Singer, had been imprisoned in Ilchester gaol for his religious views and when they moved to Frome he supported the Rooke Lane Congregational Church. Elizabeth's acquaintance with Isaac Watts began in 1706 when she read with delight his *Horae Lyricae* and about the same time Watts discovered her early poems, some of which had been published in 1696 under the pseudonym Philomena. There is a persistent local story that Watts was in love with her, but no proof. He certainly became her literary mentor in her later years and at her death in 1736 Elizabeth left him a packet of manuscript writings which he published as *Devout Exercises of the Heart in Meditation and Soliloquy and Praise* in 1737. [2]

Elizabeth Rowe's education strikingly illustrates two aspects I want to emphasize in this paper. In her early collection of poems there is a passionate outburst addressed 'To One who would persuade me to leave the Muses':

> Forgo the charming Muses! No, in spight
> Of your ill-natured Prophecy I'll write, . . .
> Yet I'm so scurvily inclin'd to Rhiming,
> That undesign'd my thoughts burst out a Chiming;
> My active Genius will by no means sleep,
> And let it then its proper channel keep.
> I've told you, and you must believe me too,
> That I must do this, or greater mischiefs do;
> And let the world think me inspir'd or mad,
> I'll surely write whilst paper's to be had;
> Since Heaven to me has a Retreat assign'd . . .³

If she had followed a conventional path she would doubtless have been sent to a typical girls' school of the period, learning little more than embroidery and French conversation. There is no evidence either way but she would surely have revolted against such a regime. Flying in the face of those who warned that 'intense thought spoils a lady's features'⁴ and that people keep their distance from 'a fair one who looks with all the gravity of a Greek professor', she was determined to become a literary writer. The second point which Elizabeth Rowe's education illustrates is that such aspiring young women were chiefly educated by their men friends. Frome is only a few miles from Longleat, the estate of the Thynne family who at this period seem to have nourished a literary coterie. It was Henry Thynne who taught Elizabeth Italian and helped her translate Tasso's poem *Jerusalem*.⁵ His learned daughter, later the countess of Hertford, was one of her closest friends while Bishop Ken, who spent some years of his exile at Longleat, widened her religious outlook. Her education was continued by her young husband, Thomas Rowe, whose father, Benoni Rowe, was an Independent minister and whose uncle was the head of the Dissenting academy at Newington where Isaac Watts had been educated. Thomas Rowe himself was a learned young man who had returned from Leiden University with a large number of books.⁶ They married in 1710 but five years later he died and Elizabeth returned from London to

Frome where she lived for the rest of her life, writing, supporting the Rooke Lane Independent Congregation, given to charitable works, conducting a large correspondence with friends, many aristocratic, and latterly retiring into a life of meditation. She died in 1737.

Elizabeth Rowe exemplifies several points which throw a significant light on provincial Nonconformist culture at this time. First, her reading, as evidenced from her writings and letters, had an astonisingly wide range. No doubt she took her husband's books back to Frome, but she read more recent literature as well, in French and Italian as well as English, literary as much as religious. There were already active bookshops in Bath but her correspondents also supplied her requests. Secondly, there was what we may anachronistically call her ecumenical outlook. This struck her first biographer forcibly: 'She continued all the latter part of her life in constant communion with some who differed from her in articles (of faith) which she thought of great importance.' This did not go down well with narrower 'persons of her adherence' but 'her friendships were founded on virtue but not on a perfect agreement in those lesser matters which divide us as Christians'.[7] Thirdly, the contemporary style in poetics is naturally fused with a genuine expression of Nonconformist spirituality. In her earlier poetry she writes easily in pastorals peopled with Silvia and Celadin, Narcissus and Daphne. In her fanciful prose romances she tells of high-born maidens in disguise, Aleander, Philander and their love affairs.[8] There is always an exemplary moral and her pastoral poetry mingles with versifyings from Job and the Psalms and a dialogue between the Soul, Riches, Fame and Pleasure. Under the influence of Isaac Watts – who, of course, was also lured into these flowery paths – she began to move away from such themes. As early as 1706 she writes 'To Mr Watts on his poems sacred to devotion'

> No more Myrtillo's fatal face
> My quiet breast alarms,
> His eyes, his air and youthful grace
> Have lost their usual charms.
>
> No gay Alexis in the grove
> Shall be my future theme:

I burn with an immortal love
And sing a purer flame.

Seraphic Heights I seem to gain,
And sacred transports feel,
While, Watts, to thy celestial strain
Surpriz'd, I listen still.[9]

She did not, however, lose her light touch in writing graceful verse, as, for instance, to her neighbour, the earl of Orrery.[10] This is a quite inadequate sketch of a most interesting woman who seems to break all the stereotypes and deserves fuller study. My reason for introducing her here is that I think she may have served as a role model for the literary women in the Steele circle who were certainly acquainted with her work.[11]

So now I move across Salisbury Plain to the village of Broughton, just over the Hampshire border. In 1680 at Wiltshire's oldest Baptist church Henry Steele had been baptized and when the Porton church moved across the border to Broughton in 1710, Henry became its pastor. His nephew, William Steele, succeeded him. He married Anne Froude (or Frowde) from a leading family in another historic Baptist church at Erlestoke.[12] Their children, William and Anne, particularly the latter, form the focus of a literary circle with ramifications spreading to Bodenham, near Salisbury, Milborne Port in Somerset, and Bratton on the northern edge of Salisbury Plain.

Like Elizabeth Rowe, Anne Steele owed her real education to her men friends, including her father and brother.[13] Perhaps more docile than Elizabeth, she did go to a girls' school where she appears to have done little but sewing and complained that 'her mind was covered with senseless stupidity'. (Reading a contemporary correspondence in the *Salisbury Journal* on girls' education fills out the 'senseless stupidity'.[14]) The Steele circle of visiting friends was narrower and less aristocratic than Elizabeth Rowe's, however, consisting largely of Nonconformist divines, but the same fusion of eighteenth-century romanticism and evangelical piety appears in their literary exchanges. Three of these friends were Jack Lavington, pastor of the Exeter Baptist church, James Fanch, a Baptist minister based in Romsey, and Philip Furneaux who became pastor of the Independent congregation at

Clapham.[15] John Ash, at the Baptist church in Pershore[16] and above all Caleb Evans, a key figure in the intellectual development of the Baptist church, centred on Bristol Baptist College,[17] were also close friends, and serious writers. The Steele papers, in the Angus Library of Regent's Park College, Oxford, record visits and other contacts with these friends and clearly there was much theological exchange. But we also get surprising glimpses of more light-hearted encounters. On an unknown date, probably in the early 1750s, Jack Lavington and Philip Furneaux were at Broughton when Anne happened to be absent. Among her poems we find the following little exchange: 'By Mr Lavington on visiting Broughton with Dr Furneaux. A parody of "My Time o Ye Muses"':

> Our time o ye Muses how happily spent
> When to visit your Favourite to Broughton we went
> Tho' absent she left us such delicate fare
> That we each of us wished we could stay there a year
> But had she been present as we fain would have had her
> I protest I believe we had stayed there for ever.

To which Anne replied:

> . . . How unlucky was I and how cruel was fate
> When the Muses designed me a favour of late
> Lysander and Lucius despatched from their seat
> A wish vouchsafed to this humble retreat
> But alas I was absent and fretting in vain
> Not one of the Nine if they heard me complain
> Would lend me her pinions to fly through the air
> Could wishes have wafted me I had been there
> This boon, o ye Muses, I've yet to implore
> Convey me their songs and I'll blame ye no more.[18]

Here we meet the first of the pen-names characteristic of this literary circle. From other evidence we can conclude that Lysander was Lavington and Lucius, Furneaux. Anne herself adopted Silviana probably in her earlier poems, but all her later published and unpublished works appear under the name of Theodosia. It is clear that Anne was the centre of attraction to these friends. There are further light-hearted and amusing verses involving Lucius and Lysander, but there must be no mistake that the main concern of this group of friends was serious writing. Furneaux championed the cause of liberty, toleration and education. Anne encouraged Fanch to publish a *Paraphrase of the Psalms of David, translated from the Latin* (1761). The Steeles read John Ash on education,[19] while Caleb Evans, apart from his own many writings, played a large part in the publication of Anne's poems.

Anne's brother William appears under the pseudonym Philander. We have a small number of his verses but his chief importance for us lies in the two commonplace books which he had specially bound for himself.[20] From these and scattered references in their poems we get a partial picture of their reading. It is somewhat surprising. Eighteenth-century poets, major and minor, occupy a central place: Pope, Chatterton, John Gay (of *Beggar's Opera* fame), William Hayley, somewhat of a ladies' poet, the Irish poet Edward Parnell, Edward Young, a court poet, Thompson and Ralph Erskine who wrote *Gospel Sonnets*. There is also an emphasis on women writers: Mary Scott, whom we shall meet shortly,[21] Anna Seward of Lichfield[22] and especially a fascinating character, Helen Maria Williams.[23] After writing an early romance, *Edwin and Eltruda*, Williams moved in a radical direction, composing a long poem about the liberation of Peru from tyranny and finally involving herself in the politics of revolutionary Paris where she survived imprisonment by Robespierre and later had a flourishing salon under Napoleon. The Steele commonplace books include her earlier works and later her translations from *Paul et Virginie*. Some of these unusual books raise the question of availability, but advertisements show that booksellers were active in Salisbury, even running circulating libraries.

In one poem Anne gives a charming picture of the Steele family cosily gathered round the fire on a winter's evening:

> When one of the Company reads to the rest
> Grave Author or Poet or what we like the best
> All soft and harmonious the hours glide along
> Conversing with Pope or with Thompson or Young . . .[24]

But was the Steeles' reading really predominantly in eighteenth-century poetry? What were the grave authors set beside the poets?

We have very little evidence. Mary Steele, Anne's niece, has left us one poem 'On reading some controversial writings',[25] but, aggravatingly she does not tell us what they were. Fordyce's *Sermons for Young Women* (still in vogue in Jane Austen's time) receive mentions but otherwise it appears that the family in which a poet chiefly known for her religious writings was brought up found its favourite reading among the classical and romantic writers of their period.

Theodosia, the poet, actually reveals to us the way in which she consciously baptizes her poetic Muse into the faith. The opening poem in her published *Poems on Subjects chiefly Devotional*, vol. 3, is an Invocation to the Muses:

> Come, sweet Urania, come, thy cheering pow'r
> Once more impart to warm my heart
> To thee I will devote this solemn, silent hour . . .

But then she continues:

> Come, heav'n-born Faith, fair seraph come:
> How weak the Muse's pow'r without thy aid!
> Thy radiant eye can pierce the gloom,
> Can guide her doubtful flight . . .
> Thy beams alone can bring my day;
> O shine with soul attracting ray,
> Till darkness, sin and doubt retire . . .
> Then shall the Muse awake the sacred lyre,
> Thus shall her sweetest notes harmonious rise,
> And bear my thoughts enraptured to the skies
> While love and thankful joy the votive songs inspire.[26]

Theodosia's unpublished poems reveal a far wider range of accomplishment than her published works. She can write a pretty conventional 'Ode to Spring', invoking Flora and all her train.[27] She can write whimsically on the 'Death of an Old Apple Tree'.[28] She can engage in witty dialogue with Lucius and her half-sister Mary, whose pseudonym was Amira.[29] In a Piers Plowman style she depicts the worldly scene as it presents itself to her imagination:

> On a verdant plain bespread with flowers
> The sons of mirth indulge their sprightly pow'rs,
> With roses crown'd, how blithsome, light and gay
> They dance and sing the flying hours away . . .

A second group appears:

> Unlike to these, yon restless tribe behold!
> Their lives, incessant toil, their idol gold
> Close on their heels attends the corroding care.
> On either side distrust and anxious fear . . .

A third group meets her eyes:

> An eager throng, the candidates for praise . . .
> To gain the envy'd height, where fame bestows
> Her fairest wreath, each panting bosom glows . . .[30]

But finally she sees a few 'of mien sedate and cheerful air' who are guided by true religion to:

> Unfading honours, pleasures all refin'd
> And riches lasting, as the immortal mind!
> There full delight, a boundless river flows!
> There unforbid the tree of knowledge grows
> And there the tree of life invites the taste
> To fruits celestial, an immortal feast.

In a half-ironical tone she lauds the solitary life:

> Lemira in her lonely cell
> Despising converse loves to dwell
> There pensive she her hours employs
> Much better than in social joys
> With deep attention counts her beads
> And sometimes thinks and sometime reads . . .
> What maid can entertainment find
> Except Lemira's noble mind
> In spending all the livelong day
> Alone, or if she deigned to stay
> With noisy mortals, silent sit
> Too wise for such low tattling wit

> Enough for her to hear the nonsense flow
> And sometimes stop to answer Yes or No . . .[31]

Far more importantly, we glimpse a powerful mind grappling with the limitations both of intellectual obstacles and feminist prejudice. Entanglement with trivialities prompts an outburst on 'Waste of Time' and a cry against 'The Fetter'd Mind',

> Ah! Why should this immortal mind,
> Enslave'd by sense, be thus confin'd,
> And never, never rise?
> Why thus amus'd with empty toys
> And sooth'd with visionary joys,
> Forget her native skies?
> The mind was form'd to mount sublime,
> Beyond the narrow bounds of time,
> To everlasting things . . .[32]

A poem addressed 'To Reason' celebrates her sovereignty, not only in individual lives, but also in public life, while the ambitions of a questing mind find further expression in a poem entitled 'The Desire for Knowledge a Proof of Immortality':

> What is this thinking pow'r, this active mind,
> Which nought on earth can satiate, nought can bind?
> Restless it roams this wide creation o'er
> In search of something more than sense can give . . .
> Surely the mind must be akin to heav'n; . . .
> Inquisitive and restless, now she soars
> Beyond the narrow bounds of earth and time.[33]

The obverse to these lofty sentiments can be seen in revealing exchanges between Anne (writing as Silviana) and 'Amira', her half-sister. Anne herself, after suffering an early tragedy through the death of her fiancé by drowning, elected to remain single. Amira married Joseph Wakeford in 1749 when she was twenty-five. A series of letters between the two in the 1750s highlights the struggles of a wife and mother to keep up with the ideals of serious reflection presented by her half-sister. Silviana recalls their conversations on 'Reason and Prudence, patience, resentment,

Benevolence and the force of example'. Amira cannot cope; in a later letter she complains that 'she cannot think anything into words' and that 'serious thoughts' only 'pass through my mind as something I remember to have heard of'. Yet she urges Silviana to go on writing high-minded thoughts to her: 'let not your candle be put under a bushel because my twinkler has gone out'. But 'dinner is coming, my work all neglected tho' it waits to be done against washing'. Silviana makes a solemn parable of the human mind as a garden to be cultivated to the glory of God; Amira replies with a funny little parable of her own house – 'ensnaring cobwebs . . . spread all around, dust, litter in every room, nothing in order and as it should be' – as a picture of the state of her own mind.[34]

Amira is the amusing one in the bunch. Half longing to be included in the precious circle, half mocking their solemn poses, she seems sometimes to be deliberately irreverent. She scandalizes Anne by calling the Nine Muses 'Old Maids'[35] and parodies different forms of verse. She scoffs at her own clumsy rhyming, as in this fragment:

> With lines so hobbling, jumping, jerking,
> Enough to make you fall a-quirking
> To read such oddities, but yet
> As I've no fame to lose or get
> I freely send you any scribble
> My pen may daintily down dribble;
> As did the pen of honest Bunyan -
> Should make you cry without an onion.[36]

(Where else is Bunyan rhymed with onion?) Perhaps her own experience lay behind a later poem of Amira's warning her niece Silvia against following the Muses:

> Dear Silvia, consider, consider in time
> The ills that await you for daring to rhyme
> A girl that's a writer, a friend of the muses,
> Almost every woman, and man too, abuses.

Then after some fine feminist lines,

> Alack the poor husband how woeful his case
> Who married a woman of genius and taste.

> Instead of a pudding you'd make him a poem
> Forgetting perhaps the observance you owe him.
> Be writing an elegy, ode or a sonnet
> When you ought to be making a cap or a bonnet . . .
> Your dress too neglected for leisure to think,
> Your tresses dishevell'd, your fingers all ink,
> Your servants unscolded, your house in a litter.
> Your husband would fret and your visitors titter . . .
> Oh humble your genius and quit your Parnassus
> For wives shou'd be stupid when husbands are asses.[37]

But Silvia, in the next generation, had every encouragement to pursue her literary inclinations. Her father, William Steele (Philander), kept copies of her poems. Her aunt, Theodosia, wrote affectionate verses to her, while her contemporary circle was widened to embrace a group of girls almost her own age. One of these was Mary Scott, born *c.*1752 at Milborne Port in Somerset, about thirty miles from Broughton. The others were three daughters of Thomas and Anna Attwater, living at Bodenham, just outside Salisbury, Marianna, Caroline and Jane. In both cases we see the Nonconformist connection at work. Mary Scott came from Independent stock.[38] Using the pen-name Myra, she played an important literary role in the Steele circle during the 1770s, exchanging letters, visits and poems with the family and, although only a little older, acting as Silvia's literary mentor. In her first important work, *The Female Advocate*,[39] she embarked on a theme which claimed considerable attention in the mid-eighteenth century, the celebration of learned women. In 1748 a poem, 'The Female Right to Literature', had appeared in a collection published by Robert Dodsley.[40] In 1754 John Duncombe published his poem *The Feminiad*.[41] Both of these were discussed in the Steele household. Indeed, Silvia wrote an enthusiastic poem about the former whose author was a canon of Lichfield.[42] Mary Scott was the first woman to enter the lists. In her prefatory 'Letter to a Lady' – almost certainly Silvia – she says: 'You and I have often read with grateful pleasure the work of Mr Duncombe', adding 'you will remember that we have also regretted that it was only on a small number of Female Geniuses that Gentleman bestowed the wreath of Fame'. So, 'being too well acquainted with the illiberal sentiments men in general hold with regard to our sex', she has been prompted to fill out the list.[43] She unearthed a fascinating collection of learned women from the Reformation onwards, many of them relatively unknown. Theodosia figures at the end of the poem and in the peroration she acknowledges her debt to Philander who preserved copies of *The Female Advocate* and her later long poem, *The Messiah*, in his commonplace books. Mary Scott eventually married John Taylor, a Unitarian who became a Quaker in 1768. She died in 1793. Shortly afterwards her husband went north to become master of the school opened by the Quakers in Manchester. Their son, John Edward, was one of the founders of the *Manchester Guardian*.[44]

The other family linked with the Steeles at this time had clear Baptist connections. Thomas Attwater had married Anna Gay from Bath, descended from Richard Gay, a Dissenting minister imprisoned for his beliefs in the reign of Charles II.[45] Their three daughters, young women in the late 1760s and the 1770s, all had literary tastes, but it was the youngest, Jane, using the pen-name Myrtilla, who was Silvia's friend from childhood. In 1771 Silvia paints an idyllic picture of early days with Myrtilla:

> Fond memory paints anew each harmless scene
> When oft we rambled o'er the daisied Green
> When oft we wasted many a Summer's Day
> In childish innocence and sprightly Play . . .[46]

Myrtilla's literary talent ran to vivid letters and a massive diary rather than to poetry, but she was a great collector of papers, especially Silvia's poetry, ultimately forming the collection now in the possession of the author. She comes over as a decidedly independent young woman who kept a suitor, called 'Mr B.' in her diaries, hanging on for nearly twenty years because she did not want to tie herself up. She even proposed at one point 'going into business' – whatever that meant. In her last poem to Myrtilla (1781) Silvia gives a hint of her active mind:

> . . . And still be thine that Cheerfulness unfeigned,
> That thirst for knowledge which empowers the Mind![47]

Her elder sister, Caroline, married Thomas Whitaker, again from a well-known Baptist family in Bratton. She appears as 'Dorinda' but nothing she wrote has survived. Her literary interest, however, appears in two unusual samplers she set her daughters to embroider, one an 'Ode to Happiness' and the other on 'Sensibility'. Neither poem is known in print,[48] so presumably they were of local authorship. Jane Attwater preserved a little manuscript book of poems by Maria – Marianna, her eldest sister. These reveal a serious-minded young woman whose long poem 'Reflections' turns away from frivolity and empty-headedness. But she could also write a shrewd and amusing poem on the rise, fall and rescue of a rake whom she calls 'Fribble'.[49] She married George Head, a clothier of Bradford-on-Avon and, though a pillar of the Baptist church there,[50] in old age was, according to family legend, accused of being frivolous for swanning around the town with the first umbrella!

There are more than fifty unpublished poems by Silvia in the Steele collection at Regent's Park College, her most productive period being 1769–75, but she went on writing poetry all her life and married Thomas Duncombe in 1779. Friendship, in poems addressed both to Myra and Myrtilla, forms a favourite theme and she can write pretty verses on conventional themes but, like her friends, she is not prepared to remain the unsophisticated maiden or the light-hearted rhymer. Poetic inspiration, she admits, cannot be confined within the limits of the simple mind, yet she longs to find 'fair Reason's sacred way' for herself.[51] But then we find her wrestling with the problem of how far critical reason can scrutinize divine truth.[52] She frets at the waste of time spent on frivolous matters in a verse 'Written while my hair was dressing' (1775):

> Can Gaudy Dress or tinsel Pomp and show
> One hour of true Contentment e'er bestow?
> Oh No! this Head now dizen'd and so smart
> Frizzell'd and Powder'd o'er with so much art
> Aches full as much as when with careless air
> The homely Night Cap hid my tumbled Hair . . .
> Then why this vain expense of time and care
> Only to ornament a little Hair?
> Why do I servile bow to Custom's rules
> Yet own her still the 'Tyranness of Fools'?[53]

The only printed work of Silvia's is a long poem called *Danebury* which, together with two odes, was published anonymously by W. Pine of Bristol in 1779. Silvia's authorship is established by an autographed copy given to Myrtilla and by copies in the Steele collection. The *Monthly Review* gave it a backhanded compliment: 'There is an excellence in this poem which few writers attain and which from a female pen especially is not always expected.'[54] Coming from this Baptist household the subject presents a real problem. The poem is set in the Anglo-Saxon period at an Iron Age earthwork, called Danebury, a few miles from Broughton; its subtitle is 'The Power of Friendship'. The peace of a rural idyll in which 'old Egbert' lives is rudely destroyed by the attacking Danes. During the battle his beautiful daughter, Elfrida, is wounded by a poisoned arrow. She is saved by her friend Emma who sucks out the poison but is then herself stricken. In the nick of time, the inevitable hermit arrives with curing herbs. The Danes, of course, are beaten and the poem ends in a sunset glow while the poet muses:

> O'er those romantic mounds whene'er I stray
> And the rude vestiges of war survey,
> Fair gratitude shall mark with smile serene
> The alter'd aspect of the pleasing scene . . .
> See smiling villages adorn the plain
> Where desolation stretch'd his iron reign.[55]

Silvia and her friends really did survey the scene, for a little manuscript poem by Miss H. More, pinned into Myrtilla's copy of the poem, records an expedition to Danebury when Hannah More saluted Silvia with a sprig of myrtle. Hannah More's contacts with the Steele family are documented in the Steele collection and it is interesting to see how the romantic passion for ruins was shared by these Baptist ladies and their evangelical acquaintance.[56] But where did Silvia find the story or, if she invented it, why did she set it in such a remote period? I have not found any answer to this question, although it is clear that, in the course of composing the poem, she used Camden's short reference to Danebury.[57]

There is one other somewhat unexpected aspect of these young women's concerns – a political one. At the end of *Danebury* another poem, 'Liberty. An Ode', is printed. Almost certainly written in 1775, it paints an idyllic picture of peaceful Britannia and asks whence its mysterious charms come:

'Tis Liberty – Her magic reign
To nature's scenes can unknown charms impart.

But what does this avail if 'civil discord wave her baleful wand',
as in the past, when 'Tyranny in sanguine garb array'd/held sway
in Albion'. She ends the ode with an appeal to heaven to avert
returning 'flames of civil discord':

> Avert it heaven! Avert th'impending storm!
> Though vengeance hover o'er a guilty land,
> When rigorous Justice lifts her awful form,
> Let Mercy still restrain her lingering hand.

The key to this agitation lies, I think, in a long and fascinating
letter from Myrtilla to Silvia dated 26 February 1775.[58] She
describes electioneering visits on behalf of parliamentary candid-
ates soliciting her brother's vote. 'My Brother desired to know
their political sentiments [and] told them he was determined to
give his vote to none who was against the Americans.' Myrtilla
then bursts into an eloquent plea for supporting 'our worthy
Brethren'. 'I wish my Silvia or Myra would draw up a petition to
present to Her Majesty . . . to be signed by all females' for her to
use

> all her interest with her Royal Consort to persuade him to adopt
> pacific measures . . . How can the father proclaim war against part of
> his once beloved offspring and those Friends who once lived in
> delightful Harmony together . . . perhaps in the same family, shall they
> now rush into the field of Battle and lift up the hostile weapon against
> those they did and those they still love? Nature recoils at the thought,
> humanity shudders at the dreaded prospect. 'A house divided against
> itself cannot stand' and I fear the fall of England is at hand.

Nonconformist support for the American colonists in 1775 is
well-known, but how did these young women, living far from
the centre of debate, acquire this political awareness? I think
one answer may lie in their intimacy with Caleb Evans who
preached and wrote eloquent pamphlets on political liberty and
the constitutional rights of the Americans.[59] More generally,
behind the specific American cause lay the whole Nonconformist

interpretation of history, focused on the glorious struggle for liberty of conscience and toleration. As further evidence one could cite the Steeles' enthusiasm for the radical Helen Williams, particularly expressed in a poem in which Silvia saluted her.[60] This political aspect of the outlook of the Steele circle is quite unexpected.

In the writings of these literary women religious aspirations and contemporary romantic themes mingle easily and naturally. They idealize Nature; they embroider their verse with the stock images of Flora and the like; they strike the current hermit pose in seeking solitude; they meditate in gardens. But they also fiercely defend their right to think, chafe at the waste of time on frivolities and ardently seek spiritual inspiration and vision through their writings. They meet the inevitable tragedies of sickness and death through pious verse, but otherwise real life seems scarcely a proper subject for literary composition. In their charitable works around the neighbourhood they must have met much poverty but in their writings villages are always 'smiling' and the dire social conditions or rural life find no place in their poetry. Nor do domestic duties, except as obstacles to high thought. Amira alone voices the frustrations of domesticity. For the rest, these literary ladies appear to have all the time in the world to pursue the Muses.

Notes

[1] Quoted, H. F. Stecher, *Elizabeth Singer Rowe, the Poetess of Frome* (Frankfurt-am-Main, 1973), 89. I acknowledge with gratitude research help for this chapter from Mrs Susan Mills, Mrs Jennifer Thorp and Mrs Madeline Barber. The two collections of family papers used here are (a) the Steele collection, Angus Library, Regent's Park College, Oxford (Ste., RPC), (b) the Reeves collection in my possession.

[2] On the life of Elizabeth Rowe, see Stecher, *Poetess of Frome*, 23–154; R. Lonsdale (ed.), *Eighteenth-Century Women Poets* (Oxford, 1989), 45–51.

[3] Stecher, *Poetess of Frome*, xxxii.

[4] *Monthly Review*, 29, 372, quoted Lonsdale, *Women Poets*, xxxii.

[5] E. S. Rowe, *Miscellaneous Works in Prose and Verse* (London, 1739), vol. i, xxxii.

[6] Ibid., xx.

[7] Ibid., p. xcvi. Stecher, *Poetess of Frome*, 13, identifies the biographer as Henry Grove, Presbyterian minister and tutor at Taunton, and Benoni Rowe's cousin.

[8] E. S. Rowe, *Letter Moral and Entertaining by the Author of Friendship in Death* (London, 1733).

[9] *The Poetical Works of Mrs Elizabeth. Rowe, including the History of Joseph in Ten Books and an Account of her Life and Writings* (London, undated, *c.*1808), 145.

[10] Ibid., 192–3.

[11] Extracts from her letters and will appear among the Steele papers, RPC.

[12] For the early history of these churches, see *Victoria County History, Wiltshire*, iii. 102–3, 110; J. H. Chandler, *Wiltshire Dissenters' Meeting House Certificates and Registrations, 1689–1852*, Wiltshire Record Society, 40 (1985), nos. 3, 38, 61, 78, 98, 125, 261; K. E. Smith, 'The community and the believers: A study of Calvinistic Baptist spirituality in some towns and villages of Hampshire and the borders of Wiltshire, *c.*1730–1830' (unpublished D. Phil. thesis, Oxford, 1986).

[13] On Anne Steele's life, see the memoir by Caleb Evans in his posthumous edn of her works, *Miscellaneous Pieces in Verse and Prose by Theodosia* (Bristol, 1780). The main source for her life and writings is the Steele collection, RPC.

[14] See, for example, *Salisbury Journal* 3 (Nov 1755; 14 May 1759; 8 July 1765, 1 April and 13 June 1763).

[15] For Lavington, see *DNB*, xxxii; for Fanch, see J. Ivimey, *History of the English Baptists*, iv (1830), 505–6 and holdings of his works, RPC; for Furneaux, see *DNB* (1908 edn), vii.

[16] For Ash, see *DNB*, ii; Ivimey, *English Baptists*, pp. 561–2; G. Nuttall, 'John Ash and the Pershore Church', *Baptist Quarterly*, 20 (1963–4), 4–22; holdings of his works, RPC.

[17] For Evans, see N. S. Moon, 'Caleb Evans, founder of the Bristol Education Society', *Baptist Quarterly*, 24/4 (Oct. 1971), 175–90; extensive holdings of his pamphlets, RPC.

[18] Anne Steele, poems, Ste. 3/3/1, RPC; cf. the original poem by John Byrom, 'My time, oh ye muses was happily spent/take heed, all ye swains, how ye love one so fair', *Spectator*, 603 (6 Oct. 1714).

[19] John Ash, *Sentiments on Education Collected from the Best Writers*, 2 vols. (London 1777), ii. 1–18, 'On female accomplishments'.

[20] For Philander's commonplace books, see Ste, 4/2, RPC.

[21] See above, p.17.

[22] On Anna Seward, see *Letters of Anna Seward, Written between the Years 1784 and 1807* (Edinburgh, 1811) and her published works; Lonsdale, *Women Poets*, 311–20, with bibl. p. 530.

[23] On H. M. Williams, see Lonsdale, *Women Poets*, 413–20, with bibl. p. 535.

[24] Theodosia, poems, Ste. 3/3/1, RPC.

[25] Silvia, poems, Ste. 5/1, RPC.

[26] Theodosia, *Poems on Subjects chiefly Devotional* (London, 1760), ii. 1–5: 'Occasional Poems. The Invocation'.

[27] Theodosia, *Poems*, (1780 edn.), iii. 1–5.

[28] Theodosia, poems, Ste. 3/3/1, RPC.

[29] Ibid.

[30] Ibid., Ste. 3/3/4, RPC.

[31] Ibid., Ste. 3/3/1, RPC.

[32] Ibid., 1760 edn, i. 245, 227.

[33] Ibid., ii. 36–8.

[34] Silviana and Amira, letters, Ste. 3/3/1, RPC.

[35] Amira, poems, Ste. 10/2, and Silviana, poems, Ste. 3/3/1, RPC.

[36] Amira, poems, Ste. 10/2, RPC.

[37] Ibid.

[38] On Mary Scott, see M. Ferguson, '"The Cause of my sex": Mary Scott and the female literary tradition', *Huntingdon Library Quarterly*, 50 (1987), 359–77; Lonsdale, *Women Poets*, pp. 320–2, and bibl., p 531.

[39] M. Scott, *The Female Advocate* (London, 1774).

[40] R. Dodsley, *A Collection of Poems by Several Hands in Three Volumes* (London, 1748), ii. 295–302.

[41] John Duncombe, *The Feminiad. A Poem* (London, 1754).

[42] Silvia, poems, Ste. 5/1, RPC.

[43] Scott, *Female Advocate*, pp. v–vi.

[44] On Mary Scott Taylor's son, J. E. Taylor, see H. McLachlan, 'The Taylors and Scotts of the "Manchester Guardian"', *Trans. of the Unitarian Historical Society*, 4/1 (Oct. 1927), 24–34.

[45] Information derived from the Reeves collection.

[46] Silvia, poems, Ste. 5/1, RPC.

[47] Jane Attwater (Myrtilla), notebook of Silvia's poems, Reeves coll.

[48] The first eight lines of 'Sensibility' are scribbled on the back page of MS Bod. Eng. Letters, d. 103, a collection of eighteenth-century letters, the author of which can be identified as Edward Young of Durnford near Salisbury.

[49] Maria, poems, notebook in Reeves coll.

[50] The Revd William Jay of Bath gave her funeral oration, *The Christian. A Sermon delivered at the Interment of the late Mrs Marianna Head in the Baptist Meeting, Bradford, March 1, 1832 . . .* Printed by George Wood, Parsonage Lane (1833).

[51] Silvia, poems, Ste. 5/5, RPC.

[52] Ibid., Ste, 5/1, RPC.

[53] Ibid., Ste, 5/5, RPC.

[54] *Monthly Review*, 61 (1779), 43

[55] *Danebury* (publ. anon. and undated, by W. Pine, Bristol). R. Watts, *Bibliotheca Britanniae*, gives the date 1779 but states that it was published in London.

[56] See W. Roberts, *Memoirs of Mrs H. More* (London, 1834), i. 186–7, 346–7.

[57] See W. Camden, *Britannia*, 2nd edn. (London, 1722), 'Hamshire', 138, col. 2.

[58] Myrtilla, letters, Reeves coll.

[59] See, in particular, 'Americus' (C. Evans), *A Letter to the Rev. John Wesley* (Bristol, 1775). See also, N. Moon, 'Caleb Evans, Founder of the Bristol Education Society', *Baptist Quarterly*, 24 (4 Oct. 1971), 186; H. Davies, 'The American Revolution and the Baptist Atlantic', *Baptist Quarterly*, 36 (3 July 1995), 132–49.

[60] Silvia, poems, Ste. 5/1, RPC.

3

Methodism and motherhood

PHYLLIS MACK

In the summer of 1997, on a research visit to the John Rylands Library in Manchester, I was overwhelmed by a letter I discovered in a box of manuscripts concerning Mary and Zachariah Taft, ministers who became notorious among mainstream Methodists for their defence of women's preaching. The letter was sent by Mary Barritt Taft to another (and more highly placed) minister, Mary Bosanquet Fletcher, on 14 May 1811.[1] Written when Taft was recovering from childbirth, the letter recounted her experience of labour and her daughter's concurrent experience of a visitation from beyond the grave.

As she told the story, Mary Taft was tending her eight-year-old daughter Mary Ann, whom she believed to be lying on her deathbed, though Mary Ann actually lived three more years. At that moment Mary Taft herself was in labour with another child, and she had been longing for a vision of her own mother, dead some eight weeks past, at the time of her delivery. When she could no longer stand up to care for Mary Ann, she lay down at the foot of the sick girl's bed, gave birth, and managed to walk out of the room, turning for what she thought was her final sight of the dying child. An hour later Mary Ann announced that she had just seen the vision Taft had longed for, the figure of Mary Taft's own mother, and in this vision the grandmother was a beautiful, winged woman, 'not an ould skinney one but a bright shining one', dressed in shimmering white and accompanied by two friends, all with crowns on their heads.

For this twentieth-century reader, the impact of the letter lay in what it implied about the physicality and emotional intensity of childbirth: the dying daughter, the birth itself – apparently unattended – on the same bed where the daughter lay, the concreteness of the visionary experience as the girl described it ('when I saw her first I thought I was going to rise on to my bottom'[2]). But for Mary Taft, the point of the story was not her own or her daughter's ordeal but the authenticity of the vision itself. The body of the letter was an attempt to build a case for those particular three women appearing together; the grand-mother had assisted one of the women's conversion and had had a vision of the other woman's untimely death. What was insignificant, barely mentioned in Taft's account, was her own experience of childbirth. Indeed, although Mary Taft had the original desire for a sight of her own dead mother, the real visionary was not the woman in labour but the sick girl. In short, here is a story of spiritual motherhood in which labour, childbirth, and nursing have no spiritual significance. It is in this double context, of the spiritual importance of motherhood and the dissociation of spirituality from bodily experience, that I want to consider Mary Taft's extraordinary letter.

Motherhood and the body

The conventional narrative of early Protestant history asserts the extreme masculinity of God, church, and family government. Because of the disappearance of the convent and the cult of Mary and the saints, and despite the new importance of mothers as educators of young children, traditions of motherhood apparently lost significance either as ways to convey religious concepts or as ways to shape spiritual and ethical experience.[3] Yet for many seventeenth-century Protestants, motherhood was immensely important in both moral and theological terms; for some women, it was also the means of imagining an unconventional apostolic authority. Drawing on the Old Testament image of the Mother in Israel as judge and provider, women assumed authority to chastize and educate followers who felt themselves in need of control as well as nurture. Adapting the New Testament image of the Woman clothed with the Sun, women spiritualized and glorified the experiences of pregnancy and childbirth. Reflecting on the pain of labour and the death of children, women transformed their personal grief into a creative and assertive spiritual energy.[4]

This capacity to relate bodily experience to spiritual energy or insight was possible because of the general understanding of spirituality as a physical, intangible force which could enter the body through the mouth or the pores, or through hearing the word of God (or the devil). Diabolical forces would contaminate the body (hence the numerous tests for witch's marks), while heavenly forces would purify it (hence the belief that saints' bodies did not putrefy after death). Because she viewed her body as a medium of spiritual perception and expression, the prophet Antoinette Bourignon, who was not a biological mother, could claim that she experienced actual, physical labour pains every time one of her disciples was saved, while the mystic Ann Bathurst, who *was* a biological mother, gave this account of her prayer for the victims of an earthquake in Jamaica:

> And my spirit was at Jamaica lying on my face at prayer . . . And I lay stretched out on the earth, licking the dust and then breathing in the earth as brooding over it for a new Creation . . . I milked milk out of my breasts on the earth . . . Still I see my spirit much on its face, with my breasts touching the earth . . . and I feel the witness of fire on my breasts . . . in my left breast, brooding, hatching as't were and nourishing a flame to break forth . . . O 'tis love's fire that burns and heals and warms! Warm, warm love, warm through blood. I am big and warm with expectation what this warm healing power will come to . . . When it breaks open it will be as sun-shine after rain. I flame, and it satisfies most of my desires.[5]

Within the Dissenting traditions of eighteenth-century British Protestantism, the figure of the spiritual mother was enhanced by the conjunction of three new cultural discourses: a general social preoccupation with motherhood and childrearing; the psychology of John Locke, which emphasized the importance of sense perception and the malleability of children; and the influence of German pietism, which focused on interiority rather than dogma or ritual, and on the concept of spiritual rebirth as a cathartic, transformative experience. So Mary Fletcher (the recipient of Mary Taft's letter), influenced equally by Lockean psychology and the theology of rebirth, wrote:

> A man who doesn't know God is like an unborn baby, without senses, who can't be said to be alive. But when he is born of God his eyes and

ears are opened. He *feels* in his heart . . . the mighty working of the
Spirit of God . . . He *feels*, is conscious of a peace which passeth all
understanding . . . No need of a divine command to make the fond
mother rejoice over her firstborn, restored to her bosom from the point
of *Herod's* sword . . . These involuntary flows of joy . . . plainly
demonstrate, the will and affections are the powerful leaders of the soul;
till, therefore, these powers are fixed on their right object, the clearest
ideas, the brightest understanding will never make a Christian.[6]

Because the concept of spiritual rebirth was centred in will and
emotion – that part of human nature that precedes and underlies
reason – the figure of the spiritual mother had the potential to
address profound human needs for forgiveness and renovation.
For if fathers controlled the education of children who had
reached the age of reason, it was mothers who responded to their
earliest emotional needs and assisted their first spiritual steps.
Images of the minister as mother and the worshipper as infant
thus gave tangible shape to the desire for renunciation, passivity
and renewal that animated pietist meditation and worship.
Indeed, for many Quakers, Methodists, Shakers, and the followers of Joanna Southcott, it was the female preacher or visionary,
not the educated male minister or theologian, who had the power
to cleanse the soul of pollution and instil a sense of primal,
inborn goodness and moral perfectability in the heart of the adult
sinner; not the complex, drawn-out experience of the Calvinist
worshipper, struggling to know herself as a member of the Elect,
but an instantaneous transformation. Letters written to Methodist women ministers spoke of conversion as a birth trauma, and
dwelt on the writer's abjection and struggle and the transformative power of the mother's prayer. 'D/ea/r and honoured Mother
and sister in the Gospel', wrote Joseph Bakewell to Mary Taft,

> . . . I write to acknowledge the debt of gratitude I owe to you for I owe
> you more than worlds can repay for it was you that in the hands of
> God was the honoured instrument of my conversion 40 year ago . . .
> you may have forgot that when you was leading the class at Mansfield
> at a time when I should think there was 100 persons present there was
> a poor criple there which you prayed with while in the pangs of the
> new birth I am that criple and surely if there was then a happy being
> upon the earth it was I . . . This is 40 years since this very day so that
> this is my spiritual birth day in my fortieth year.[7]

It is surely no accident that those groups which affirmed women's spiritual leadership – Quakers, Arminian Methodists, Shakers – were also those groups which combined a conviction of human unworthiness with the promise of universal spiritual rebirth.[8]

But if the concept of spiritual motherhood was enriched by the new discourses of maternity, psychology and religion, it was also limited by those same discourses, particularly in new attitudes about the body. For Methodists, and indeed for many others who absorbed the principles of Lockean psychology, the body was understood not as a container of spiritual forces but as a system of nerve fibres which transmitted sense perceptions to the brain. Because the accuracy of sense perceptions was essential to the formation of accurate ideas, John Wesley linked damnation to the consumption of caffeine, arguing that drinking tea unsettled the nerves and distorted intellectual perception and spiritual health:

> If you drink any, drink but little tea, and none at all without eating, or without sugar and cream . . . Every day of your life take at least an hour's exercise, between breakfast and dinner . . . If you cannot ride or walk abroad, use, within, a dumb bell or a wooden horse . . . Let nothing hinder you. Your life is at stake. Make everything yield to this.[9]

In a similar vein, Mary Fletcher counselled her followers to remember that 'the mind is the mouth of the soul, therefore the food my mind receives is that on which my soul must feed whether it be healthful or poisonous. And that all my success in the spiritual life depends on this.'[10] While bodily pain might be interpreted as a visitation of divine instruction or punishment – a chance for mind to triumph over matter – pain itself had no inherent spiritual significance either as a source of knowledge or an opportunity for heroic martyrdom. As a perceiving organism, the body could be fine-tuned (by not sleeping too much or avoiding tea), but it could never be perfected or transformed from a carcass into a transparent vessel.[11] One Methodist account of a friend's mastectomy without anaesthetic is both understated and excruciating in its depiction of the women's attempt to be stoic in the face of their own bodies' weakness:

> When the inside of her breast was taken out she ask'd if they had done cutting; I answer'd yes, and some thread being call'd for, she

immediately said there is some in my work basket on the table: while they sewd up the blood vessel, she said this pain is very great, she call'd on the Lord to strengthen her and said I'm faint, and while she was going to receive some drops from the hands of a friend: I fainted away: the cause of my fainting is quite hid from me at present: For during the whole time I found my soul entirely stay'd on the Lord, . . . and being confident that every pain she endur'd wou'd be sanctified to the good of her soul, I felt no degree of fear. I was entirely happy.[12]

Thus the emotion of the eighteenth-century Methodist who wept at her conversion was different from the ecstasy of the seventeenth-century Quaker whose body shook in readiness to receive and absorb the Holy Spirit.

The body of the eighteenth-century mother was not merely despiritualized; it was also desexualized. Ruth Perry has written eloquently about the ideal of bourgeois motherhood which became the new cultural norm:

> . . . in the eighteenth century, maternity came to be imagined as a counter to sexual feeling, opposing alike individual expression, desire, and agency in favor of a mother-self at the service of the family and the state . . . by the middle of the eighteenth century they were increasingly reimagined as belonging to another order of being: loving but without sexual needs, morally pure, disinterested, benevolent, and self-sacrificing . . . this was a colonization of women far more thoroughgoing than any that had preceded it . . . an unprecedented cultural use of women and the appropriation of their bodies for procreation.[13]

Celibacy and motherhood

Mary Taft was born into a Methodist community whose teachings emphasized both the authority of spiritual motherhood and the necessity of restrained and respectable motherly behaviour.[14] In fact, from the perspective of the Methodist leadership, the ideal spiritual mother was not an actual mother at all, but a celibate woman – often a very young woman – in whom the desire for biological motherhood had been sublimated into a concern for all those unborn souls waiting to be helped into existence. Mary Taft fulfilled that role more successfully than any of her peers; too successfully, according to some Methodist leaders.

Educated by her mother in Methodist values and worship, she experienced conversion at age twelve and began walking from house to house to pray with neighbours. By age seventeen she was organizing her own prayer meetings, despite threats by the Wesleyan superintendent, local preachers (who saw their congregations leaving them to follow her), and her own (non-Methodist) father. Saving souls, she maintained, was 'the one talent God hath give me'. After preaching with her brother, also a minister, on the Isle of Man, she returned to Lancashire during the revivals of 1792 and resumed her local ministry. Feeling in low spirits, she was prodded by another female minister, 'Praying Nanny', to join her as an itinerant preacher. Their fame increased after they held a joint meeting which lasted from 9.00 a.m. till midnight, and for the next several years she received regular invitations to preach in distant villages in Yorkshire and Lancashire, speaking in chapels, town halls, cottages, and out of doors. The minister William Bramwell, comparing her to himself, said, 'You do more work in less time', and (writing to a male minister), 'I never knew one man so much blessed as this young woman is in the salvation of souls'.[15]

The Methodists' advocacy of a celibate female ministry reflected their conviction that respectable and devoted mothers were the ones who stayed at home.[16] It also reflected a desire to protect the autonomy and mobility of the itinerant minister. 'Fully understand me', Mary's mentor William Bramwell wrote when she was contemplating marriage to Zachariah Taft,

> I do not mean that it is wrong to marry, but I think it would prevent in you the answering [of] that great end of your call . . . your situation would become local . . . You would soon become in a great degree useless . . . I conceive you can only think of altering your state upon one ground – and that is, 'I am become obsolete! My work is done! I am shut out! I can do no more! I am called to give it up!' If you think so, I think differently.[17]

Indeed, the ideal of a celibate ministry applied to men as well as women; when Bramwell himself married in 1787, John Wesley temporarily suspended him from the itinerant preaching circuit. But by the time of Mary's marriage to Zachariah Taft in 1802, the Methodist leadership was putting greater emphasis on formalized chapel services and discouraging informal lay preaching (Wesley died in 1791). Women had benefited from the fact that the line between prayer, exhortation and formal sermonizing was blurred, especially in more intimate class and band meetings, so that women might preach without claiming to be members of an established clergy. But because of the new formalism in Methodist worship and church organization, the pressures against women (married or celibate) escalated, and – partly in response to the Tafts' own campaign in defence of women's authority – the central Conference of 1802 formally disavowed female preaching.

Thus by 1811, when Taft composed her letter to Mary Fletcher, the Tafts had already set themselves against the Methodist establishment, first by marrying and then by becoming activists in defence of women's preaching and popular revivalism.[18] It is with these conflicts in mind that we should read the second part of her letter to Mrs Fletcher, building a case for the authenticity of Mary Ann's vision. This account may have worked to vindicate Mary Taft's own ministry by establishing a genealogy of visionary women or spiritual mothers. Yet it was not their own embodied experience that validated their spiritual authority, but their capacity for *out* of the body, supernatural experience:

> It is amasing what exceeding littal we know or can know while hear, conserning the invisabal world especaly the Spirate of the just maid perfect there knowledge of & intrests in our conserns & yeat I am persweded *it is even so*, & on some particlors occason *& to some persons this is reveld so far* as flesh & Blood can bear such discoveryes . . .

The fact that Mary Taft did not, indeed *could* not emphasize the connection between physical childbirth and her own spiritual authority, tells us a great deal about the role of cultural discourse in shaping religious behaviour, but it tells us little about the role of discourse in shaping subjective experience. However reticent she was in rendering her own experience of childbirth as spiritually significant, I find it hard to believe that Mary Taft did not connect the two in her own mind. She was active as a religious leader (and revered as a spiritual mother) when she was nearly nine months pregnant, and she took her baby with her on preaching trips.[19] She wrote to friends and family about the glories of the second birth and (delightedly) to her husband about the surfeit of milk in her breasts. She prayed in the night while she nursed.[20] Surely the pain and joy of her own labour and nursing resonated at some level with her emotional praying for the sinner's spiritual transformation; and surely her charismatic authority as a minister resonated with the knowledge of her own mother's apotheosis and her daughter's visionary insight.

Certainly she believed that her vocation as a minister would be best served as a wife and a biological mother. And in fact, if marriage and motherhood did not redirect or enhance women's focus on the spiritual life of the body, they did give religious women new possibilities for preaching to heterogeneous groups and humanizing their own spiritual authority. When John Fletcher married Mary Bosanquet, he announced to his followers, 'I am going to take an important step . . . I am going to marry a wife, not so much a wife for myself as a mother for you.' Certainly married women's public behaviour was more conventional (though no less emotional) than that of more radical, working-class, celibate prophets like Ann Lee or Joanna Southcott. Women ministers usually deferred to male authority by standing beside the pulpit, not in it (Taft ignored this convention), or by asking the advice of the male leadership on the presentation and content of their sermons. Yet these ministers routinely preached alongside or immediately following their husbands, and this suggests a popular tolerance for the spiritual authority of sexually mature women. I know of no earlier cases of men marrying their spiritual mothers (the women who had converted them), much less of men joking about it, as Zachariah Taft recounted in 1809: 'The late pious and useful Mr Jonathan Cousins was awakened [to God] by hearing his wife. Hence he would often pleasantly say that he had married his mother!'[21]

The Tafts never disavowed their allegiance to traditional Methodism. They remained in the north of England, where Mary continued to preach, admonish, and, as the years went on, to fuss over her spiritual children in endearingly physical ways. Benjamin Gregory, who had read Taft's autobiography when he was four years old, visited her as a young minister:

> . . . the old lady, who was reckoned somewhat hard and stern, treated him like a son. She made him take a teaspoonful of friar's balsam on a piece of sugar before he went into the pulpit, and stood over him, with eyes and hands uplifted, exclaiming, 'God bless it to you!'

When he was ill she paid for him to consult a doctor, and when he was ordained at the Conference of 1844 (she was seventy-three), she brought him a present: 'You used to suffer from cold feet. I've brought a pair of stockings knitted on purpose for you, such as you could not buy anywhere.'[22] She died in 1851, aged seventy-nine. The *Methodist Magazine*, which regularly published extended biographies of eminent ministers, gave her a paragraph.

Conclusion

I want to conclude with some general – and very tentative – statements about spiritual women in general and spiritual motherhood in particular. Most students of religious behaviour associate female preachers or visionaries with movements celebrating liminality or the absence of structure. This is true of traditional scholars, who denigrate women as hysterical or over-sexed; it is true of social theorists, who view women as marginal figures who achieve status as charismatic leaders in periods of social dislocation; it is true of feminists, who are understandably more interested in women's intrusion into the public sphere than women praying in their closets or teaching Sunday school; and – perhaps most important – it is true of religious actors themselves, who celebrated women's authority as evidence of a world turned upside down, a world in which the last would finally be first.[23]

Indeed, all popular movements where women held positions of spiritual leadership (as opposed to that of patron to male leaders) were both universalist and unstructured. But within those movements that were ultimately successful (Quakers, Methodists), the male leaders who supported women were also the great organizers: George Fox, John Wesley.[24] Especially in periods of social upheaval, they saw women as upholders of order, providers of shelter, negotiators with magistrates, pastoral counsellors, and as a kind of moral police, who were effective precisely *because* they had no formal status, no place in the structures that were being attacked. The presence of women in leadership roles allowed those movements to see themselves as radical or innovative, while ensuring that what needed to be done in order to make the movement cohere would in fact be done; women symbolized social reversal, but they also provided a hidden structure. The purely charismatic movements like the Ranters or communist movements like the Diggers did not give women authority; nor did they survive.

Both these aspects of female spiritual authority (the liminal, charismatic visionary and the upholder of values and provider of continuity) were most often expressed by the dual figure of the mother: the woman in childbirth and the Mother in Israel. At her most exalted, the woman in spiritual childbirth became a kind of shaman, who travelled between the living and the dead and claimed the power of viewing souls in purgatory; thus the Shaker leader, Mother Ann Lee, envisioned herself sprouting wings at the ends of her hands and flying to the realm of the dead.[25] At her most magisterial, the mother in Israel was notable for the thoughtful cruelty with which she instilled in her children the techniques of bodily discipline that would enable them to experience sanctification; thus John Wesley's revered mother Susanna taught her children to cry quietly by whipping them from the moment they were one year old.[26]

Both aspects of spiritual motherhood were replicated in Mary Taft's self-presentation and in the language used by her followers. Both as a spiritual midwife who assisted in the rebirth of sinners, and as an old lady 'somewhat hard and stern', she participated in a tradition of female spiritual authority stretching back to medieval times.[27] Thus, to my mind, motherhood is more important than sexuality or status anxiety in understanding women's religious behaviour and their spiritual importance for men. We need a history of motherhood and its relation to popular religious movements, an effort to trace the changing relationship between biology, language, and spiritual authority as religious men and women struggled through their own transition from spiritual death to rebirth.

Appendix

Taft Papers, 104.5.1

Dear Mrs Fletchor:

I hope you will pardon us for not writing soonor. sevral have been our reasons but the greatist is. I have not recovored so fast as formerly – but thank the Lord I am now in a likely way to get

strong in a littal time I hope If all is well with us, Since we wrote
Last some have been our exercises both of body & mind but far
greator our mercies

Next Friday it will be 6 weeks since I was delivored of a
Daughter which praise the Lord coms on finley but I have
something pirticuler to relate It often crost my Mind that if my
Lord would permit my Dear Departed Mothor who died at our
house 8 weeks back would pay me aviset a bout the time of my
Delivery. but be it Remerked our Daughter Mary Ann was the
saime Day sick unto Death to all appearance I waited upon her as
long as I was able & then was delivord at her bed feet & walked
into the next Room, at the same time taking my last looke as I
thougt at her, but it pleased our good god that night to give her
comeplaints a favourabel turn I was delivourd about 6 in the
Evning and about an Hour after as my Servant & an othor young
Woman stood by the Bed of our Doughtor our Sirvant obsirved
her look over her shouldor & smiled as she muttored something,
our sirvant said Mary Ann what dou you smile at, do you see
something. yes, says she, I do, I see a Womon & she is not an
Ould skiney one but a Bright shining one, She is drest all like
Silver I heard her & said Praise the Lord fuly beliveing who it
was, the next Day she begd to be Carried in to my room & when
they had fixed her in the Big chair with pillows she said Mother it
was my granmother that I saw last night. I said was it my Dear,
she said yes She was dresed in shining like silver & she had a
Wing upon each shoulder & a Crown on her head – I tould her if
we did but sirve the Lord we should be Crowned also with God
to praise him for ever.

but on the Sabath day night following she had a dreame & did
not think of it after till near noon the next day when she came in
& said Mother I dreampt of my granmother last night I said did
you, yea said she & I thought I saw her in the saime place I saw
her stand on friday night – & when I saw her first I thought I was
going to rise on to my bottom but I thought she said Mary Ann it
is only me do not be afrad she replyed is it you Granmother I am
not afraid of you; continued she my Mothor has got a littel one
since you was hear & if you stay till it is light I will go in with you
to look at it – she said has she, but she said to me Mother there
was not only my Granmother but there was 3 of them & my
Granmother stood first & shone the Brightest, but they was all

drest in white shining like silver – & there was a Book said she, over there heads & it was larg & open & there I saw my Granmothers naime first then Mrs Hay & then Dorothy Babb

This to me is remarkeabel Dorothey Babb Died the weeke after my Mother & was at her own request Buried by my Mother but Mrs Hay Died 4 years since this Month at Burnley in Lancashire & my Dear Mother under God was maid an instrument of her being more fuly a wakend & it was on this wise, one day my Mother said to her Mrs Hay you will never be convirted unless it is in a good shouting prayer meeting this she dispised, but the Lord maid it as a nail in a sure place & sum time aftor one night I had to speake & after this we had 2 prayer meetings one after an other as there was several undor distress & she was one that would not go a way till the Lord had spoken Peace to her soul, but he heard her cry & that of others & saived her she met in Class with us & got more fuly saived so that for the last month not a cloud save one over spread her skey. she Died a witness of Gods Pour to saive, my Mother while at Burnley had a sever affliction it was much worse appearantly then that she died of but when I asked her how she was she said Mary come forwards I have some thing to say to thee: bad as I am, Mrs Hay must die before me I have had a visionary sight of her, she came & stood upon nothing but a white cloud drest in a garment of white shining mist waved her hand for me to come, so says she I shall not die but get better & Mrs Hay will die before me but she will come to welcome me when I die Mrs Hay was then in tolarabl helth but soon after her afflictions increased a pease till she died, but my Mother recovered & on the Evening of her death Mr Taft & me was encirageing her & saying that such & such of her frinds would meet & shout her wellcome to glory. yea said she, & Mrs Hay will meet me to, now it being near 4 years since Mrs Hay died & our Daughter not then 4 years of Age she could have no pirsnal knowlidge of her but by reading the naims she saw wrote in the Book which she said was not wrote with pen & Inke but with Brite shining lettors: O that we may all shin to all Etirnety. It is amasing what exceeding littal we know or can know while hear, conserning the invisabal world especaly the Spirate of the just maid perfect there knowledge if & intrests in our conserns & yeat I am persweded *it is even so*, & on some particlors occason *& to some persons this is reveld so far* as flesh & Blood can bear such

discoveryes, *hear in* I know that my honourad frind is like minded
with my unworthy self – We shall be happy to hear from you soon
& more espeshaly to hear that the Lord continus your helth &
strength enebels you to atend your regulor meetings & continue
to speake & act for *God* O that the Lord would condesend more
fuly to bless us, & cause his face continualy to shine up on us, &
more fuly so stamp his Image *with in* & *on us*, & that he would
more fully own our labours of Love which we have showd to ward
his naime. My Dear Mr T unites me in love to you Miss Tooth &
all under your Hospitabal Roof & your Dear Preachers & to all
that still Remember us & we beg anintrest (?) in ther *Prayers* & I
hope you will still Remember us & write soon though unworthy

Dear Mrs Fletchar
    I remain as ever & for ever
        your frind & sister in Christ
        Mary Taft
Castle Donington May 14: 1811

Notes

This essay was completed with the generous assistance of the Center for
Advanced Study in Behavioral Sciences, Stanford, California, and the
Andrew W. Mellon Foundation.

[1] See Appendix.

[2] The letter describes the presence of a servant and another young
woman an hour after the delivery, but does not mention a midwife or
physician.

[3] Lyndal Roper discusses the absence of a rhetoric of motherhood in early
Protestantism in *Oedipus and the Devil: Witchcraft, Sexuality and Religion
in Early Modern Europe* (London and New York, 1994), 40, 42. On
images of motherhood in Calvinist writing, see Jane Dempsey Douglass,
'Calvin's use of metaphorical language for God: God as enemy and God
as mother', *Archive for Reformation History*, 77 (1986), 126–39. Calvin
wrote, 'that comparison of a labouring woman [to God] might
somewhat degrade the majesty and power of God . . . So far then as
relates to love, [Isaiah] says that God resembles a mother; so far as
relates to power, he says that he resembles a lion or a giant.' (*Com. Isa.
C.O.* 37, 70, quoted Dempsey Douglass, 'Calvin's use', 134)

[4] Phyllis Mack, *Visionary Women: Ecstatic Prophecy in Seventeenth-
Century England* (Berkeley and Los Angeles, 1992).

[5] Diary of Ann Bathurst, 1692, Rawlinson Manuscripts, D.1262–63/480.

[6] Mary Bosanquet [Fletcher], *An Aunt's Advice to a Niece, in a Letter to Miss ***** (Leeds, by J. Bowling, 1780), 28–29, 38.

[7] Joseph Bakewell to Mary Taft, Mansfield, 14 May 1840, Rylands Library, Mss. 104.1.4. Another man wrote to her, 'While you was use to be speaking and Praying in York it was to my soul as though I was on the boarders of heaven . . . [I] do oppose all that come in my way bouth people and preachers that speak against you . . . I begin to tell how you was the means of my conversion . . . Your son in the Lord, George Lees' (5 April 1803, 104.1.10). And see the letter from Mary Anderson (13 Oct. 1811, 104.1.3). In 1841 Mary Taft wrote that a preacher came up to her saying 'I am glad to see you I never did before – But I have been sorounded with your chldren wear ever I have traveld' (Mary Taft to Miss Tooth, 8 Nov 1841, 104.5.13).

[8] The prominence of women in early Methodism was largely due to John Wesley, who also championed the wing of Methodism which rejected predestination. The followers of George Whitfield, a predestinarian, opposed women's public role.

[9] John Wesley, 'Thoughts on nervous disorders', *The Works of John Wesley*, 3rd edn, xi: *Thoughts, Addresses, Prayers, and Letters* (Grand Rapids, MI, 1996), 520. And see 'A letter to a friend concerning tea', Newington, 10 Dec. 1748, xi 504–15.

[10] John Wesley, letter 'To a friend', Newington, 10 Dec. 1748, *The Letters of the Rev. John Wesley, A.M.*, ed. John Telford (London, 1931, repr. 1960), ii. 158–70. Mary Tooth's Account of her Life and Journal, vol. 15 (1840–1842), 31 Dec. 1840 (Rylands Library, Fletcher-Tooth Collection, Box 14).

[11] On sleep, see 'Thoughts on nervous disorders', 518–19. 'And if we lie longer in bed, though without sleep, the very posture relaxes the whole body; much more when we are covered up with clothes, which throw back on the body whatever perspires from it. By this means it is stewed in the moist vapour . . . and the flesh is, as it were, parboiled therein . . . and the nerves suffer.'

[12] 'An account of Mrs Davis' behaviour during the operation of her breast being cut off', to Charles Wesley, 1 July 1758, 'Early Methodist Volume', No. 48, John Rylands MSS.

[13] Ruth Perry, 'Colonizing the breast: sexuality and maternity in eighteenth-century England', *Journal of the History of Sexuality*, 2, No. 2 (1991), 209, 216, 231.

[14] Mary Barritt was born in Hay, Lancashire, in 1772. Her mother converted to Methodism shortly after her birth. Biographical information on Mary Taft is taken from Deborah M. Valenze, *Prophetic*

Sons and Daughters: Female Preaching and Popular Religion in Industrial England (Princeton, 1985), 55–64.

[15] Ibid., 56.

[16] At least one woman gossiped about Mary Taft because she travelled away from her husband to preach (Mary Taft to Zachariah Taft, 19 June 1803, 104.4.14): 'She may speake a against me being so much away from you . . . as if I had little respect for *you* but be ashurd my Dear this has Ever had an opesit Efect on me the more willing you have been to let me go and the more abundantly I have Lovd *you* seeing you could give up *your owne will* for the good of *Souls*.'

[17] W. Bramwell to Miss Barritt (n.d.), quoted in Valenze, *Prophetic Sons and Daughters*, 58–9. Mary Fletcher and John Wesley both wrote in defence of the celibate life.

[18] In 1803, just after Mary Ann was born, Mary had written to her husband, 'I do feel fully willing to wash my Hands of Methedisam for a lie to them – I have Ever Been willing to be turnd out for Labouring for God . . . and though I feel a weke body at Present no changes of Season or Place has maid aneny Chaing in my mind' (5 July 1803, Rylands Library, 104.4.15).

[19] Zachariah Taft wrote, shortly before his wife expected to give birth, 'circumstanced as we are my wife has a good oppertunity of getting out, the best of all is God is with us, we are doing I trust and getting good' (Z. Taft to Mrs Fletcher, 2 Oct. 1809, Rylands Library, 104.5.6). And see Mary Taft to 'My dear Mr Taft', 5 July 1803, Rylands Library, 104.4.15. See above, n. 4, citing adulatory letters to her as a spiritual mother, written in the years when she was the mother of young children.

[20] 'I have Recovrd gradialy a littel strength Evry Day but hav so much suck for young Mary scarce now what to Do with it but she coms on wondrfuly. I tell her what you say and she lookes and smils all redy – we shall be wonderful glad to see Father come into this Roome I Praid for you much this Morning evry time Mary waked me . . . I have ever been willing to be turnd out for labouring for God . . . me thinkes the would like to see our Dear Littl Mary God Bless her she is viry good and I hope will be better evry day . . . she has rested and slept 4 ours at a time and then suckd and slept again . . . Lord over rule all for thy glory and the good of Preshous souls and let not thy enemeys escape that have this year oposed thee in the house of thy *frends* . . . Lord save me from ever looking to much after this world' (5 July 1803, 104.4.15).

[21] Zachariah Taft to 'Dear Brother', Birstal near Leeds, July 1809, printed, in Rylands Library, Taft documents, Box 104.5.3.

[22] Dr Waller and the Editor, 'A Famous Lady Preacher', 1907, 538–44.

[23] See, for example, Paul Hazard, *La Crise de la conscience européenne (1680–1716)*, 2 vols. (Paris, 1935), ii. 272–5; I. M. Lewis, *Ecstatic Religions: An Anthropological Study of Spirit Possession and Shamanism* (Harmondsworth, 1971); Christina Berg and Philippa Berry, 'Spiritual whoredom: An essay on female prophets in the seventeenth century', in Francis Barker et al. (eds.), *1642: Literature and Power in the Seventeenth Century* (Colchester, 1981).

[24] On the struggle over women's public authority in Quakerism, see Mack, *Visionary Women*, chap. 8, 'The snake in the garden: Quaker politics and the origin of the women's meeting', 265–304.

[25] 'I felt [my disciple's] lost state and laboured for him . . . and I felt the power of God come upon me, which moved my hand up and down like the motion of wings; and soon I felt as if I had wings on both hands; and I saw them, and they appeared as bright as gold. And I let my hands go as the power directed, and these wings parted the darkness to where souls lay in the ditch of hell; and I saw their lost state' (sayings of Mother Ann Lee, quoted in Jean M. Humez (ed.), *Mother's First-Born Daughters: Early Shaker Writings on Women and Religion* (Bloomington and Indianapolis, 1993), 22–3).

[26] 'As self-will is the root of all sin and misery, so whatever cherishes this in children ensures their after-wretchedness and irreligion . . . This therefore I cannot but earnestly repeat: break their wills betimes . . . Whatever pains it cost, conquer their stubbornness: break the will, if you would not damn the child . . . Let a child from a year old, be taught to fear the rod and cry softly . . . if you whip him ten times running . . . Let none persuade you it is cruelty to do this; it is cruelty not to do it. Break his will now, and his soul will live, and he will probably bless you to all eternity' (Susannah Wesley to John Wesley, 24 July 1732, in Charles Wallace, Jr. (ed.), *Susanna Wesley: The Complete Writings* (New York and Oxford, 1997), 370–1).

[27] The literary scholar Barbara Newman describes the apostolic authority of medieval visionaries, whose suffering gave them the power to ransom dead souls from purgatory. Barbara Newman, *From Virile Woman to WomanChrist: Studies in Medieval Religion and Literature* (Philadelphia, 1995), chaps. 3 and 4.

4

Gospel and culture in Victorian Nonconformity

DAVID BEBBINGTON

The relationship of gospel and culture, the undergirding theme of this set of studies, is itself the topic of the present paper. It is a subject that has received increasing attention since the Second World War. In 1948 T. S. Eliot argued that every religion necessarily has a cultural expression, and that the two are ultimately indistinguishable.[1] A more nuanced analysis by H. Richard Niebuhr, *Christ and Culture,* published in 1951, is still a work of influence. Niebuhr examined a variety of ways in which gospel and culture can interact, and have interacted, pointing out the merits and pitfalls of each.[2] Missionary studies have scrutinized the relationship with great thoroughness. A whole discipline has been created to explore it: transcultural missiology.[3] Perhaps the best-known recent venture designed to explore the issue in its Western setting was the Swanwick Conference of 1992, the culmination of 'The Gospel and our Culture' project sponsored by the British Council of Churches. The collected conference papers, edited by Hugh Montefiore, were published as *The Gospel and Contemporary Culture.*[4] The relationship constitutes a theme of recognized importance.

This paper takes a case study in the field: Victorian Nonconformity. Like the Swanwick Conference, it is concerned primarily with England and Wales, but it turns to the past for its content. It considers a self-contained period, the longest reign in English history, and a self-contained community, the world of Protestant Dissent. Yet the paper is indebted to missionary studies for its definition of 'culture'. The word is used here in the broad sense that missiology has taken over from anthropology. The term refers not just to 'high culture', the expressions of civilization in art, music and literature. Although that has been the most common British usage during the twentieth century,[5] the word is deployed here to mean something more. Nor is this analysis merely adding to high culture what is often called 'popular culture', the expression of folkways, traditional customs and mass enthusiasms. That usage is standard in the United States and has become widespread among British historians in recent years.[6] Here, however, the term is being employed in a third sense that is much wider. It is not a synonym for civilization, high or low, but rather a word for the web of attitudes and behaviour characterizing a particular group. This is the sense in which it is used, for example, in the Lausanne Covenant;[7] it has become familiar in Britain in the recent past through the popularization of the phrase 'enterprise culture'. Because it is so broad, this usage encompasses both élite and popular culture, aspects of each of which will be considered in due course. But its primary meaning is nothing less than the whole range of human thought and activity.

It is clear that there has been, in every age and every society, a two-way interaction between gospel and culture. The gospel shapes the culture and the culture modifies the expression of the gospel. Sometimes one process predominates, sometimes the other. The aim in this chapter is to study both directions of influence in the case of Victorian Nonconformity. There are therefore two central questions. How did the Nonconformist version of Christianity mould Victorian Britain? Conversely, how did Victorian Britain affect the Nonconformist version of Christianity? We begin with the former process, the gospel shaping culture.

In *The Age of Atonement* (1988), Boyd Hilton has argued that, from the end of the eighteenth century to the middle of the nineteenth, Britain was deeply swayed by evangelical religion. Economics, social policy, politics, even aspects of science were transformed by this energetic spiritual force. Although there may be reservations about points of detail, the overall picture is generally accepted. Down to about 1860, themes associated with the atonement had a powerful resonance in the public arena.[8] It was not just the Anglican evangelicals that Hilton emphasizes who were responsible for this impact of their faith, though William Wilberforce and his friends of the Clapham Sect were among the more notable agents of the process. Evangelicals were never a majority in the nineteenth-century Church of England, even at the peak of their influence around mid-century. Evangelicalism was much more widespread in Nonconformity, which was also re-creating society in its own image. Chapel strength is demonstrated by the results of the 1851 Religious Census, the only official survey of religion ever undertaken in Britain. Estimates of the proportion of attendants from the various denominations show that the Church of England had 52 per cent, a bare majority of churchgoers. The Roman Catholics, with 4 per cent, still formed only a small community, despite the recent influx of Irish immigrants. The tiny group of others outside Nonconformity, with 0.5 per cent, consisted chiefly of Latter Day Saints, most of whom were soon to depart to Salt Lake City. The Unitarians, at 0.5 per cent, constituted an equivalent body of unorthodox Dissenters, about whom more will be said later. Evangelical Nonconformists represented fully 43 per cent of attendants, and so were not far behind the Church of England as a whole.[9] They had been gaining ground steadily for over half a century in a heroic age of rapid expansion recently documented by Michael Watts in the second volume of his work *The Dissenters*.[10] Growth relative to population continued after 1851 for another quarter-century or more.[11] In the later Victorian period, a time when churchgoing was the norm, chapel was rightly thought to represent roughly half the people at worship.

Furthermore, evangelical Nonconformity was believed to be well adapted to the trends of the times. This was the message of *The Age of Great Cities* (1843) by Robert Vaughan, appointed president of Lancashire Independent College in the same year. A new industrial age was dawning, drawing people into the mushrooming urban areas. According to Vaughan, the peasantry, with its vice and vulgarity, was being superseded by burghers of civic spirit. The Church of England was shackled by hoary restrictions, but evangelical Nonconformists, especially Vaughan's own Independents, were free to cater for the religious needs of the enterprising population.[12] It was an idealized image, but it embodied a great deal of truth at the time: nearly half the cotton manufacturers of Lancashire, the standard-bearers of the new age, were Nonconformists.[13] Two years later Vaughan founded *The British Quarterly Review* so that Nonconformity could have a cultivated organ alongside the *Quarterly*, the *Edinburgh* and the *Westminster*. Here was a voice of evangelical Nonconformity that was usually as weighty in its pronouncements as *The Christian Observer*, its evangelical Anglican counterpart, and often more so. Chapel was not just reaching the masses with popular revivalism, though it was doing that effectively. Rather it was sharing in the spread of evangelical values at all cultural levels in the earlier part of the Victorian era.

In the later part of the Queen's reign, according to Hilton, evangelical influence waned. Its characteristic stress on Christ crucified was superseded by an emphasis, put in different ways by High and Broad Churchmen, on the incarnation – the person rather than the work of Christ. The atonement was no longer the central metaphor of the civilization. Again it seems that this general picture is valid. Michael Ramsey, the former archbishop of Canterbury, for example, showed how, from Charles Gore in the 1880s to William Temple in the 1930s, the typical focus of Anglican theology was the incarnation.[14] There was, as Hilton suggests, a transition from an age of atonement to an age of incarnation in the 1860s. Yet this process, which affected the Church of England so drastically, had relatively little impact on Nonconformity, at least during the nineteenth century. Nonconformists remained overwhelmingly evangelical and so cruci-centric in their theology. Thus *The Baptist Magazine* for June 1866 criticized the American Congregationalist Horace Bushnell:

> According to Dr Bushnell, the life of Christ, His incarnation, His submission to the lot of humanity, His sympathy and fellow-feeling with man, are everything. His death is the mere accident of His condition, and was a sacrifice to the malice and cruelty of man, and not a sacrifice to God at all . . . But in the sacred Scriptures the death or blood of Christ is everywhere prominent.[15]

For this commentator the cross was clearly still the dominant doctrinal motif. Although in England a few advanced thinkers, especially among the Congregationalists, took the path charted by Bushnell, they did not gain the ascendancy. Only at the very end of the century is a shift of theological opinion detectable. The Wesleyan Scott Lidgett, in his book *The Spiritual Principle of the Atonement* (1897), moved towards an incarnation-centred scheme. Even then, however, he was censured for the change of emphasis by the president of Conference.[16] In the main late

Victorian Nonconformists remained as attached to the centrality of the atonement as their predecessors in the faith.

Consequently during the late nineteenth century evangelical influence on society was more Nonconformist than Anglican. It was evident in a variety of fields, of which three instances may be given. First can be their place in literature. Early nineteenth-century chapel folk had normally – though by no means universally – been suspicious of novels as worldly. In the later part of the century, however, many Nonconformists themselves wrote novels. Silas Hocking, a minister of the United Methodist Free Churches, became the best-selling author of the turn of the century. It is true that his first novel, called *Alec Green* (1879), had encountered some misunderstanding. One elderly member of his Burnley congregation suggested that Alec Green should be invited to address a missionary meeting![17] The practice of writing fiction became almost a fashion in the ministry. Joseph Parker, the Congregational minister of the City Temple, regularly published novels from 1868 onwards; John Clifford, the leading General Baptist, issued one in 1874.[18] These writings were often marked by conviction of sin and deep repentance. It has to be admitted, in fact, that they often enter the realm of melodrama. Yet the whole genre, often chapel-based, has been largely lost to the literary memory and deserves recovery. It forms a clear instance of evangelical Nonconformist cultural influence.

Another instance relates to the role of women. It has been argued that evangelicalism was substantially responsible for the early nineteenth-century articulation of separate spheres ideology, which depicted home as the proper place for women while men entered the public arena of business and politics.[19] This contention seems well established, notwithstanding the antiquity of many elements of the domestic ideology and notwithstanding the fact that this division of labour was seen, not least by most women themselves, as a desirable goal, enabling them to find fulfilment in their own sphere. It has been less noticed that evangelical Nonconformist opinion in the later nineteenth century was closely aligned with feminist aspirations. In particular, the Anti-Contagious Diseases Acts movement sprang largely from Nonconformist roots. The Contagious Diseases Acts were passed in the 1860s to provide for health inspection of prostitutes in the vicinity of naval bases and military barracks. From 1869 there existed a movement aiming for the repeal of the Acts, with a Ladies' National Association in the van. Although its leader, Josephine Butler, was the wife of an Anglican clergyman, its support was chiefly Nonconformist. Sixteen of the twenty-two members of the central committee whose religious allegiance is known were Nonconformists, twelve of them Quakers.[20] The movement gathered momentum on Christian grounds. The Wesleyan Hugh Price Hughes contended that the policy of the Acts, apart from discriminating against women while ignoring the guilt of their male clients, was based on a moral error: the legislation was recommended by a utilitarian ethic that assessed behaviour according to results (military efficiency) rather than a Christian absolutist ethic.[21] The campaign achieved the suspension of the Acts in 1883. Many of those who had been involved went on to advocate further changes that would benefit women, several, including the Congregationalist MP and Bristol coalowner Handel Cossham, becoming advocates of female suffrage. The movement which was the seed-bed of later feminist efforts was predominantly an evangelical Nonconformist enterprise.

A third example of Nonconformist influence was the broader political scene. Hugh Price Hughes's evangelical style of politicking was the herald of a new mode of Nonconformist engagement with public issues that lasted from the 1870s to the Edwardian period, the phenomenon of the Nonconformist conscience. The very name, coined in 1890, shows that it was distinctive to Nonconformity. The style possessed a number of characteristic features. Its targets were what Nonconformists identified as intrinsic wrongs, whether gambling or the sufferings of the Irish that led to support for Gladstone's policy of Home Rule. Consequently its policy was negative. The conscience did not offer constructive proposals but instead called for the abandonment of existing practices. Campaigns were often explicitly 'anti-', whether embodied in the Anti-Contagious Diseases Acts movement or in the Anti-Gambling League, and typically there were demands for change to be immediate, since there could be no loitering with sin. The conscience was at its most assertive when it was able to vent its wrath on government policy, and so, since Nonconformists were overwhelmingly Liberals, it was usually directed against Conservative administrations.[22] The resulting tone was shrill and the *ad hominem* censure seems distasteful, perhaps all too similar to the late twentieth-century *Sun* on a bad day. Yet often the conscience selected worthy targets to attack. It denounced, for example, the popular jingoism that fuelled the spread of empire without regard to the status of indigenous peoples. That policy, if not the technique, ranged the conscience against the chauvinism that has sometimes blemished the *Sun*. Certainly the Nonconformist conscience generated widespread attention and at times it achieved results. It is a further illustration of the impact of Nonconformity on Victorian England and Wales.

If Nonconformists were exerting an influence on the whole of their society in these and other diffuse ways, they were also creating their own micro-culture: the world of the chapel. Again it reflected evangelical values. The family Bible on the parlour table symbolized its centrality to this way of life. Yet chapel was different from the Anglican version of the evangelical ethos. Within the Church of England there was a profound deference for established authority, typified by long subscription lists headed by aristocracy (or even royalty) followed by the gentry and ending with the mere people. Evangelical Nonconformity, by contrast, was moulded by its experience of being outside the centres of power. Only since 1828, when the Test and Corporation Acts were repealed, had Nonconformists ceased in law to be second-class citizens and during the Victorian era they remained acutely conscious of their continuing disabilities. Their social composition in the period confirms that they were not among the great of the land. Michael Watts has convincingly shown that, far from being wholly bourgeois institutions, the chapels, at least in the early Victorian period, contained a large number of the poor. The Methodists, for example, were predominantly working-class. It is often supposed that, while the Primitive Methodists were working-class, the Wesleyans were middle-class. That turns out not to have been the case: all branches of Methodism had a majority of members drawn from the working classes.[23] Even at the end of the century the Baptists were similar, though Congregationalists were on average slightly higher in the social scale.[24] Nonconformity enjoyed the support of many artisans and their families. From the 1870s, with the growth of the tertiary sector of the economy, there was a mushrooming of clerks and small shopkeepers in Britain. Many of these lower middle classes were Nonconformists. The chapels of London were thronged with them, but the pattern was reproduced in the provinces. Even among the Primitive Methodists of Ashton-under-Lyne, the proportion of lower middle-class members quintupled between about 1860 and about 1900.[25] The strength of Nonconformity therefore lay among the working classes and, increasingly towards the end of Victoria's reign, the lower middle classes.

The self-image of the Nonconformist was therefore that of the common man. It is well established in the secondary literature on nineteenth-century Wales that Nonconformity thought of itself as representing *y gwerin*, 'the people'. But Welsh Nonconformity, despite the language barrier, was very close in spirit to English Nonconformity, and the same view prevailed east of Offa's Dyke. A Welsh instance is David Davies, a Baptist minister who doubled as a farmer in a remote area of Radnorshire. He despised formal dress, finding difficulty in manipulating his own neck-tie. Once at an ordination when he spied a minister of another denomination daring to wear a dog collar, he preached on John the Baptist, who, he said, did not look like a preacher. 'Some people', he exploded, 'seem to think a man can't preach unless he's got a silk hat and frock coat and *a collar without a beginning!*'[26] Affecting a clerical collar, in Davies's eyes, was to distance the preacher from the congregation, to create a barrier against the free communication of the gospel. Exactly the same attitude, however, is evident in England in Davies's hero Charles Haddon Spurgeon. He too denounced pretensions of dress in the pulpit, dismissing the wearing of black kid gloves by a preacher as 'effeminate vice'.[27] Each preacher he trained at his college, he insisted, must remain 'one of the people'.[28]

Hence Nonconformists were characteristically critical of the élite. Robert Vaughan, though in many respects a moderate man, was unsparing in a book of 1842: 'The wrongs privately inflicted on English congregationalism at this moment, by large classes of the wealthy and the powerful, are many, widely diffused and too often merciless – such as might well excuse . . . almost any measure of retaliation.'[29] Seven years later his fellow Congregationalist Edward Miall saw what he called 'the aristocratic sentiment' as the chief factor inhibiting the mission of the British churches.[30] The typical class consciousness of the nineteenth century was not that of the working people by themselves against

their middle-class employers, as so much *marxisant* historio-
graphy has supposed. Rather it was the stance of the 'industrious
classes', the middle and working classes together, against the
aristocracy and gentry who still dominated state and society.[31]
There was a strong affinity for the United States, where, it was
believed, the shackles of the aristocracy had already been thrown
off. The sturdy Nonconformists, retaining close links with their
American co-religionists, contributed a sharp edge to this temper.

The exaltation of the hard-working common man against the
corrupt upper classes explains much about the best-known critique of chapel culture penned during the nineteenth century. In
1869 Matthew Arnold published *Culture and Anarchy*. Arnold,
the son of the great headmaster of Rugby, had long been an
inspector of the voluntary schools run by the undenominational
British and Foreign School Society whose institutions were often
attached to chapels. In his book, which did so much to popularize
the use of the word 'culture', he vented his distaste for the
Hebraists of Nonconformity whose exaggerated religiosity was
not compensated for by any fostering of the Hellenic virtues of
sweetness and light.[32] Arnold was perceiving that the chapels did
not share his values. He appreciated all that the study of ancient
Greece had to offer: respect for art and poetry, etiquette and
good manners, and the ideals of the gentleman. By contrast
Spurgeon, whom Arnold singles out for censure, was bored by
Italian art galleries and announced that he hated the fashions of
society.[33] Against the ideal of the gentleman, like Elizabeth
Gaskell in *North and South*, Spurgeon set the image of the man.
'Manliness', he once declared, 'must never be sacrificed to
elegances.'[34] In one sense Arnold's assault was entirely unfair. He
was criticizing Nonconformists for not sharing the values
inculcated by the ancient universities. Until two years after the
publication of *Culture and Anarchy*, however, they were unable to
take degrees at Oxford or Cambridge. As a result, Spurgeon once
remarked that the motto of the University of Oxford should be,
not *Dominus illuminatio mea* (The Lord is my light), but *Aristoteles
meae tenebrae* (Aristotle is my darkness).[35] Nonconformists were
suspicious of the ancient English universities and what they
represented because they were excluded from them. In another
sense, nevertheless, Arnold hit the mark precisely. It was true
that in the 1860s chapelgoers rarely aspired to classical ideals.

Although later in the century a growing number would attend Oxford and Cambridge, the bulk of Nonconformity did represent a culture hostile to the ancient universities because they catered for the élite.

The greatest campaign of Victorian Nonconformity was a striking expression of its anti-élitism. During the Queen's reign the disestablishment movement rose in a mighty crescendo before falling away in a gradual diminuendo. The pressure group aiming for the separation of church and state, the Liberation Society, was the most powerful of political organizations, receiving around 1870 a higher annual income than the Liberal Party. In 1847 there had been a Dissenters' Parliamentary Committee to promote the return of anti-state-church MPs. Its address to Nonconformist electors captures something of the motivation behind the campaign. There was, first, an evangelical, or even evangelistic, concern. State policy, in upholding an established church, the committee claimed, was degrading 'God's appointed instrumentality for the regeneration of the world, into a mere system of police'. Then, secondly, there was a passionate sense of being put down by the existing establishment, in state as well as church: the Nonconformists' aim was to show Parliament that there were electors 'who have sufficient self-respect to resent gratuitous insult; [and] attachment enough to their principles to stand by them against any and every political confederacy'.[36] The first of these considerations reflected the evangelicalism of the chapels, the desire that the word of God should have free course, unimpeded by association with state power. The second showed that the chapels were also committed to their Nonconformity, objecting to the superior pretensions of the landed politicians who managed church and state. They were evangelical Nonconformists.

The chapel subculture in Victorian England and Wales was therefore firmly opposed to the established order and itself populist in tone. It possessed the strength of weakness: like the people among whom it conducted its mission, Nonconformity was not identified with status and power. There were therefore fewer unnecessary obstacles to its evangelistic effectiveness among them. The idealization of the common people, the rejection of élite values, created shared ground with those outside the chapel doors. That helps explain the continuing spate of church growth for much of Victoria's reign. In other apparently successful episodes in Christian history, the authority of the state was invoked to assist the work of the church: it was so under Constantine in the fourth century, under Ethelbert of Kent in 597 and in many a tribal kingdom of nineteenth-century Africa. Victorian Nonconformity, by contrast, consisted of self-conscious outsiders who eschewed, as much as Lord Acton, the corrupting use of power. Perhaps it therefore has more than most phases of the past to teach Christians in the West during the early twenty-first century, increasingly outside the centres of power in a secular age.

We can now turn to the second of the two main questions addressed in this chapter. How was Nonconformity itself moulded by its context? Three aspects of the cultural setting of Victorian Britain warrant consideration, one being a form of popular culture and two being versions of high culture. The prevailing popular culture, first of all, consisted partly of the customs inherited from the eighteenth century and the remoter past among the mass of the people. This was the plebeian culture presented by E. P. Thompson, marked by neighbourliness, respect for fair dealing and rough yet vibrant ways.[37] But this pattern had been modified by the increasing wealth associated with industrialization. During the Queen's reign people possessed more of the Victorian things that Asa Briggs has described in the book of that title.[38] There could be a print on the wall of the humblest cottage. There was a complex blend of the old and the new affecting the lives of the lower strata of society. Although a significant proportion of the lower working classes maintained some connection, perhaps only nominal, with the parish church, at least as many normally attended no place of worship. They entertained many non-Christian values, but they were generally far from secularist in their attitudes. On the contrary, there was a great deal of superstition in the countryside, and, as Sarah Williams has recently shown, an amalgam of Christian teaching and eclectic supernaturalism was also common in urban society at the end of the century.[39] Such popular cultural forms can have an influence outwards and upwards, affecting peer groups and those of higher standing in society. How then did these styles of life impinge on Nonconformity?

There could be a mingling in day-to-day life of plebeian themes with chapel culture. The popular supernaturalism, for example, could readily mesh with the evangelical awareness of divine

purpose in events. Thus members of Nonconformist congregations could be found opening their Bibles at random in quest of
spiritual guidance, much as their ancestors had observed animal
behaviour in order to assist in the making of choices. Yet there was
an ideological barrier between the plebeian and the chapel worlds:
justification by faith. It was axiomatic in traditional lore that God,
who pities the hardships of the poor, would welcome to a heavenly
rest all those who had done their best on earth. Faith in Christ as a
matter of personal allegiance found no place here. City missioners
commonly reported that conversations with ordinary folk would
go smoothly until they challenged them with calls to individual
trust in Christ. Chapelgoers were at a distance from popular
assumptions created by doctrine. There was also a practical
barrier. Chapel symbolized respectability, self-improvement and
getting on in the world. For those to whom these values meant
nothing, a Christian profession was a form of treachery to one's
mates. At Woolwich Arsenal at the end of the century, according to
a Congregationalist, a worker who was religious was a marked
man, rejected for implicitly claiming moral superiority.[40] From the
point of view of the chapelgoer, on the other hand, the rough
pleasures of plebeian life were viewed with distaste. They formed a
species of Vanity Fair that had detained so many but from which
the earnest Pilgrim had to escape. Between worldliness and
discipleship there was a great gulf fixed.

Consequently the influence of plebeian culture on the chapels
was primarily a matter of repulsion. The focus of sociability for
many of the poor was the ale-house. There were enormous
numbers of drink outlets. As late as 1905, by which time licensing
regulations were more stringent than they had once been, there
were in Lambeth 172 places of worship but as many as 430 drink
outlets.[41] Furthermore, public houses were usually close to
chapels. Both flourished in areas of divided landownership where
direction from above was insufficient to exclude both kinds of
nuisance from orderly Anglican communities. Drunkenness
seemed the enemy most resistant to the gospel. There was therefore Nonconformist sympathy for the anti-spirits societies that
arose from the early 1830s, the Primitive Methodists being
particularly attracted to the temperance cause. Total abstinence
took much longer to make headway, so that it was only from
the 1870s that chapels in general began to endorse it.[42] The

drunkard, it was hoped, would put away his bottle and then, in a less befuddled state, he might respond to the gospel. It is right to see this development as an extreme measure against the greatest rival to the chapels. Plebeian culture was less a moulder of the chapel world than its antagonist.

Our attention can move to the high cultural developments of the period. Was Nonconformity being influenced from above? Novel currents among nineteenth-century intellectuals certainly did have an impact. Most fall under the broad heading of romanticism. By that term is meant not merely the philosophy of the Lake Poets at the start of the century. Rather it is used here to encompass their cultural attitudes but also to denote the ethos that gradually spread to a wider public as the nineteenth century progressed. It represents the temper that emphasized mystery, intuition and history, the spiritual against the rational, the relative against the rigid and the natural against the artificial. How did these currents flow into Nonconformity?

The greatest impact was on the Unitarians. Before Victoria's reign this denomination had been dominated by the theology of Joseph Priestley, necessitarian, progressive, an extreme product of the eighteenth-century Enlightenment. A change began in the 1830s with the teachings of John Hamilton Thom and James Martineau, both ministers in Liverpool.[43] They upheld views similar to those of W. E. Channing and the New England Transcendentalists, the epitome of American romanticism. The chief source of inspiration for English Unitarians, however, was Germany, in the advanced thinkers who blended the latest idealist metaphysic into theology. This was the 'neology' so hated equally by Dr Pusey and the orthodox Nonconformists. Yet this version of Unitarianism was not far from orthodoxy: although Christ was portrayed as only human, his exalted spiritual consciousness was presented as giving him unique access to the divine. It is significant that the deepest inroads of romanticism into Nonconformist theology took place among the Unitarians, the nearest equivalent to a religious élite outside the Church of England. Their congregations, full of prosperous businessmen and professionals, maintained high educational standards. It was the Unitarians who were the most open to the latest ideas.

Within evangelical Nonconformity a much smaller proportion had their thinking profoundly affected by romantic trends. One such figure was J. Denholm Brash, a Wesleyan minister who in his last years around the end of the century professed to believe in the innate goodness of man and the ultimate salvation of all. He acknowledged his debt to Martineau.[44] It was slightly more common for Congregationalists to be swayed in a similar more liberal theological direction. The typical contemporary emphasis on the spiritual eroded traditional doctrinal convictions and generated broader religious views. Thus James Baldwin Brown, in his work *The Divine Life in Man* (1859), expounded the fatherhood of God, human freedom and the law of righteousness, dwelling on the standard romantic motif of human growth. Again he was from the élite of Nonconformity: one of the first to receive a degree from London University in 1839, he went on to serve one of the most prosperous of suburban congregations, the Independent church at Brixton.[45] Closely associated with cultural relativism, another feature of romantic thought, was biblical criticism. The so-called higher criticism, though accepted in principle by most Nonconformist scholars by the 1890s, was also embraced more readily by those with higher educational standards.[46] The least resistance was once more among the Congregationalists, whose average status was higher than that of other evangelical Nonconformists. So liberal theological tendencies generated by romantic patterns of thought did impinge on Nonconformists, but chiefly on some of those with greater intellectual attainments rather than on the mass of the occupants of the pews.

The same cultural setting, however, also pointed certain Nonconformists in a conservative direction. From the late 1820s the romantic frame of mind had encouraged Edward Irving, J. N. Darby and their disciples to engage in prophetic speculations. Their premillennial teaching that Christ would soon return gradually spread within evangelicalism. Its influence was far greater in the Church of England than in Nonconformity, but it penetrated the Baptists through their imprecise frontier with the so-called Plymouth Brethren. In 1868 a correspondent of *The Baptist Magazine* wrote with assurance of the different 'dispensations', a buzz-word of the followers of Darby. Yet it is more significant that another correspondent complained that the term was incomprehensible.[47] Premillennialism had little appeal for the Baptists and was almost non-existent elsewhere in mainstream Nonconformity. Likewise there arose from the late 1860s a distinctive form of holiness teaching that mirrored romantic sensibilities. Chiefly focused on the Keswick Convention, the movement drew in a few Nonconformists, the best known being F. B. Meyer. Spurgeon, however, was more typical in his robust reaction: 'One thing I notice,' he remarked, 'when a brother gets perfectly holy he becomes perfectly useless.'[48] The conservative impact of romantic attitudes on popular Nonconformist theology was even more marginal than its liberal equivalent. The fresh cultural influences of the century, we may conclude, reshaped Unitarianism, modified the thinking of a number of the more educated evangelical Nonconformists in a liberal fashion and of a few others in a conservative manner, but were distinctly limited in their inroads.

Hence the bulk of Nonconformity remained a bastion of inherited values rather than a sponsor of the innovations of the nineteenth century. Victorian Nonconformist leaders frequently warned against the rising tide of romantic sentiment. Thus J. P. Mursell, as chairman of the Baptist Union in 1864, cautioned against undue sympathy with the aesthetic spirit exemplified by tendencies in architecture and worship towards 'the imposing and ornate'.[49] There was a deep aversion among Nonconformists to the sense of mystery cultivated by the disciples of the Oxford Movement around the Eucharist. It caused a reaction among them away from the residual Calvinistic theology of the Lord's Supper as a distinctive means of grace towards a form of memorialism that sometimes gloried in the real absence of Christ from the feast.[50] Spurgeon indiscriminately denounced Gothic for chapels, organs for worship and gowns for preachers. His famous resistance to theological innovation in the Down Grade controversy of 1887–8 must be placed in this context. Spurgeon was not, as is sometimes supposed, attacking Arminianism in defence of the Reformed faith. Rather, he was rejecting the theological reformulation in a romantic idiom undertaken by men such as Baldwin Brown as an inadequate statement of the gospel. The change, Spurgeon pointed out, had gone further among the Congregationalists than among the Baptists.[51] The foes of the gospel, as he had put it in an article of 1876, were modern culture, intellectual preaching and aesthetic taste.[52] Spurgeon was a champion of the older cultural synthesis still upheld by Nonconformity as a whole.

The legacy from the past was a deposit shared alike by Calvinists such as Charles Spurgeon and Arminians such as John Clifford. It was deeply indebted to the high cultural phenomenon of the eighteenth century usually labelled the Enlightenment. The rise of the evangelical movement in church and chapel during that century had been closely associated with the Enlightenment.[53] Wesley had exalted the role of reason as much as Voltaire. Evangelicals therefore displayed many of the characteristics of Enlightenment thought and practice as they entered the nineteenth century, and the Nonconformists among them retained these qualities during the Victorian epoch. They believed, for instance, in empirical method. Joseph Angus, the principal of Regent's Park College, the Baptist institution then sited in London, taught in the 1860s that theology is an inductive science. The theologian must proceed on Baconian lines, taking the texts of scripture as its factual building blocks.[54] The Nonconformist theological colleges, as much as their counterparts in America, used the common-sense philosophy of the Scottish school as the foundation of their instruction.[55] Although it held that first principles have to be assumed, it was essentially empirical, not deductive. It was easy to wed this philosophy with science by means of natural theology, a resilient British tradition of apologetic. The evidences in the world, it was argued, confirmed the existence of a designing purpose and therefore of a Creator. One of the chief works by the leading mind in early nineteenth-century Congregationalism, John Pye Smith, fell into this tradition. His book *On the Relation between the Holy Scriptures and Some Parts of Geological Science* (1839) sought to establish a harmony between revelation and recent discoveries.[56] Later in the century, natural theology remained the tradition within which it was possible for Nonconformist writers such as John Clifford to come to terms with the Darwinian revolution. Purpose, they contended, could still be discerned in an evolutionary world if it was not presumed from the start to be absent.[57] An essentially Enlightenment framework remained immensely useful.

In a similar way the optimism of the Enlightenment was still embodied in Victorian Nonconformity. It has been recognized that in America the idea of progress, so powerful during the nineteenth century, was strongly indebted to postmillennial theology,[58] and the same needs to be appreciated for England.

Postmillennialists held that the peace and prosperity of the millennium would be attained by the steady spread of the gospel and the consequent extension of Christian values. Thus *The General Baptist Magazine* for 1854 carried an article on 'The Millennium', arguing that the triumph of the gospel would usher in an end to war, famine, oppressive taxes, crime, drunkenness, slavery, scandal, loose talk and false teaching. Because all this would take time, the writer calculated that their completion could be expected only in 2016![59] Secular advocates of progress such as John Stuart Mill possessed no grander vision.

The supreme characteristic of the Enlightenment was its pragmatism. Traditional institutions, however venerable, must be reformed if they did not work effectively. Victorian Nonconformists still gloried in their own adaptability. The whole Methodist structure, it was authoritatively claimed, existed simply to serve the spread of the gospel most efficiently.[60] Hence late Victorian Methodist revivalists, Thomas Champness among them, had no hesitation in introducing entirely new methods such as Gospel Mission Cars.[61] Perhaps more surprisingly, Baptists, whose *raison d'être* depended on an ecclesiology deduced from scripture, were prepared to modify their polity drastically by admitting to communion those unbaptized as believers. A small party, the promoters of *The Primitive Church Magazine*, resisted the innovation, but *The Baptist Magazine*, the denomination's semi-official organ, maintained a neutral stance on the issue, refusing to condemn an increasingly popular practice.[62] Change was possible because pragmatism took precedence over principle, another triumph for the spirit of the Enlightenment. That was the chief cultural factor moulding Victorian Nonconformity.

The two sides of this examination can, in conclusion, be brought together. The gospel created in the chapels a community that was deeply committed to the values of the common man: it looked down on, not up to, the élite. Because evangelical Nonconformity was not identified with the trend-setters of the time, nor was it readily swept along by the incoming tide of romantic ideas, Nonconformists as a whole adhered to the assumptions of a previous generation of cultural leaders, the commonplaces of the Enlightenment. That stance served them well in the Victorian age. Because society at large was deeply imbued with rational, pragmatic values, Nonconformists found a natural place within it and attracted many of their contemporaries to join them. Victorian Nonconformity represents a success story. It achieved a close identification with the common people without any sacrifice of the substance of the faith, a true indigenization of the Christian religion.

Notes

[1] T. S. Eliot, *Notes Towards the Definition of Culture* (London, 1948).

[2] H. R. Niebuhr, *Christ and Culture* (New York, 1951).

[3] The most illuminating contribution in this field is perhaps A. F. Walls, *The Missionary Movement in Christian History: Studies in the Transmission of Faith* (Edinburgh, 1996).

[4] Hugh Montefiore (ed.), *The Gospel and Contemporary Culture* (London, 1992).

[5] The classic analysis of this aspect of the subject is Raymond Williams, *Culture and Society, 1780–1850* (London, 1958).

[6] For example, Peter Burke, *Popular Culture in Early Modern Europe* (London, 1978).

[7] J. A. Loewen, 'Evangelism and culture', in C. R. Padilla (ed.), *The New Face of Evangelicalism: An International Symposium on the Lausanne Covenant* (London, 1976).

[8] Boyd Hilton, *The Age of Atonement: The Influence of Evangelicalism on Social and Economic Thought* (Oxford, 1988).

[9] D. M. Thompson, *Nonconformity in the Nineteenth Century* (London, 1972), 152–3.

[10] M. R. Watts, *The Dissenters*, ii. *The Expansion of Evangelical Nonconformity* (Oxford, 1995).

[11] A. D. Gilbert, *Religion and Society in Industrial England: Church, Chapel and Social Change, 1740–1914* (London, 1976), 39.

[12] Robert Vaughan, *The Age of Great Cities* (London, 1843).

[13] Anthony Howe, *The Cotton Masters, 1830–1860* (Oxford, 1984), 62.

[14] A. M. Ramsey, *From Gore to Temple: The Development of Anglican Theology between 'Lux Mundi' and the Second World War* (London, 1960).

[15] *The Baptist Magazine* (June 1866), 365.

[16] J. Scott Lidgett, *My Guided Life* (London, 1936), 157.

[17] S. K. Hocking, *My Book of Memory* (London, 1923), 71–2.

[18] Valentine Cunningham, *Everywhere Spoken Against: Dissent in the Victorian Novel* (Oxford, 1975), 59–60.

[19] Leonore Davidoff and Catherine Hall, *Family Fortunes: Men and Women of the English Middle Classes, 1780–1850* (London, 1987).

20 J. R. Walkowitz, *Prostitution and Victorian Society: Women, Class and the State* (Cambridge, 1980), 122.

21 D. W. Bebbington, *The Nonconformist Conscience: Chapel and Politics, 1870–1914* (London, 1982), 38–42.

22 Ibid., 15–17, 153–7.

23 Watts, *Dissenters*, ii, 319–27; C. D. Field, 'The social structure of English Methodism: eighteenth–twentieth centuries', *British Journal of Sociology*, 28 (1977), 199–225.

24 Hugh McLeod, *Class and Religion in the Late Victorian City* (London, 1974), 33.

25 Field, 'Social structure', 209.

26 Edward Davies and Rhys Davies, *The Life of the Late Revd David Davies, Maesyrhelem* (Brecon, 1914), 64.

27 C. H. Spurgeon, *Lectures to my Students* (London, 1954), 301.

28 C. H. Spurgeon to Mr Sawday, sen., 12 Apr. 1862, in Charles Spurgeon (ed.), *The Letters of Charles Haddon Spurgeon* (London, 1923), 191.

29 Robert Vaughan, *Congregationalism: Or, the Polity of Independent Churches, Viewed in Relation to the State and Tendencies of Modern Society*, 2nd edn (London, 1842), vii.

30 Edward Miall, *The British Churches in Relation to the British People* (London, 1849), chap. 4.

31 This recognition is most apparent in Patrick Joyce, *Visions of the People: Industrial England and the Question of Class, c. 1848–1914* (London, 1991).

32 Matthew Arnold, *Culture and Anarchy and Other Writings*, ed. Stefan Collini (Cambridge, 1993), chap. 4.

33 Patricia S. Kruppa, *Charles Haddon Spurgeon: A Preacher's Progress* (New York, 1982), 218; Spurgeon, *Lectures*, 21.

34 Spurgeon, *Lectures*, 299.

35 Ibid., 78.

36 Edwin Hodder, *The Life of Samuel Morley* (London, 1887), 104.

37 E. P. Thompson, 'The patricians and the plebs', in his *Customs in Common* (London, 1991).

38 Asa Briggs, *Victorian Things* (London, 1988).

39 James Obelkevich, *Religion and Rural Society: South Lindsey, 1825–1875* (Oxford, 1976), chap. 6. S. C. Williams, 'Urban popular religion and the rites of passage', in Hugh McLeod (ed.), *European Religion in the Age of Great Cities, 1830–1930* (London, 1995).

40 Geoffrey Crossick, *An Artisan Elite in Victorian Society: Kentish London, 1840–1880* (London, 1978), 144.

41 Jeffrey Cox, *The English Churches in a Secular Society: Lambeth, 1870–1930* (New York, 1982), 24.

[42] Brian Harrison, *Drink and the Victorians: The Temperance Question in England, 1815–1872* (London, 1971), chap. 8.

[43] R. K. Webb, 'John Hamilton Thom: Intellect and conscience in Liverpool', in P. T. Phillips (ed.), *The View from the Pulpit: Victorian Ministers and Society* (Toronto, 1978), 210–43. Ralph Waller, 'James Martineau: the development of his thought', in Barbara Smith (ed.), *Truth, Liberty, Religion: Essays Celebrating Two Hundred Years of Manchester College* (Oxford, 1986), 225–64.

[44] W. B. Brash, *Love and Life: The Story of J Denholm Brash*, 2nd edn (London, 1913), 79–80, 105.

[45] M. T. E. Hopkins, 'Baptists, Congregationalists and theological change: some late nineteenth-century leaders and controversies' (Oxford D.Phil. thesis, 1988), chap. 1.

[46] W. B. Glover, *Evangelical Nonconformists and Higher Criticism in the Nineteenth Century* (London, 1954).

[47] The exchange between R. Govett of Norwich and Samuel Green of Hammersmith is in *The Baptist Magazine* (July 1868), 461–4; (Aug. 1868), 528–30; (Dec. 1868), 792–5.

[48] *The Freeman* (20 Apr. 1883), 245.

[49] *The Baptist Magazine* (May 1864), 278.

[50] Michael Walker, *Baptists at the Table: The Theology of the Lord's Supper amongst English Baptists in the Nineteenth Century* (Didcot, 1992), chap. 3.

[51] *The Sword and the Trowel* (Sept. 1887), 464.

[52] *The Sword and the Trowel* (July 1876), 306.

[53] D. W. Bebbington, *Evangelicalism in Modern Britain: A History from the 1730s to the 1980s* (London, 1989), chap. 2.

[54] Joseph Angus, *Theology: An Inductive and Progressive Science* (London, n.d.), 20–1.

[55] Spurgeon's institution, the Pastors' College, for instance, used Sir William Hamilton's *Lectures on Metaphysics* from 1870: *Annual paper descriptive of the Lord's work connected with the Pastors' College, during the year 1870* (London, 1871), 19.

[56] J. Pye Smith, *On the Relation between the Holy Scriptures and Some Parts of Geological Science* (London, 1839).

[57] John Clifford, 'Charles Darwin: or evolution and Christianity', *Typical Christian Leaders* (London, 1889), 233.

[58] T. L. Smith, *Revivalism and Social Reform: American Protestantism on the Eve of the Civil War*, 2nd edn (New York, 1965), chap. 14.

[59] *The General Baptist Magazine* (July 1854), 308–11.

[60] J. H. Rigg, *A Comparative View of Church Organizations, Primitive and Protestant* (London, 1887).

[61] Josiah Mee, *Thomas Champness as I Knew Him* (London, n.d.), chap. 6.

[62] *The Baptist Magazine* (Apr. 1846), 237–8; (Apr. 1857), 240.

5

Politics and the pulpit: Robert Hall and the 'Signs of the Times'

JOHN BRIGGS

The context of the sermon

'The Signs of the Times', an expressive phrase from Matthew's gospel,[1] has commanded the attention of many preachers over the ages.[2] In 1820, nine years before Thomas Carlyle wrote his famous article for the *Edinburgh Review* under that title,[3] Robert Hall delivered a sermon in Bristol which was similarly titled. The beneficiary of the sermon was the Bristol Auxiliary of the British and Foreign Schools Society at a time when Church and Dissent were in dispute over national education. Lord Brougham had produced a bill to effect this, but it seemed to please neither party. The Anglicans did not like the emphasis on simple Bible instruction and the Dissenters the requirement that the schoolmaster be a communicant of the Church, or the fact that the children, unless parental consciences dictated otherwise, were to be catechized in church on Sundays.[4]

On another occasion, Hall had this to say on the issue:

> To contend for the legal monopoly of religious instruction, under pretence of securing the morals of the people, is a similar kind of policy with that of the papists, who withhold the Scriptures from the common people, lest they should be betrayed into heresy.[5]

Even though Baptists were committed to the idea of universal educational provision, they were not prepared to support it, if the price to be paid was a substantial extension of the establishment principle. That then was the immediate context for Hall's address, but the language of 'Signs of the Times' had a particular intellectual pedigree.

'Signs of the Times' writings

In fact, expositors of 'Signs of the Times'[6] can be classified into two broad categories: on the one hand, those who penned millenarian calendars of great precision and, on the other, more practical kingdom-watchers who sought to realize their eschatology by persuading themselves that in the unfolding patterns of history in their own day they could discern undeniable signs of the establishment of the rule of God. Whilst the former were in danger of programming God to a timetable of their own devising, the latter could easily become secularized, as indeed in Carlyle's use of the phrase, or in the writings of liberal Nonconformists later in the century. A second line of division would separate optimists from pessimists: did the signs of the times invite believers to embrace change confidently, or did they threaten disaster to the Christian inheritance? Were they signs in fact of the threshold of Armageddon or some similar fate? Or could Christians by such a device sanctify Whig hopes of progress?

Sometimes the several genres merged into one. James Bicheno (*c.*1752–1831),[7] a Bristol College man who came from Robert Robinson's church in Cambridge, had a twenty-seven-year ministry at the Particular Baptist church at Newbury in Berkshire (1780–1807). In 1793 he penned a fascinating volume entitled *The Signs of the Times: or the Overthrow of Papal Tyranny in France, the prelude of the Destruction to Popery and Despotism; but of Peace to Mankind.* This he published privately, though successfully, for the work went into several editions.[8] The great questions posed by the French Revolution were: 'Is it one of those commotions produced by the conflicting passions of men, that rise and sink, and are soon forgotten? Or is it one of those events which mark the great eras of time, and from which originate new orders of things?' Reading the French Revolution in the light of Jesus' eschatological discourses, and the prophecies of the Book of Daniel and the Book of Revelation, the events of 1789 were seen to be those foretold in scripture. Bicheno easily identified Louis XIV as the beast of Revelation 13 and saw the fall of the French royal house as heralding a millennium to be ushered in in 1864. These events were significant not only for heralding the coming of liberty to the French but, from an English Protestant perspective, as the sure and certain commencement of the fall of papal power. More positively Bicheno rejoiced in the manifestation in his day of the two witnesses of Revelation 11 identified by him as the joint ministry of 'gospel truth' and 'civil liberty'.

This was not an uncommon reaction among Baptists to the traumatic events in France. For example, the deacons of the Maze Pond Particular Baptist Chapel in Southwark wrote to their pastor, noting 'the wonderful Revolution, that a neighbouring nation hitherto groaning under ecclesiastical and civil Tyranny' has recently experienced as also 'the ardor for Liberty extending itself to other Countries'. Both were causes for thanksgiving to God, and as such were to be seen 'as links in that great chain of Events foretold in Scripture which will finally issue in [Christ's] glory and the happiness of Mankind'. However, at home there was still much persecution and as yet an inadequate measure of freedom accorded to Dissenters. The pastor, who is complimented on his 'repeated exertions to advance the cause of Humanity and Universal Freedom', was consequently requested by his fifteen deacons to prepare a series of winter lectures 'on the principles of Nonconformity, and of civil and religious Liberty'.[9]

In contrast to such Dissenting optimism, several prelates on the episcopal bench were much more inclined to pessimistic hypothesizing.[10] The suggestion was that events in Europe were part of some great international conspiracy against the Christian religion which was at the end of the eighteenth century unfolding in accordance with apocalyptic predictions. No one was more eloquent on this theme than Samuel Horsley, successively bishop of St David's, Rochester and St Asaph, whose writings were on several occasions the trigger to such of Hall's polemical responses as his *Apology for the Freedom of the Press* and his *Defence of Village Preaching*. Horsley, a convinced believer in the Divine Right of Kings, saw the execution of Louis XVI as directly the consequence of English precedents: 'O my Country! Read the horror of thy own deed in this recent heightened imitation! Lament and weep, that this black French treason should have found its example, in the crime of thy unnatural sons!'[11] In the charge which accompanied his primary visitation of the Rochester diocese following his translation in 1793, he identified the contemporary situation as one of the most potentially dangerous that the Christian church had had to face 'since its first struggles with the powers of darkness in the first centuries': 'The signs of the times are such as may create an apprehension that the hour of trial is not far distant.'[12]

Horsley owed nothing to Dissenting millenarians in his psychedelic use of language. Not fearing to speak of the Anti-Christ, now identified with the republican supplanter of kings, Napoleon, he anticipated the rising 'out of the raging sea of Anarchy and Irreligion' of 'the dreadful Apocalyptic Beast . . . in its ancient form'.[13] Apocalyptic was as much a part of the mental coinage of conservative churchmen in the late eighteenth century as of that of radical Dissenters.

John Gill, eighteenth-century London's leading high Calvinist amongst the Baptists, was not highly regarded by Robert Hall, who spoke of his voluminous works over-contemptuously as 'a continent of mud'. Whereas Gill's view of election has long been taken as an impediment to effective evangelism, his eschatology is championed by James de Jong as being 'strongly evangelistic', which 'undoubtedly contributed' to the rebirth of missions among the Particular Baptists.[14] His vision of *The Glory of the Church in the Latter Day* (1753), was of

> a sett of gospel ministers . . . discharging their office with great readiness and swiftness, and in the most public manner in the church of God; 'having the everlasting gospel', not a little dry morality, but the gospel of the grace of God, the good news of life and salvation by Jesus Christ.

These ministers will be 'very diligent and industrious', taking advantage of 'an open door set' which 'no man can shut'; an opportunity of 'preaching the gospel everywhere', activity which Gill predicted would be blessed by 'very large conversions everywhere' from those previously Roman Catholic, Moslem and pagan. Thus arguably there was a duality about the legacy of John Gill, a belief in the global claims of God's kingdom but accompanied by a belief that the timetable for extending its boundaries was his sovereign prerogative. When in the generation after his death

> the impetuous William Carey tried to force the divinely determined pace for history in his famous sermon to the Northamptonshire Association, he was duly reminded of this truth. But with the outbreak

of the French Revolution it appeared to many that God had begun that decisive battle against AntiChrist for which they had been waiting.[15]

Some of Andrew Fuller's reported preaching, for example, is presented in the language of apocalyptic as demonstrated by De Jong, who refers to Fuller deploying the language of Babylon, the four beasts and the anticipation of the marriage of the Lamb.[16]

Hall's exposition of *The Signs of the Times*, which is two decades later than Bicheno and Horsley, is far less alarmist. He affirmed from Matthew's text that, whilst engaging in any kind of futurology was dangerous, there was a moral duty, incumbent on all Christians, to discern the significance of events and developments in the world that was contemporary to them, though he does not underestimate the difficulty of the task. Thus Hall described the Book of Revelation as 'a composition distinguished above all others by a profusion of obscure, figurative diction; delineating by a sort of hieroglyphics, the principal Revolutions destined to befall the Christian church, from the earliest times till the consummation of all things'. 'This portion of scripture', he continued, 'is a fertile mine of erroneous, extravagant conjecture, and supplies, by its injudicious interpretation, more gratification to a heated imagination, to a taste for the marvellous and the incredible, than the whole of the New Testament beside' (*Works*, iv. 348). Notwithstanding the dangers of such prejudiced and unbalanced deductions, perceiving God's purposes in history, Hall argued, not only provided critical insight into the divine character, but provided a basis for both intelligent prayer and responsible action.[17] Moreover this kind of exercise put the events of human history in a proper context:

The welfare of a nation depends much less on the refined wisdom of the few, than on the manners and character of the many; and as moral and religious principles have the chief influence in forming that character, so an acknowledgment of the hand of God, a deep sense of his dominion, is among the first of those principles. While we attend to the operation of second causes, let us never forget that there is a Being placed above them, who can move and arrange them at pleasure, and in whose hands they never fail to accomplish the purposes of his unerring counsel.[18]

In his sermon Hall eschews the extensive citation of scripture: the text from Matthew 16 is the only identified scripture in the whole sermon, though several others are glossed as it progresses. Hall's vision was more for contemporary life, which he saw as offering six signs of divine providence at work in the historical process.

'Signs of the Times' identified

1. 'The great increase of mental exertion'

The first sign he perceived was in 'the great increase of mental exertion', which he later identifies with 'an age of universal curiosity'. This he identifies as standing over against lengthy periods of intellectual stagnation and decline. In this respect, the Reformation marked a new beginning when ordinary men 'began to investigate truth for themselves'. In true Whig fashion he continues, 'they started to that career of genius and science which has ever since been rapidly advancing'. After paying tribute to Isaac Newton, Hall identified advances in chemistry, moral and political philosophy, and legislation towards liberty of conscience as marks of intellectual advance. Outward signs of this could be seen both in the architecture of the modern Bristol and in the extensive circulation of literature and ideas amongst its population.[19]

This was a subject on which Hall had already elaborated in a sermon preached on behalf of the infant Stepney College.[20] He was careful not to claim too much for collegiate education: it could not 'make' a minister, only help those whom God had called to exploit more effectively the gifts he had given them. 'An unconverted ministry we look upon as the greatest calamity that can befall the church; nor would we be supposed to insinuate . . . that education can ever be a proper substitute for native talent much less real piety' (*Works*, vi. 363–4). The demand for the new college was itself a testimony to changes in society which demanded a better equipped ministry, through 'enlisting literature in the service of religion'. Whilst affirming 'the absolute sufficiency of the Scriptures' (*Works*, vi. 362), Hall believed that to secure a proper understanding of the sacred writings, it was necessary to engage in supplementary reading to illuminate both treasure and obscurity within that record. Beyond this the serious scholar has to contemplate the nature of the biblical record itself, which Hall defined as

> A collection of writings, composed on various occasions, and at remote intervals of time, including detached portions of history the most ancient, and of poetry awfully sublime, but often obscure, – a book containing continual allusion to matters unknown in this part of the world, and to institutions which have long ceased to exist. (*Works*, vi. 362)

Reason, educated to the limitations of its capacity, was not to be opposed to revelation, for truth must always be consistent with itself. Moreover revelation must necessarily communicate itself through the human intelligence. The diffusion of knowledge in society at large in the early nineteenth century, put a new premium upon an educated ministry, which was even more a necessity because of the circulation of much literature in this new urban world which was hostile to the interests of true religion.

2. 'An increased attention to the instruction of the lower orders'

The second hopeful development, which developed quite closely from this, was 'an increased attention to the instruction of the lower orders'. This topic he had contemplated in greater detail ten years previously in his consideration of knowledge and the lower classes.[21] The arguments for such activity Hall himself found compelling: 'when you have given the poor the habit of thinking, you have conferred on them a much greater favour than by the gift of a large sum of money, since you have put them in possession of the principle of all legitimate prosperity' (*Works*, vi. 152). Negatively, a lack of education must leave the poor in a situation of wretchedness and misery. Hall swiftly dismissed the argument that the education of the poor, by lifting them above their station in life and thereby making them dissatisfied with their lot, represented a threat to the tranquillity of the state. On the contrary, 'Nothing in reality renders legitimate governments so insecure as extreme ignorance in the people. It is this which yields them an easy prey to seduction . . .' Thus, 'The true prop of good government is . . . a settled conviction . . . of it being a public good' (*Works*, vi. 153). In the annals of the French

Revolution it was the uneducated masses who took the Revolution into the excesses of murderous bloodshed.

Hall's concern for the poor was not confined to their education: the over-taxation of their modest wages not only prevented them from educating their children but made even the provision of daily bread for their offspring problematic. Moreover, the poor laws confined them to locations where they were unable to secure that employment which would enable them to make proper provision for their families:

> Were industry allowed to find its level, were the poor laws abolished, and a small portion of that expense which swells the tide of corruption, the splendours of the great, and the miseries of war, bestowed on the instruction of the common people, the happy effects would descend to the remotest posterity, and open a prospect which humanity might delight to anticipate.

But in fact England's governors had been 'deaf to the complaints of the poor', whilst they mindlessly observed 'ignorance, wretchedness and barbarity multiply at home, without the smallest regard' (*Freedom of the Press*, in *Works*, iv. 120).[22]

Teaching was, in Hall's judgement, part of the dominical command to the disciples which, in large measure neglected by the Church of Rome, was reinstituted as a Christian priority by the Reformers. Since reason was the distinguishing feature of the human species, it would be a scandal to neglect the cultivation of this most human attribute in persons of all classes. Such an emphasis was proper, even though, from the beginning of church history, the cultivation of the mind seemed to be most easily achieved by the urban middle orders amongst whom it has been found the easiest to establish Christian churches. This appeal to rationality was a constant theme in Hall's writings, suggesting a desire to appeal to an 'Age of Reason' rather than to attack its aspirations: it explains why Hall underwrote the general terms of Paley's argument from design, which he lays out quite clearly in his sermon on 'Modern Infidelity'.[23]

At the heart of all knowledge, however, was that religious knowledge which was essential to both salvation and the living of the godly life. Thus Hall commended the Sunday school movement which he saw as contributing so much both to the diffusion of knowledge (*Works*, vi. 163) and the improvement of the lower

orders. But that was not enough. He exhorted the teachers of the
Sunday school not to be content with the knowledge of the Bible
in academic isolation without seeking the Spirit of Christ to apply
the written word to the needs of the individual.

> While the philosopher wearies himself with endless speculations on
> their physical properties and nature, while the politician only
> contemplates the social arrangements of mankind, and the shifting
> forms of policy, fix your attention on the individual importance of
> man, as the creature of God, and a candidate for immortality. . . . Let
> the salvation of these children be the object, to which every word of
> your instructions, every exertion of your authority, is directed. (*Works*,
> vi. 162)

Such work was of vital importance: 'while a spirit of giddiness
and revolt is shed upon the nations . . . , the improvement of the
mass of the people will be our grand security' (*Works*, vi. 163).

3. 'The improved state of preaching and the more abundant supply of the means of grace'

Thirdly, Hall noted 'the improved state of preaching' and 'the
more abundant supply of the means of grace'. Dating this change
to the latter part of the eighteenth century, he paid particular
tribute to the renewed piety and diligence of many of the clergy
of the Anglican Church. Moreover, looking beyond the shores of
Britain, it was pertinent to recognize the period in which he was
writing as 'the very era of missions' (*Works*, vi. 188–9). Home and
overseas missions, as well as the growth of the great religious
societies of the turn of the century, were part of the one
movement of renewal here noted.

Hall had much to say about this in his critical response to an
anonymous volume, hostile to Dissent, entitled *Zeal without
Innovation*, published in 1808. Hall's extensive review appeared
in *The Eclectic Review*.[24] He, like so many other Dissenters of his
age, was unpersuaded of the efficacy of the articles of the
established church in protecting its orthodoxy when the message
of those articles seemed more revered outside the boundaries of
the Church than within them. 'A long course of experience has
clearly demonstrated the inefficacy of creeds and confessions to
perpetuate religious belief. Of this the only faithful depository is,

not that "written with ink", but [that] engraved on the "fleshly tables of the heart"' (*Works*, vi. 278). The debate turned on the issue of form and reality; whereas the defender of establishment bemoaned the empty pews in many parish churches and the popularity of Dissent, Hall argued that empty pews were not simply caused by infidelity among the people but rather, when the pattern of preaching was so variable, by people's discernment as to where they could find the gospel faithfully proclaimed: there were many churches which rightly ought to be empty!

As over against the dismal diagnosis of the author of *Zeal without Innovation*, Hall writes,

> we have no doubt of the kingdom of Christ making sensible advances; and in support of this opinion, we adduce the wider extension of religious truth, the multitude of places where the gospel is preached in its purity, the general disposition to attend it, the establishment of Sunday schools, the circulation, with happy effect, of innumerable tracts, the translation of the Scriptures into foreign languages, and their more extensive communication to all nations, the formation of missionary societies, the growing unanimity among christians, and the prodigious increase of faithful ministers in the established church. (*Works*, vi. 290)

To such a catalogue of achievement, which constitutes 'the distinguishing features in the aspects of the times' (*Works*, vi. 291), the would-be defender of establishments was apparently blind. In fact this list of missionary developments anticipates fairly closely the marks he identified a decade later in *The Signs of the Times*, though by 1820 the signs perceived embrace aspects of cultural development that are not exclusively religious.

Challenging the utility of subscribing to articles of religion, Hall argued that such articles only had a validity when, as in Cranmer's day, they reflected the faith of the people. But subsequent developments, identified by Hall as the intrusion into church doctrine of a low Arminianism, the intolerance of Laud, and the occupation of the pulpit with a species of moralistic scholasticism rather than the challenge of the peculiar teachings of the Christian gospel, had failed to nurture faith. 'The consequence was', Hall argued, 'that the creed established by law had no sort of influence in forming the sentiments of the people . . . and the English became the most irreligious people upon earth'

(*Works*, vi. 294). Indeed Reformed doctrine, that is the faith of the articles, was more clearly to be found among the Dissenters than amongst those who formally subscribed to them. Here was the irony: 'that the doctrines of the church, with or without subscription, are sure to perpetuate themselves where they are faithfully preached; but that the mere circumstance of them being subscribed, will neither secure their being preached nor believed' (*Works*, vi. 278).

The evangelical clergy, whose growth in numbers Hall warmly applauded, were, however, diligent in preaching the faith of the articles, 'the doctrines which relate to the way of salvation, or the method of a sinner's reconciliation with God' (*Works*, vi. 297), but for their pains were in danger of being labelled Methodist by the great majority of the clergy. If their preaching was to be censured then in consistency the articles of the church, rather than being subscribed to, ought to be cancelled.

In fact, the impact of the evangelical party, both within and beyond the established church, had been the means of reviving the fortune of the Christian religion in Britain to such an extent that Wesley and Whitfield could with justice be acclaimed as 'the second Reformers of England' (*Works*, vi. 294). This movement, though properly concentrating on a spiritual ministry, was not wanting in its encouragement of practical Christianity. Though 'they ascribe their transition from a state of death to a state of justification solely to faith in Christ previous to good works actually performed, yet they equally insist upon performance of those works as the evidence of justifying faith' (*Works*, vi. 301). Such an emphasis was evidenced by the support the Evangelical clergy gave to 'the excellent work of Mr Wilberforce, which is not more conspicuous for the orthodoxy of its tenets than for the purity and energy of its moral instruction' (*Works*, vi. 302).[25] In short, the evangelical clergy were Christian ministers who were in earnest about 'a visible reformation in society at large' (*Works*, vi. 302).

4. 'The advancement of the Bible as the great and only standard of Christian faith and practice'

Fourthly, there was 'the advancement of the Bible as the great and only standard of Christian faith and practice' (*Works*, vi. 189). On numerous occasions Hall preached on behalf of the Bible Society and its local auxiliaries.[26] The whole enterprise impressed Hall greatly, with its ambition not just to circulate the scriptures around the world as best they could, but 'to lay them open, if possible, to all classes of society in every nation', that is to say, the Bible Society's programme was a democratic one, targeting not just an élite but all members of society.

Hall vigorously argued against those who believed that the Bible should only be circulated with a commentary, indicating the right interpretation of the text, for the scriptures themselves would necessarily need to be the test of that commentary. Similarly he attacked the notion that 'people must be content to derive their religious information through the medium of priests'.[27] By contrast, the scriptures freely available to ordinary people were a liberating agency. The consequences of their free dissemination would not only be spiritual, in inculcating a knowledge of gospel truth, but would also be highly desirable in promoting a higher morality and improvements through the exchange of rational argument.

The Bible Society had secured unique patronage:

> This idea of the Bible Society has [been] nobly realized by taking pledges from the statesmen, the senators, the nobles of the land, of their devoted attachment to the Word of God: they have publicly lifted up their voice, and declared in the face of all Europe, that the Bible is the religion of Great Britain.

Hall was not, perhaps, persuaded that all the good and the great knew exactly what they were doing, for he adds,

> It is not too much to hope that the attachment to the gospel, avowed by those who have co-operated in the measures of this society, will be followed by an increased attention on their part to explore its contents, to imbibe its spirit, and to regulate their lives by its precepts; and that thus the interests of vital christianity, may keep pace with the more extensive promulgation of revealed truth. (*Works*, vi. 341)

Such action, he believed, writing in 1812, would afford to the nation more protection than all its military and naval preparations.

5. 'The increasing harmony which prevails among the genuine disciples of Jesus Christ'

Fifthly, Hall identified the 'increasing harmony which prevails among the genuine disciples of Jesus Christ', which work for the Bible Society had done much to promote: indeed Hall predicted that the birth of the BFBS would be seen to inaugurate a new era in religious history which he over-optimistically styled 'the era of unanimity'.[28] The Bible Society had had a unique influence through its ability 'to promote a good understanding among Christians of different denominations' as it offered them 'a common ground of co-operation, a centre of union without a sacrifice of principle' (*Works*, iv. 340). He further believed that the challenge of modern infidelity provided an additional reason for Christian churches to act in unison:

> In such a crisis is it not best for christians of all denominations, that they may better concentrate their forces against the common adversary, to suspend for the present their internal disputes; imitating the policies of wise states, who never failed to consider the invasion of an enemy as a signal for terminating the contests of party?

In reality the controversies that separated Christians, which mainly concerned issues of church government, were trivial by contrast with the task of common mission.[29] 'The idea of a plurality of true churches', whether in communion with one another or not, was, in Hall's view, wholly abhorrent to the biblical view of the church: thus Christian schism and the creation of so many separate churches 'is by far the greatest calamity' recorded in church history, being productive of incalculable evil (*Works*, iii. 7–8).

Hall's appeal for unity was thus strongly advocated. The history of the last 300 years was sufficient demonstration of the evils of disunity:

> While Protestants attended more to the points on which they differed than to those on which they agreed; while more zeal was employed in settling ceremonies and defending subtleties, than in enforcing plain revealed truths; the lovely fruits of peace and charity perished under the storms of controversy. (*Works*, ii. 13)

For its part, controversy bred uncertainty which in turn was the parent of infidelity. It was the sacredness of the unity of the

church that made Hall such a doughty defender of open communion as over against that closed communion which he regarded as sectarian: biblical teaching about brotherly love as
adduced in the First Epistle of John made no allowance for
divisions in the church; by contrast Christ prays for the unity of
his disciples 'that the world might be furnished with a convincing
evidence of his mission'.[30] The breadth of his vision here is
remarkable for his period: 'Even protestants and catholics,
influenced by a kindred piety, can now cordially embrace each
other . . . The most enlightened, the selectest christians in every
denomination, are ready to cultivate an intercourse with kindred
spirits, with all who hold the same essential principles in any
other' (*Works*, vi. 191). In particular he cited the animated
correspondence between a Roman Catholic professor and the
Protestant Foreign Secretary of the British and Foreign Bible
Society in the interests of disseminating the scriptures.

6. 'That extension of civil and religious liberty by which the present times are distinguished'

Sixthly, Hall focused on 'that extension of civil and religious liberty
by which the present times are distinguished'. This represented a
perennial concern throughout Hall's ministry. What is remarkable
here was the way in which his two great analyses of the 1790s –
Christianity Consistent with a Love of Freedom (1791) and *The
Freedom of the Press* (1793) – were repeatedly reprinted for the next
twenty to thirty years, even against the will of their author.

a. 'A defence of worldly Christianity'

In the 1790s, events in Europe divided society in a new and more
radical fashion. The rather aristocratic minister of the Congregationalist King's Weigh House Church in London, John Clayton,
senior, in a context in which Dissenters were all too easily
construed as harbouring republican sentiments, preached an
extremely conservative sermon on *The Duty of Christians to
Magistrates* which *inter alia* suggested that defence of the principles of freedom was tainted because of its association with
advocacy by those of unitarian outlook. In particular, he attacked
the reputation of Joseph Priestley, whose person and possessions
had been violated in the Birmingham riots of the summer of
1791. The most effective answer to Clayton was a youthful piece

by Robert Hall, his *Christianity Consistent with a Love of Freedom,* which he penned and published in September 1791, very shortly after his settlement in his Cambridge pastorate.[31]

Clayton's sermon, fortified by Paul's teaching in Romans 13, basically advocated a strict 'No Politics' line (pp. 25–7), unless exceptionally the pulpit be used 'in defence of the measures of government' (p. 7), or 'to counteract the spirit of faction raised by persons who seem born to vex the state' (p. 19).[32] By contrast, Hall argued,

> The profession of religion does not oblige us to relinquish any undertaking on account of its being worldly, for we must then go out of the world; it is sufficient, that everything in which we engage, is of such a nature, as will not violate the principles of virtue, or occupy so much of our time or attention, as may interfere with more sacred and important duties. (*Works,* iv. 9)

Indeed, Olinthus Gregory says that Hall

> regarded a government chiefly worried about the emoluments of office, or aiming to consolidate its own power at home and to aid the efforts of despots abroad, while it neglected the welfare of individuals in middle or lower life, whose burdens it augmented by a mistaken course, as a government that should be constitutionally opposed by every lawful means. (*Works,* i. 38)

Hall dismissed Clayton's appeal to Jesus' own non-involvement in political affairs, arguing that his life on earth was not in this sense a model life. Indeed, if abstention from such involvement had been required of Christ's followers then there would necessarily have been very specific teaching to this end.

Freedom of conscience, of opinion and of rights to worship were all essential prerequisites to the nurture of an evangelical faith, but they also had larger implications, leading Hall to pose the question, 'can the rights of private judgement be safe under a government, whose professed principle is, that the subject has no rights at all?' This was no mere hypothetical question but reflected the situation in more than half the nations of Europe, and if Clayton's advice were followed could soon characterize all. In fact, the freedom of a society would never be safe until it was no longer dependent upon the mere goodwill of prince or minister or church establishment, but rather was enshrined within a constitution, in which, ideally, 'every individual becomes its guarantee', with everybody's arm ready to rise to its defence (*Works*, iv. 12). Christianity, far from 'weakening our attachment to the principles of freedom . . . renders them doubly dear to us, by giving us an interest in them, proportioned to the value of those religious privileges which they secure and protect' (*Works*, iv. 12).

Historical precedent, it was believed, was on the side of a faithful engagement by committed Christians with the political process: 'in the reigns of Charles the First and Second, the chief friends of freedom were the puritans of whom many were republicans, and the remainder zealously attached to limited monarchy'. The puritans were as zealous in their attachment to defence of freedom as to their defence of the doctrines of grace; there was, therefore, no necessary connection between unitarianism and the defence of freedom (*Works*, iv. 12–13). Denying the association that Clayton tried to establish between heresy and the advocacy of civil freedom, Hall made the positive affirmation that: 'The knowledge and the study of the Scriptures, far from favouring the pretensions of despotism, have almost ever diminished it, and been attended with a proportional increase of freedom.'

b. 'A critique of government'

To promote the discussion of the role of the government it was necessary to address the substance of government activity in the contemporary world. Accordingly Hall argued,

> He who breaks the fetters of slavery, and delivers a nation from thraldom, forms, in my opinion, the noblest comment on the great law of love, whilst he distributes the greatest blessing which man can receive from man: but next to that is the merit of him, who in times like the present, watches over the edifice of public liberty, repairs its foundations and strengthens its cement, when he beholds it hastening to decay. (*Works*, iv. 14)

By contrast comes his judgement, 'The boasted alliance between church and state, on which so many encomiums have been lavished, seems to have been little more than a compact between the priest and the magistrate, to betray the liberties of mankind, both civil and religious' (*Works*, iv. 18).

The last section of *Christianity Consistent with a Love of Freedom* concerns the operation of the Test Act which surprisingly Clayton defended as protecting the doctrines of the church, by which he presumably means the Reformed faith in England and Wales. The Test Act specifically motivated an individual to conform to the sacramental test, which Hall calls 'a solemn act of religious deception' (*Works*, iv. 36), for reasons of office rather than out of genuine faith. In fact whilst Reformation doctrines were treated with contempt by those who subscribed to the articles in the established church, in Dissent those same teachings 'have found a congenial soil and continue to flourish with vigour' (*Works*, iv. 38). In practice this legislation proscribed Dissenters 'as unfit to be trusted by the community to which they belong'; for them it represented 'a political annihilation'; whatever their talents, they were debarred from deploying them in the service of their fellow citizens 'in the administration of their country'. Clayton had argued against political activities as 'secularizing the gospel' and putting at risk its evangelistic power. Hall boldly counters: 'human ingenuity would be at a loss to contrive a method of secularizing the gospel more completely, than by rendering it the common passport of all who aspire to civil distinctions' (*Works*, iv. 39). Hall argued that until the Dissenters rightly raised the issue of the Test Acts, Dissenters and churchmen lived together in relative harmony enjoying 'the mildness of the times'. When however Dissenters began to campaign for repeal this was construed as an uncalled for 'attack on church and state' which found its worst manifestation in the Priestley riots in Birmingham (*Works*, iv. 108–9).

c. 'On the French Revolution'

Hall's arguments were clearly contexted by events in France: he notes Priestley's 'satisfaction on the liberation of France: an event which, promising a firmer establishment to liberty than any recorded in the annals of the world, is contemplated by the friends of arbitrary power throughout every kingdom of Europe with the utmost concern' (*Works*, iv. 22–3). Hall's sense of the progress of history is clearly articulated in the final paragraphs of his sermon:

the present is a period more interesting, perhaps than any which has been known, in the whole flight of time. The scenes of Providence thicken upon us so fast and are shifted with so strange a rapidity, as if the great drama of the world were drawing to a close. Events have taken place, of late, and revolutions have been effected, which, had they been foretold a very few years ago, would have been viewed as visionary and extravagant; and their influence is far from being spent. Europe never presented such a spectacle before, and it is worthy of being contemplated, with the profoundest attention by all its inhabitants. The empire of darkness and of despotism has been smitten with a stroke which has sounded through the universe. When we see whole kingdoms, after reposing for centuries on the lap of their rulers, start from their slumber, the dignity of man rising up from depression, and tyrants trembling on their thrones, who can remain entirely indifferent, or fail to turn his eye towards a theatre so August and extraordinary! (*Works*, iv. 41–2)

Hall's sympathies were quite clear:

That fond attachment to ancient institutions and blind submission to opinions already received which has ever checked the growth of improvement, and drawn on the greatest benefactors of mankind danger or neglect, is giving way to a spirit of bold and fearless investigation. Man seems to be becoming more erect and independent . . . The events which have already taken place, and the further changes they forbode,[33] will open to the contemplative of every character, innumerable sources of reflection . . . The devout mind will behold in these momentous changes the finger of God, and, discerning in them the dawn of that glorious period in which wars will cease, and unchristian tyranny shall fall, will adore that unerring wisdom, whose secret operation never fails to conduct all human affairs to their proper issue, and impels the great actors on that troubled theatre, to fulfil, when they least intend it, the counsels of heaven, and the predictions of its prophets. (*Works*, iv. 43)

In this Hall reflected an attitude common to Dissenters, perhaps best expressed by David Bogue who argued that, as Satan had raised up Louis XIV to expel the Protestant religion from France, so now 'the present zeal for liberty' was to be the instrument 'designed by the great Governor of the world as a preparatory step to the extending of the Redeemer's kingdom'.[34]

History, however, did not develop quite as Hall foresaw it in 1793. Accordingly his evaluation of the Revolution by the end of the 1790s is much more qualified: the Revolution is now called God's 'work' (*Works*, ii. 81), in which he was seen to be exercising judgement by allowing the search for liberty to give birth to a ferocity which ended its career by giving birth to 'the most unrelenting despotism'. In self-congratulatory tone, in which the excellence of the British constitution was extolled, Hall reflected 'that at a period when the spirit of giddiness and revolt has been so prevalent, we have preferred the blessings of order to a phantom of liberty, and have not been so mad as to wade through the horrors of a Revolution to make way for a military despot' (*Works*, ii. 80).[35]

The impact of atheism amongst the agents of the Revolution and the fallenness of human nature were now more obvious to him. Thus whilst the French Revolution was to be seen as 'a grand experiment on human nature', that self-same human nature proved inadequate to the Revolution's high ambitions. Its progress was, therefore, crucified by the forces of passion, vanity and the lack of education of those called to implement its development. Thus it all too soon lapsed into a chaos of disorderly and godless barbarity and violence, which was, perhaps, no more than to be expected of those whose minds had been shaped by the writings of Voltaire, D'Alembert, Diderot and Rousseau, all 'avowed enemies of revelation'. This led Hall to argue that History demonstrated that 'the principles of infidelity facilitate the commission of crimes, by removing the restraints of fear'. From this it had to be deduced that religion was 'the pillar of society, the safeguard of nations, the parent of social order, which alone has the power to curb the fury of the passions, and to secure to everyone his rights'.[36] Hall thus sees the process at work in European history: the unleashing of atheism but contemporary to this a revival of true religion. These parallel developments are seen as true 'signs of the times': 'To an attentive observer of the signs of the times, it will appear one of the most extraordinary phenomena of this eventful crisis, that, amidst the ravages of atheism and infidelity, real religion is evidently on the increase' (*Works*, iv. 56).

In the process of the Revolution was to be traced the working out of principles of divine judgement:

While it [the Revolution] confined itself to the exposure of the corruptions of religion and the abuse of power, it met with some degree of countenance from the wise and good in all countries, who were ready to hope it was the instrument destined by Providence to meliorate the condition of mankind. How great was their disappointment when they perceived that pretensions to philanthropy were, with many, only a mask assumed for the more successful propagation of impiety and anarchy.

The ensuing strife witnessed a cataclysmic conflict of principles,

On one side an attachment to the ancient order of things, on the other a passionate desire of change; . . . a jealousy of power shrinking from the slightest innovation, pretensions to freedom pushed to madness and anarchy; superstition in all its dotage, impiety in all its fury: whatever, in short, could be found most discordant in the principles, or violent in the passions of men, were the fearful ingredients which the hand of divine justice selected to mingle in this furnace of wrath.[37]

Such was his perception of the significance of developments in France that he did not hesitate to resort to apocalyptic language to describe them.

d. *'Pitt and the British scene'*

The consideration of such topical developments necessarily led Hall to pass judgement on contemporary British politics and politicians and to declare himself on basic political theory as it applied to the modern British state. Thus he argues: 'the violence and injustice of the internal administration keeps pace with our iniquities abroad. Liberty and truth are silenced. An unrelenting system of persecution prevails' (*Works*, iv. 47).[38] Of Pitt he wrote,

A veteran in frauds while in the bloom of youth, betraying first, and then persecuting, his earliest friends and connexions, falsifying every promise, and violating every political engagement, ever making the fairest professions a prelude to the darkest actions, punishing with the utmost rigour the publisher of the identical paper he had himself circulated, [Mr Holt of Newark then in prison in that town for printing an address on Reform certainly sanctioned by Pitt and even possibly written by him], are traits in the conduct of Pitt which entitle him to a fair preeminence in guilt . . . The contempt we feel for his meanness and duplicity, is lost in the dread of his machinations, and the abhorrence of his crimes. (*Works*, iv. 48–9)

After the end of the French Wars it came to be suggested that Hall had repented of his earlier radicalism. To refute this Hall authorized the publishing of a new edition of the *Apology,* printed in 1821. In this Hall removed his earlier attack on the character of Bishop Horsley as a youthful extravagance, but very deliberately made no apology for his attack on Pitt,

> because he feels the fullest conviction that the policy, foreign and domestic, of that celebrated statesman, has inflicted a more incurable wound on the constitution, and entailed more permanent and irreparable calamities on the nation, than that of any other minister in the annals of British history. A simple reflection will be sufficient to evince the unparalleled magnitude of his apostasy, which is, that the memory of the Son of Lord Chatham, the vehement opposer of the American War, the champion of Reform, and the idol of the people, has become the rallying point of toryism, the type and symbol of whatever is most illiberal in principle and intolerant in practice. (*Works,* iv. 60)

He also attacked Pitt for reneging on political reform which at the beginning of his ministry he had supported (*Works,* iv. 86). All this, it should be noted, is the censure of a man who is on record in 1803–4, after citing Romans 13, as saying: 'At this season especially, when unanimity is so requisite, every endeavour to excite discontent, by reviling the character, or deprecating the talents, of those who are entrusted with the administration, is highly criminal.'[39]

e. 'Basic political assumptions'
Hall derived his political theory from a number of calculations. Very basically he argued that since scripture made no specific allocation of 'the right of dominion', it was right to assume that all matters relating to it should be 'settled by the consent and approbation of mankind' or 'the acquiescence of the people'. 'Government', he more particularly affirmed, 'is the creature of the people, and that which they have created they surely have a right to examine'. Thus there should be a right to free discussion of matters of state, and indeed the power to participate in determining them. 'Free enquiry will never endanger the existence of a good government; scarcely will it be able to work the overthrow of a bad one'.[40]

On a more practical note he argued that 'the real danger to every free government is less from its enemies than from itself', that is by resisting appropriate reforms and obstinately maintaining abuses, in particular relying on a system of informants 'turning every man into a spy'. This accusation he supported by referring also to 'those insurrections and plots, of which no traces have appeared, except in a speech from the throne' (*Works*, iv. 69). Hall further refers to the way in which reactionary associations had been able to avail themselves 'of an alarm which they had artfully prepared, in order to withdraw the public attention from real grievances to imaginary dangers' (*Works*, iv. 73, a theme that he returns to on p. 115).

But there were further considerations. 'From the known perfection of God, we conclude he wills the happiness of mankind'; therefore 'that kind of civil polity is most pleasing in his eye which is productive of the greatest felicity' (*Works*, iv. 53), which seems like an argument in favour of a species of sanctified Benthamism. Contrariwise, not to allow some role to those governed allows too much arbitrary liberty to those who govern: 'Is it best for the human race that every tyrant and usurper be submitted to without check or control?' (*Works*, iv. 53). In his judgement it could clearly be observed that free governments uniformly impart a greater share of happiness to those who live under their rule than do arbitrary governments. All citizens, therefore, had a duty to be actively engaged with the affairs of state. A response by way of passive obedience was insufficient; to neglect to exercise that right was a crime against society. If in England, 'the state of things continues to grow worse and worse, if the friends of reform, the true friends of their country, continue to be overwhelmed by calumny and persecution, the confusion will probably be dreadful, the misery extreme, and the calamities that await us too great for human calculation' (*Works*, iv. 57). The future of the whole empire was at stake in the defence of free opinions and democratic actions at such a time as this.

f. Arguments for parliamentary reform

The inadequacies of parliamentary representation in 1793 were obvious: whatever else one might want to say it was clear in Hall's view that the House of Commons had ceased to be capable of accomplishing 'the design of its functions as a representative assembly' (*Works*, iv. 143). Reflecting a more general Dissenting concern for parliamentary reform (*Works*, iv. 109), he focused his criticism on a House of Commons which lacked independence because of an extremely limited and capricious franchise, over-long parliaments, the corruption of undue Treasury influence, the 'roar of faction' supplanting both conscience and 'the still voice of Liberty', and the over-representation of the rural south at the expense of the wealth-creating areas of industrial England. By contrast, a system of household suffrage would not only be truly representative but it would also create an electorate too large to be swayed by bribes (*Works*, iv. 76–8). His opponents represented this as advocacy of annual parliaments and universal suffrage and Hall did not deny this, adding his desire for the secret ballot as well (*Works*, iv. 137–8). But as long as no action was taken, discontent continued to fester:

> In the extension of excise laws, in the erection of barracks, in the determined adherence to abuses displayed by parliament; in the desertion of pretended patriots, the spread of arbitrary principles, the tame subdued spirit of the nation, we behold the seeds of political ruin quickening into life.

The original *Apology* was given in 1793 but was reprinted in 1822 and provoked the charge from an anonymous writer in the *Christian Guardian* that it ill-behoved a minister of the gospel to meddle with party politics as Hall's address appeared to do. A bemused Hall replied by referring to the way in which, at the beginning of the Revolutionary Wars, military banners had been consecrated in churches, how the bishops sat in the House of Lords and how clergy meetings sent up petitions to Parliament against Catholic emancipation. 'The plain state of the case is, not that the writer is offended at my meddling with politics, but that I have meddled on the wrong side.'

Unfulfilled Prophecy?

Hall's six points are an invitation to make a positive assessment of the progress of society in the 1820s. He was not, however, universally optimistic in his historical judgement. When he reprinted his *Apology for the Freedom of the Press* almost thirty years after its first publication, he had to relate to what hostile reviewers took to be certain unfulfilled dooms that had not occurred, for example, in the absence of parliamentary reform. The writer to the *Christian Guardian* spoke instead of years of improvement, provoking Hall's rhetorical response:

> Where is this improvement to be found? Is it in the augmentation of the national debt to three times its former amount; in the accumulated weight of taxes; in the increase of the poor rates; in the depression of land to half its former value; in the ruin of the agricultural interest, in the thousands and tens of thousands of farmers who are distrained for rent, and they and their families reduced to beggary? Has this writer already forgotten the recent distress of the manufacturing class, who, from failure of employment, and the depression of wages, were plunged into despair, while numbers of them quitted their homes, and sought a scanty and precarious relief, by dragging through the country loaded wagons and carts, like beasts of burden? Is it in the rapid and portentous multiplication of crimes by which our prisons are glutted with malefactors? (*Works*, iv. 141)

I had hoped that my readings in Hall's rhetoric would have led me more clearly into Carlyle's analysis of 1829.[41] Clearly Hall would not have been worried at Carlyle's mocking of an established church bereft of Test and Corporation Acts and of a shackled Catholicism (p. 58); and he could well have shared in Carlyle's mirth at the expense of millenarians prophesying out of scripture and Millites predicting out of Bentham, though there would be no sympathy for construing the Bible Society as a religious machine. Carlyle sees as the essential sign of the times the fact that the contemporary world reflects a 'Mechanical Age . . . the age of Machinery, in every outward and inward sense of that word' (p. 59). Such a system clearly brought material advantage but, infecting social relations and spiritual perceptions, it appeared a less certain gain: 'Men are grown mechanical in head and in heart, as well as in hand' (p. 63). Thus whilst Mechanism might have aided man's material welfare, it is not clear that it had significantly added to his happiness.

The machinery metaphor is very telling, but this is prophecy and not analysis. By 1829 England had not yet entered into a Mechanical Age: pioneering entrepreneurs in certain advanced industries were moving in that direction, but mechanization was not in 1829 a widespread or universally present phenomenon: if human relations had deteriorated into calculations of profit and loss that reflected a spirit of commercialization not mechanization. The framework knitters, to the betterment of whose lot Hall was passionately committed, were not yet the victims of machinery. In 1820 that was still a generation into the future. The industry had, however, been capitalized with a structure of 'manufacturers', middlemen and workers, some of whom worked in overcrowded workshops in the city, others working in their homes in the surrounding villages. Most workers had to hire their frames, which in itself became a cause of exploitation. What the workers were suffering from was a glutted labour supply working to the demands of a more or less finite market. Various developments in the late eighteenth century meant that more workers were attracted into the hosiery industry than could be consistently supported, with a consequent depression of payments. Accordingly, men were working a full working week to receive a wage that would not support their families without the assistance of the parish. Whereas in the past, hosiers had handed out orders to be completed, the bagmen in the trade now began to work speculatively ahead of securing orders.

Government, though passing in 1815 a Corn Law to protect agriculture, was unwilling to intervene in the framework knitters' plight. Hall pointed out the partisanship: 'The vaunted maxim of leaving every kind of production and labour to find its own level', that cherished doctrine of *laissez-faire*, had only been partially adhered to. It ought not to be selectively invoked against combining workers in an oppressed industry when it was studiously not deployed against the agricultural interest on whose behalf the state all too readily intervened. In a glut situation, argued Hall, the employer withdraws his stock, or some part of it, until trade has recovered; why should the framework knitters not do the same with their labour, for if this is not allowed 'a small surplus of labour . . . . becomes an engine for effecting a deep and universal depression [of wages]'.[42] In such a situation it was not simply the individual employee that suffered but the whole district, including the parish which had to supplement wages, tradesmen who lost custom and local farmers whose market was reduced. Hall's promotion of the interests of the Leicestershire Framework Knitters' Fund lent support to a practical way of seeking to mitigate the worst abuses of the trade, and illustrates his consistent support of the plight of the poor. It also illustrates the way that his life was contexted by a society that was increasingly becoming capitalized if not yet industrialized. But the 'Signs of the Times' were changing rapidly.

Hall's 1820 *Signs of the Times* and his other writings of political and social analysis still essentially reflect a pre-industrial world of some religious confidence: the problem that the framework knitters in Hall's congregation faced was not industrialization but imperfect commercialization. In 1820 mechanization still lay some thirty years into the future, and even in Carlyle's day was a fear and a threat rather than an experienced reality for most workers. But Carlyle had the vision to see the way in which manufacturing was developing: accordingly his analysis and his remedies are very different from Hall's, not only contexted by the coming of the machine but also by a humanism that makes his *Signs of the Times* a type of secularized apocalyptic.

Mechanization was the new tyranny which threatened to imprison man at just that time when Hall's revered divinity was crumbling in men's hands:[43] 'Thus is the Body politic more than ever worshipped and tendered; but the Soul-politic less than ever' (p. 6). 'The time is sick and out of joint'; accordingly, 'The thinking minds of all nations call for change' (p. 81). But Carlyle was fearful that nineteenth-century man, replete as he might be with his 'faith in Mechanism', lacked the moral capacity to effect that change; 'while civil liberty is more and more secured to us, our moral liberty is all but lost. . . . . Free in hand and foot we are shackled in heart and soul with far straiter than feudal chains' (p. 79). For all the elegance of the analysis, Carlyle's piece ends with a whimper rather than a war-cry: 'To reform a world, to reform a nation, no wise man will undertake; and all but foolish men know, that the only solid, though a far slower reformation, is what each begins and perfects on *himself*' (p. 82). But that leaves all the weight of moral obligation on the shoulders of the individual, and Robert Hall, loose as he sat to Calvin's *Institutes,* knew quite well that that was a burden no man could bear. By contrast his piece ends with the act of God, but God acting through human agency: 'He does not christianize the world by magic; we are not to expect religion to descend from heaven, or to arise upon earth like a beautiful vision.' These things will happen, but only as men and women allow themselves to become the vehicles of God's purposes. That for Hall was the crucial understanding: the decisive enpowering was 'a spirit within us which must be imparted from above', giving Hall the last say on the mechanistic metaphor when he affirms: 'The machinery [of Christian organization] is provided, but the Spirit alone can move the wheels'.[44]

Notes

[1] Matthew 16:1–3.
[2] Standard bibliographies yield a variety of titles under this heading which range from the futuristic prophetic to more immediate political tracts, to trade journals in the advertising business. *Signs of the Times* was also favoured as a title for periodicals, particularly those of an Adventist tone. For example, in the UK a slight variant, *The Signs of Our Times* (1867 following), was the forerunner of *The Christian Herald. Signs of the Times* was also the title of the periodical of the Old School Baptists in the USA from 1832.
[3] In the same year, 1829, Edward Irving, subsequently the founder of the Catholic Apostolic Church, penned a tract under the same title. Ironically he had earlier been tutor to Jane Welsh, Carlyle's future wife: in 1821 Irving and Welsh fell deeply in love with one another but a union was not forthcoming because Irving had since 1812 been engaged to Isabella Martin whom he reluctantly married in 1823. 'If I had married Irving', Jane Welsh later retorted, 'the tongues would never have been heard.' *The Blackwell Dictionary of Evangelical Biography*, ed. Donald Lewis (Oxford, 1995), i. 595–6.
[4] The lecture was given, as was to be expected, to the British and Foreign Schools Society and not the National Society as erroneously appears in Gregory's edition of Hall's *Collected Works*: Robert Hall, *Collected Works*, ed. O. Gregory, 6 vols. (London, George Routledge, 1866), vi, 181–95, a misattribution which falsely set me on this research as an example of remarkable ecumenical sharing at this date! See the announcement of the lecture in *Felix Farley's Bristol Journal* (Saturday, 25 Nov. 1820), and a report of the lecture in *The Bristol Mirror* (Saturday, 2 Dec. 1820). The emphasis of the newspaper reporter is slightly different from the printed sermon as reconstructed from notes taken down by the Revd Thomas Grinfield:

> An uneducated, ignorant and irreligious populace, he described as a volcano, which, however it might be for a time overgrown with beautiful verdure, was liable to an explosion more dangerous than any that ever burst from Vesuvius or Aetna. The promulgation of the

Gospel was intended as a promulgation of light; the humblest individual, however obscured by exterior circumstance, possessed a soul capable, by instruction, of diffusing that light; to communicate to another the power of reading a Bible was parallel only to the obligation of preaching the gospel to the Poor. The Rev Preacher then ably and convincingly refuted the absurd notion that Education rendered mankind less loyal and tractable subjects. Whatever might be the inconvenience in a progress from ignorance to knowledge, there was no comparison in the observance of order or propriety after the possession of knowledge – How common was it to hear persons exclaim that such and such conduct could not be the conduct of well-informed individuals – Why not then make them well-informed? We heartily wish that every opposer of the Education of the Poor could have heard the convincing arguments, the powerful pathos, and the brilliant declaration of the revered, pious and eloquent preacher. The Society for which he pleaded could do no better in our opinion than procure, if possible, a Copy of his Sermon, to disperse among their opponents.

I am grateful to the Revd Ruth Gouldbourne for providing me with the Bristol references. The Revd Thomas Grinfield (1788–1870), the son of another Thomas Grinfield, a Moravian minister, was educated at Trinity College and ordained into the Church of England in 1813. Although serving the title of rector of Shirland, Derbyshire, 1827–47, he seems to have resided for most of his life in Clifton, Bristol. Not given to much social involvement, he is described as 'an accomplished scholar, and poet and well-known hymnwriter' (Julian, Boase, Venn and Venn, *DNB*).

[5] *Fragments on the Defence of Village Preaching etc.* (1801–11), vi. 398.

[6] For a discussion of the genre of such prophetic writings see J. A. Oddy, 'Bicheno and Tyso on the prophecies: a Baptist generation gap', *Baptist Quarterly (BQ)* (1993), 81–9.

[7] *Dictionary of Evangelical Biography*, i. 91; Bicheno's prophetic studies also took him into Zionism, forecasting *The Restoration of the Jews, the Crisis of All Nations,* in 1800.

[8] Oddy refers to a 3rd edn published in 1799, *BQ* (1993), 84, and Hywel M. Davies, *Transatlantic Brethren: Revd Samuel Jones and His Friends: Baptists in Wales, Pennsylvania and Beyond* (Bethlehem, Pa., 1995), 184–5, refers to a digest of Bicheno's work being made available in Welsh by Morgan Rhys of Penycarn, Monmouthshire, to settlers in the USA. Davies shows how relativist 'Signs of the Times' interpretations could be: alienated from the British state, persecuted Welsh Dissenters believed that 'the Signs of the Times predicted awful

portents for Britain' (p. 186). Both R. A. Soloway, *Prelates and People: Ecclesiastical Social Thought in England, 1783–1852* (London, 1969), 34, and M. Watts, *The Dissenters*, ii. *The Expansion of Evangelical Nonconformity* (Oxford, 1995), 8, place Bicheno in a broader intellectual context, but Soloway conflates into one person the biographies of James Bicheno and his son, James Ebenezer Bicheno, 1785–1851. It was the latter who from 1842 was Colonial Secretary in Van Diemansland, and who espoused an extreme puritanism which insisted that it was essential that every individual should be made to exert himself in order to secure his daily wants, and which made him an enthusiastic supporter of Malthus in *An Inquiry into the Nature of Benevolence, Chiefly with a View to Elucidate the Principles of the Poor Laws, and to Show their Immoral Tendency* (1817).

⁹ 'A diaconal epistle, 1790', *BQ* (1936), 216. The letter is to the Revd James Dore, is signed by fifteen friends and is dated October 1790.

¹⁰ E.g. Pretyman of Lincoln, van Mildert of Durham and Huntingford of Gloucester, in addition to Horsley of Rochester.

¹¹ S. Horsley, *A Sermon Preached Before the Lords Spiritual and Temporal . . . January 30 1793, Being the Anniversary of the Martyrdom of King Charles I. With an Appendix Concerning the Political Principles of Calvin* (1793), 22–3, cited by Soloway, *Prelates and People*, 32.

¹² S. Horsley, *The Charge . . . Delivered at his Primary Visitation . . . in 1796* (1796), 33, 52, cited by Soloway, *Prelates and People*, 39.

¹³ S. Horsley, *The Charge . . . Delivered at his Second General Visitation in . . . 1800* (1800), 3, cited by Soloway, *Prelates and People*, 40.

¹⁴ James de Jong, *As the Waters Cover the Sea: Millennial Expectations in the Rise of Anglo-American Missions, 1640–1810* (Kampen, 1970), 156, referring to Gill's 1753 sermon, *The Glory of the Church in the Latter Day*.

¹⁵ Ibid., 156–7, 198, 202.

¹⁶ Ibid., 181.

¹⁷ Hall, *Works*, ed. O. Gregory, vi. 182–3; cf. his judgement in his 1802 sermon, *Reflections on War*: 'To acknowledge the hand of God is a duty indeed at all times: but there are seasons when it is made so bare, that it is next to impossible, and therefore signally criminal, to overlook it. It is almost unnecessary to add that the present is one of those seasons.' Contemporaries had witnessed 'a crisis so unexampled in the annals of the world; during which scenes have been disclosed, and events have arisen, so much more astonishing than history had recorded or romance feigned, that we are compelled to lose sight of human agency, and to behold the Deity acting as it were apart and alone' (*Works*, ii. 75). A speech delivered at the Guildhall, Leicester, on 15 July 1817, at the seventeenth anniversary of the auxiliary Bible Society, *Works*, iv. 348.

18 R. Hall, *Sentiments Proper to the Present Crisis*, 2nd edn (1802–3), *Works*, ii. 105.

19 Ibid., vi. 183–6.

20 'Address on behalf of the Baptist Academical Institution at Stepney, Written 1811 or 1812', in Hall, *Works*, iv. 361–6.

21 'The advantage of knowledge to the lower classes', a sermon preached on behalf of a Sunday school at Hervey (Harvey) Lane, Leicester, 1810, in Hall, *Works*, ii. 149.

22 Hall was not simply opposed to war in general terms: he was particularly anxious to discern the policy behind military action, thus the question whether the Revolutionary Wars were the result of treaty obligations or in defence of national honour, both of which were honourable motivations: 'But if the re-establishment of the ancient government of France be any part of the object; if it be a war with freedom, a confederacy of kings against the rights of man, it will be the last humiliation and disgrace that can be inflicted on Great Britain.' See 'An Apology for the Freedom of the Press and the General Liberty, to which are prefixed remarks on Bishop Horsley's Sermon, preached 30 January 1793', pp. 120–3. This was first published in 1793, and went through successive editions. Gregory includes in *Works*, iv. 45–146, the article, several prefaces and notes, a review in *The Christian Guardian* of 1822 and Hall's reply to this.

23 'Modern Infidelity Considered with Respect to its Influence on Society, a Sermon Preached in the Meeting house, Cambridge, November 1799, Preface January 1800'. See Olinthus Gregory's footnote on p. 7 where Paley's *View of the Evidences of Christianity* is described as 'probably, without exception, the most clear and satisfactory statement of the historical proofs of the Christian religion ever exhibited in any age or country'. The argument from design is most fully worked out in Paley's *Natural Theology* (1802).

24 'Review of Zeal without Innovation'. Gregory prints, in *Works*, ii. 269–320, what he calls the second edition of a review which originally appeared in *The Eclectic Review*. No dates are given, but presumably the original review appeared soon after the volume reviewed which was published in 1808.

25 Hall deploys the same distinction between 'real' and 'nominal' which is at the heart of Wilberforce's great tract, his *Practical View of the Prevailing Religious System of Professed Christians* (1797), in his 'Modern Infidelity Considered' (1799) in *Works*, ii. 1–60, where he argues that the attacks of infidelity were in fact purifying the church: 'nominal christians will probably be scattered like chaff. But has real Christianity anything to fear? Have not the degenerate manners and corrupt lives of multitudes in the visible church, been, on the contrary,

the principal occasion of scandal and offence?' (p. 55). See also his 'Fragments on Village Preaching', 'On Toleration, 1801 or 1802', in *Works*, vi. 381, 383–6, and *'Sentiments Proper to the Present Crisis'* (1803), *Works*, ii. 119–20:

> The truths and mysteries which distinguished the christian religion from all other religions, have been little attended to by some, totally denied by others . . . The doctrines of the fall and of redemption, which are two grand points on which the christian dispensation hinges, have been too much neglected . . . This alienation from the distinguishing truths of our holy religion accounts for a portentous peculiarity among christians, their being ashamed of a book which they profess to receive as the word of God.

In fact Hall pays tribute to Wilberforce's volume in a footnote as 'an inestimable work, which has, perhaps, done more than any other to rouse the insensibility and augment the piety of the age'.

[26] 'An Address circulated at the Formation of the Leicester Auxiliary Bible Society' (19 Feb. 1810), *Works*, iv. 329ff.

[27] 'A Speech delivered at the 7th Anniversary of the Leicester Auxiliary Bible Society' (15 July 1817), *Works*, iv. 350.

[28] 'An Address . . . Formation of the Leicester Auxiliary Bible Society' (1810), *Works*, iv. 330–2, and 'A Speech delivered at the Second Anniversary of the Leicester Auxiliary Bible Society' (13 Apr. 1812), *Works*, iv. 333ff.

[29] Preface to 'Modern Infidelity Considered with respect to its Influence on Society' (Cambridge, Nov. 1799), *Works*, ii. 6: first preached in Bristol (October 1799), 10.

[30] 'On Terms of Communion with a particular view to the case of Baptists and PaedoBaptists' (1815), in *Works*, iii. 58–9.

[31] R. Tudur Jones, *Congregationalism in England, 1662–1962* (London, 1962), 185. 'Christianity consistent with a Love of Freedom' (1791), *Works*, iv. 2–43. Hall did not initially identify Clayton by name; he regarded this as a rather immature offering and would not consent to its being reprinted, but Gregory produces evidence of its being reproduced on several occasions notwithstanding this.

[32] Hall's comment is, 'It is easy to brand a passion for liberty with the odious epithet of faction; no two things, however can be more opposite . . . Every tory upholds a faction; every whig in so far as he is sincere and well-informed, is a friend to the equal liberties of mankind' (*Works*, iv. 31).

[33] Significantly, Olinthus Gregory, in editing this address, refers to the appositeness of Hall's 1790 analysis to the situation in 1830 when once more France was experiencing a Revolution (*Works*, iv. 41).

³⁴ D. Bogue, *A Sermon Preached at Salter's Hall, 30 March 1792, before the Correspondent Board in London of the Society in Scotland for Propagating Christian Knowledge* (1793), 46–8.

³⁵ 'Reflections on War', p. 80; Hall was not always so persuaded of the excellence of the British constitution. In the advertisement to the 3rd edn of *An Apology for the Freedom of the Press, and for General Liberty: in which are prefixed Remarks on Bishop Horsley's Sermon, preached 30 Jan. 1793*, he complains about British troops being sent to France on the command of the prime minister, the younger Pitt, acting in the name of the king 'without the previous consent of Parliament':

> If this doctrine be true, the boasted equilibrium of the constitution, all the barriers which the wisdom of our ancestors have opposed to the encroachments of arbitrary power are idle, ineffectual precautions . . . Our constitution, on this principle, is the absurdest system that was ever conceived; pretending liberty for its object, yet providing no security against the great antagonist and destroyer of liberty, the employment of military power by the chief magistrate.

The fault was not so much with the theory of the constitution but with current practice: 'Theory tells us the parliament is free and independent; experience will correct the mistake by showing its subservience to the crown . . . The principal remedy for the diseases of the state is undoubtedly a reform in parliament' (*Works*, iv. 47–8, 85, 118–19).

³⁶ 'Modern Infidelity Considered' (1799), in *Works*, ii. 30, 36, 51.

³⁷ 'Reflections on War', *Works*, ii. 76–8 (Cambridge, 1 June 1802, 'being the day of thanksgiving for a general peace', preached on behalf of a Benevolent Society), 78.

³⁸ Advertisement to the 3rd edn of 'An Apology for the Freedom of the Press and for General Liberty to which are prefixed remarks of Bishop Horsley's Sermon' (preached 30 Jan. 1793), *Works*, iv. 47.

³⁹ 'The Sentiments Proper to the Present Crisis' (1803), *Works*, ii. 109.

⁴⁰ 'An Apology for the Freedom of the Press etc.' (1793), *Works*, iv. 66–8.

⁴¹ T. Carlyle, 'Signs of the Times', *Edinburgh Review*, 98 (1829), 56–82.

⁴² R. Hall, 'An Appeal to the Public, on the Subject of the Frame-work Knitters' Fund' (1819), *Works*, iv. 167–84, at 174.

⁴³ Carlyle, 'Signs of the Times', 81.

⁴⁴ R. Hall, 'Signs of the Times' (1820), *Works*, vi. 195.

6

Nonconformists, economic ethics and the consumer society in mid-Victorian Britain

JANE GARNETT

The year 1862 was a critical focus of self-examination for Victorian Nonconformity. In the first place, it was the bicentenary of the ejection of the Puritan clergy from the Church of England. In 1862 a plethora of lectures and publications debated the implications of this anniversary for the mid-nineteenth century. By modern historians it is often discussed straightforwardly as a potent stimulus to the movement pressing for disestablishment of the Church of England, and as a context within which the *particularity* of the Nonconformist inheritance was reinforced. It certainly did offer such opportunities. It also, however, suggested more open-ended questions about where Nonconformity was going, and helped to highlight common evangelical principles, extending on either side of the Nonconformist–Anglican divide. Revived enthusiasm for 'Puritan' heroes – Bunyan, Milton, Baxter – was manifested not just by Nonconformists but also by evangelical Anglicans. The qualities stressed by both could be common ones of principle, character, charity, fidelity to conscience.[1] This was especially true for those nineteenth-century evangelicals who wanted to assert the relevance of these figures as models for the development of sound religious and ethical principles in modern commercial life. The 1850s, 1860s and 1870s saw the proliferation of a complex and interdenominational evangelical literature devoted to economic ethics, on which this chapter is focused. Sermons, tracts, pamphlets, biographies, exemplary studies of particular business enterprises and periodical articles were produced by evangelical ministers and laymen working in industrial and commercial communities. Lectures were delivered in town halls and music halls, as well as in specifically evangelical venues like Exeter Hall in London, which regularly accommodated 3,000 businessmen at one sitting.[2]

The year 1862 also saw a major international exhibition, which built on the example of the 1851 Great Exhibition, and gave rise, as that occasion had, to debate about the nature of industrial and commercial progress and of Britain's place relative to other countries. As one evangelical put it: 'The International Exhibition is a representation on a colossal scale . . . of man's power and capacity to mould the crude materials of nature into forms of grace and beauty, grandeur and elegance, utility, comfort and convenience.'[3] It was easy to see signs of Britain's providential status in being able to produce and to enjoy such a cornucopia of wonderful things. The reality of an intimate relationship between Protestantism and the development of capitalism and the trappings of modern civilization was widely assumed, and could lead to massive rhetorical distortion and complacency, especially when it acquired a patriotic form. In 1858, the Wesleyan Robert Spence Hardy had cast himself in the role of Ezekiel in urging his country to beware, 'for if there be iniquity in thy traffic, the same calamity shall overcome thee [as the ruin of Tyre], though now thou callest thyself, in thine arrogance, the Ruler of the Waves'.[4] Whilst Britain's industrial and commercial status and her Protestantism were simply assumed to be mutually reinforcing, there were many reasons, in practice as well as in theory, why the two might not fit together so neatly. Each side of the assumption could be used to prop up the other, without there being any critical interaction between the two. Many evangelicals saw that Protestant principles which were held to have been conducive to economic success and to have supported a structure in which the trust and mutuality necessary to the continuation of that development could operate, were in danger of being thoroughly commercialized themselves. If this happened, both commerce and religion would lose. In a climate of intensifying commercial pressures, there was a need to come down from the realms of abstraction and to discuss in tangible terms where individually held principle could meet practical circumstance and to construct relevant role-models for behaviour. The removal of commercial restrictions had opened up new markets for industry and fields for speculation, and were seen to have suggested a complete readjustment of notions of what constituted success. The moral perils of business life had never seemed so great. The middle-class and especially lower middle-class community which evangelicals principally addressed was faced by a particularly grey area of decision-making, and was simultaneously bombarded by a new variety of secular success and self-help literature, some of which – like Samuel Smiles's *Self-Help* (published in 1859) – adopted a beguilingly simplified religious position. To win over – and to support – such a constituency, it was felt necessary to reinforce specific Protestant principles and to strike a positively Protestant note of challenge and inspiration.

The final resonance of 1862 on which I want to focus is the association with the earlier St Bartholomew's Day – the massacre in Paris in 1572, an event which had been both a source of shock and a reminder of the force of Protestant solidarity to sixteenth-century English Protestants. In 1862 rhetorical reference was made both to this event and to the earlier sixteenth-century Protestant martyrdoms at Smithfield. Mid-nineteenth-century Britain might seem to represent a total contrast – a period both of Protestant supremacy and of evangelical confidence. But in his Baptist Union address in 1864, 'The influence of the present times on personal religion', C. M. Birrell argued that

> To refuse to speak blasphemy before the instruments of torture did not require half so much spiritual power as it does to ascertain how to act in the midst of a society professedly on good terms with Christ, but unconsciously imbued with a spirit completely devoid of His . . .[5]

The prominent evangelical Anglican Hugh Stowell made the same point: 'For a man to dare to do justly at whatever risk or cost, requires an amount of heroism which would bear no un-favourable comparison with the intrepidity of the Christian hero who fell at Sebastopol, or the Christian martyr burned at Smithfield.'[6] That there was a concerted and systematic attempt in the mid-nineteenth century to invoke such heroism and to root it in both a Nonconformist and a broader Protestant evangelical tradition has been remarkably lost sight of in the twentieth century. In part this results from taking too much at face value George Eliot's, Dickens's and Matthew Arnold's characterizations of Nonconformist narrowness and hypocrisy. In part it comes from the influence of the early twentieth-century social critique of capitalism from a High Church Anglican and Christian Socialist perspective. R. H. Tawney's *The Acquisitive Society* (1921), in its passionate call for the revival of a sense of Christian duty and community to combat faith in materialism, helped powerfully to re-establish a pejorative image of the eighteenth and nineteenth centuries, in which period, he asserted, 'The Churches made religion the ornament of leisure, instead of the banner of a Crusade.' The Church of England – in his view – ceased to speak its mind, and Nonconformity failed to take up the challenge. 'Individualist in their faith, they were individualist in their interpretation of social morality' – by which he meant to indicate that they allowed religion and economics to operate in entirely separate spheres. Between the Church of England and Nonconformity a vacuum was created into which rushed the self-confident, militant gospel proclaiming the absolute value of economic success.[7] Such a perspective has been worked into deeply misleading twentieth-century myths about supposed 'Victorian values', which have certainly *not* been held to include the posing of new questions about the moral challenges of the market or attempts to reformulate and reassert ideals of character for the commercial community. Moreover the recent historical focus on the development of a consumer mentality has been rather detached from a relationship to the *ethos* of producers and those in the retail trade who served consumers. Thus the tensions between different goals and areas of responsibility and the ways in which these tensions were exacerbated by an expanding market have not properly been considered.

In the mid-nineteenth-century context it was not in fact surprising that the concern to revitalize a moral dynamic to confront such tensions should have come from the evangelical churches. Evangelical ministers and churchmen were strongly represented in commercial and industrial areas and often had direct experience of commerce themselves. Hence, of course, their identification with this constituency by those contemporary critics who tainted them with the slur of commercialism. In this sense they saw their mission as to combat both the slur and whatever justification might lie behind it. Evangelicals in this period were also moving into a new phase of their development as a religious movement. Looking back in 1889 over his career as a

Congregationalist, the Birmingham minister R. W. Dale recognized a shift within evangelicalism from a greater preoccupation with the ultimate state of the individual soul in relative isolation from the general order of human society, to a greater emphasis over recent decades on practical ethical engagement.[8] This was a common perception. The evangelicalism of the eighteenth-century revival was widely seen as having tended to deprecate the significance of moral instruction and discipline, in reaction both to the classical morality which had dominated latitudinarian sermons, and to the Catholic emphasis on works. The spiritual discipline of evangelicalism had been open to the charge of excessive subjectivity. Dale and others applauded the shift of emphasis. But there was concern, too, to stress the importance of balance and of the maintenance of the critical and creative tensions between sin and grace which constituted the ethical impulse of evangelicalism. The spiritual and the dogmatic had to be united with the moral in *all* aspects of Christian teaching; otherwise there was a danger, not of focusing too much on the details of moral conduct, but of focusing too little on the greater forces and aims which gave strength to moral life. Hence the stress on life as both discipline and probation. The balance which needed to be struck was a delicate one. Optimism about human creativity needed to be encouraged in order to prevent a timid retreat from the challenges offered by the increasing complications of economic life. On the other hand, the instilling of a due appreciation of human frailty was necessary in order to reinforce recognition of the need for a religious and moral basis for this economic life. In developing this dialectic, evangelicals self-consciously referred to what they termed 'Puritan' qualities of manliness and individuality and to an evangelical sense of vitality and usefulness.

In the debates around 1862, of course, Nonconformists had a particular concern with defining the positive connotations of both 'Puritanism' and Nonconformity. The inheritance of Puritanism was a contested one. It could be equated (both pejoratively and favourably) with extreme plainness and abstinence from pleasure. It could be identified with qualities of self-discipline and courage, which could seem to be all too easily detached from specific doctrinal foundations (as by Carlyle, for example).[9] Nonconformity too could bear different emphases – not just historical, doctrinal and ecclesiological, but also social. Had too much pity been expressed for the men of 1662 in their loss of social position and income? Were such material deprivations in fact felt much more keenly in 1862 than in 1662?[10] Did this signify a drift towards a dangerous conformity with the social mores of the establishment? In what did the essence of Nonconformity reside? Samuel Martin, chairman of the Congregational Union in 1862, developed in his spring address to the annual assembly an elaborate rhetorical defence of Nonconformity, which drew on three topical paintings by Millais, exhibited in 1852, 1853 and 1860 respectively, the first two of which had already been published in popular engravings.

> PEACEABLENESS seems to stand before us like that pale, passionate, imploring woman in Millais' Huguenot . . . SOCIAL ELEVATION draws near to us like that flushed and queenly woman in the 'Order of Release' . . . our fingers are interlaced with hers, our arm is about her neck, we are starting to occupy the higher places of conformists; but we retrace our steps . . . THE PRAISE OF MEN takes hold of us like that gay and beautiful damsel in 'The Black Brunswicker' – she holds the door of a place of revelry into which we have strayed, and tries to prevent our exit. But we cannot listen to her entreaties . . . for we hear the noise of a holy war arising from at least two thousand good soldiers of Christ . . .[11]

There are multiple points of reference in this extended simile. In its appropriation for particular purposes of more general Protestant icons, the assumption is confidently made that Martin's listeners would know these images well. Pre-Raphaelite painting had, of course, established itself as offering moral and religious insights, and as such had become open to variant readings in the Protestant religious world, of which Martin's own Westminster Chapel formed a central part. His own preaching, like that of many other prominent urban Nonconformists, was dedicated to distinguishing the fundamental principles of Nonconformity – and specifically of congregational cohesion. Only then could a sense of responsibility be sustained in those who were in fact moving materially and socially in a world of conformists, in all the different senses of that word.

The difficulty was to distinguish the fundamental from the transient in a way which could carry conviction. The controversy surrounding the publication in 1853 of the Congregationalist Thomas Binney's *Is it Possible to Make the Best of Both Worlds?* showed how fine the line was between apparent conformity to the world and the challenge to act with integrity *in the world.*[12] Binney's work, which was aimed specifically at young people entering commercial life, sold a hundred copies a day (excluding Sundays) for the first year after publication, and went into fifteen editions. Its title was deliberately provocative. Binney felt, as Dale did, that evangelicals had laid too much stress on the future life, at the expense of the present world. He surmounted criticisms that he was simply preaching a gospel of getting on. But some of his evangelical colleagues continued to feel it necessary to correct possible misunderstandings of his message. The Baptist Alexander Maclaren, who regarded himself as a disciple of Binney, argued that it was possible to 'make the most of both worlds', but reiterated that true religion would keep men back from many things which '"the world" thinks "the best" that it has'.[13] William Landels was more trenchant:

> If there were no possibility of our having to exchange profit for probity
> . . . Christ would never have said 'Ye cannot serve God and Mammon'
> . . . obviously men of integrity *are* successful. But success is not so
> uniform as to furnish a ground of appeal to those to whom success is
> the only motive.[14]

At a time of both Catholic and Anglo-Catholic revival, the Baptist W. T. Rosevear drew on anti-Catholic prejudice to define the essence of Puritanism. He contrasted the Ritualists' aim to reproduce both the spirit and the form of the medieval age with the Baptists' desire to reproduce the spirit and *not* the form of the Puritan age. Thus the key events of Puritanism to be reinforced were the importance of personality, of prayer and the adaptation of eternal truths to the needs of the present day.[15] Tradition was rhetorically distinguished from traditionalism in a way which was open to all Protestant evangelicals.

One of the most direct ways in which Puritan and evangelical qualities were to be regenerated and made to strike home in the contemporary world was through a new genre of exemplary biographies of merchants and manufacturers[16] and a literature which related biblical figures like Nehemiah very specifically to details of commercial casuistry.[17] These became part of a conscious answer to the Catholic resurgence of hagiography, and both recalled the immediately post-Reformation tradition of Protestant casuistics, and represented a development of the biographical tradition of holy lives and happy deaths particularly characteristic of Methodism. The Revd Thomas Pennington asserted his exemplary heritage in a line which he traced from Nehemiah through David to Richard Baxter to Joseph Williams, the eighteenth-century Nonconformist merchant. By relating Baxter and Williams, Pennington signalled his intention to develop a more dynamic combination of moral casuistry and biography.[18] In the eighteenth and early nineteenth centuries any biographies of businessmen-'saints' which existed had tended to point out merely that work in the commercial world need not *undermine* a man's spiritual life. They were rarely devoted to arguing through a positive case for the spiritual potential of a constructive Christian involvement in trade.[19] The detailed challenges and dilemmas of business life needed to be addressed in order to invest that life with the potential for chivalry and heroic virtue. It was all too easy to portray acts of benevolence which could be seen as compensatory for the activity of the rest of life. As the Wesleyan Methodist William Arthur observed, even when biographers had taken up the life of a commercial man, 'they have dropped business as a leaden thing, a dead weight, that would sink the book; and so you float away on a fragrant cargo of philanthropy and public life'.[20] Arthur himself was the author of the best-selling biography of the exemplary Wesleyan commodity merchant Samuel Budgett, which was published in 1852 under the title *The Successful Merchant*. This book had gone into forty-three editions by 1885, and had sold over 84,000 copies by the end of the century. It was translated into Welsh, Dutch, French and German, and extracts from it were printed in American commercial periodicals. Arthur reconfigured the secular self-help success model within a Christian framework. At the beginning it appeared as if Budgett was going to follow the typical success-story pattern. He was said to have started his commercial career by picking up a horse-shoe in the road and selling it. But as the story developed, the reader saw him constantly giving away his savings so that he had to start all over again, thus permanently gaining the Wesleyan habit of making, saving and giving. Arthur described the particular areas of temptation in Budgett's commercial life – adulteration of goods, speculation, the offering of loss-leaders to attract custom – emphasizing that these were continual challenges even for the truly Christian merchant. In this context Arthur stressed how crucial it was for a preacher living amongst people engaged in trade to know in detail the life they were leading. Ignorant of the specific temptations, causes of depression, anxieties, and ambitions 'which outweigh the claims of truth and right', he would be unfit to act as any sort of guide or support.[21]

There were many biographical collections, which placed exemplary merchants alongside figures in the established Puritan and evangelical canon – Bunyan, Owen, Tersteegen – as well as alongside widely admired nineteenth-century philanthropists or Christian military heroes such as Major-General Havelock.[22] Analogies were made especially with military heroism to point up the ways in which the language of the market could delimit public recognition of commercial virtue:

> The soldier is called by all his pledges to forget himself and seek alone the good of his country. The man of science has before his eye the splendid service he may render to mankind . . . the only form public success can wear for the man of commerce is that of remuneration, and general approbation attends him in proportion as he 'does well to himself'.[23]

Real heroism lay in clarifying personal motivation, in continuous, scrupulous attention to the concealed selfishness which might lie behind 'doing well to oneself'. Professed Christians often failed to relate broad ethical precepts to particular circumstances. Evangelical moralists emphasized that it would not be an excuse to say that they were forced into wrong-doing only under the extreme pressure of a moment. As R. W. Dale said: 'What man would dream of raising money in dishonest ways who was not in difficulties? It is only when the difficulties come that the test of honesty assumes this form.'[24] He stressed the importance of *intelligence* and *understanding* in grasping the necessary integration of the religious and secular spheres. Just because a man was a Christian, he would not automatically have a nobler idea of moral duty. The injunction to take regular account of where one stood had an interlocking religious and economic significance. Just as in business one could easily go wrong without noticing it, if one had not instituted systematic stock-taking, so in morals it was possible to go astray without marking the stages by which it had happened. 'The 11th Commandment', Dale urged, was 'Thou shalt make a balance-sheet'.[25] William Arthur emphasized that 'love of system was as rooted in Budgett's character as perseverance'.[26] The example of a fixed, ordered, Christian pattern of life could also provide inspiration for others and could often do more than pulpit sermons to propagate the gospel. The motives of publicly professed Christian merchants were naturally more suspiciously scrutinized – and consistency of character was necessary to earn respect and to reinforce the role of Christian principle in commercial life.[27]

Such systematization and interrelation of different aspects of life were crucial in guarding against covetousness and the spirit of worldliness. Although complaints about worldliness were as old as time, the context in which it could develop was seen to be changing. Was the progression by which the luxuries of one day became the necessities of the next inherently to be condemned? Where was the line to be drawn between a man's pecuniary obligations to his business and family and his wider charitable obligations to society? By its very nature, covetousness could not be defined in a single way, because it was an attitude of mind which could reveal itself in any number of manifestations. The very fact that it took so many forms – and represented the illegitimate exaggeration of desires which were not in themselves necessarily wrong – meant that people could often reassure themselves by believing that because they were free of one form, they were innocent of all.[28] Since worldliness was generally connected exclusively with unbecoming splendour and extravagance, those who refrained from ostentation were apt to regard the term as irrelevant to them, though they were guilty of other forms of worldliness, such as meanness and avarice. 'The snare of another may lie in what he considers the neat, quiet, gentlemanly taste with which he does things; this is his world. Vulgarity and refinement are but the accidental form in either case.'[29] Thomas Binney pointed out the scope for sanctimoniousness in the argument that spiritual perfection was to be attained by stripping life of all beauty.

Because once there were no carpets, nor curtains, nor rosewood chairs, nor beautiful engravings, to be seen in the houses of certain classes . . . that is no reason why it should be thought wrong to have them now . . . If a man can keep a carriage, let him keep it; and let him *call* it a carriage, and not attempt to sophisticate his soul by describing it with the Quakers as only a 'leathern convenience'.[30]

The relevant point to establish was the necessary relationship between such expenditure and all the other areas of responsibility.

To this end Binney and others from all evangelical denominations came together to promote what they described as *systematic beneficence*. A volume of essays, *Gold and the Gospel*, was published in 1853 and in 1860 a national society was formed with active branches in the major commercial centres.[31] The aim was to urge people to organize their lives in such a way that sums would be set aside regularly to meet all commitments. The obligation to set aside a tenth of one's income for religious use was reinforced by reference to the Old and New Testaments and again to the seventeenth-century casuistical tradition. Binney adopted the rhetorical device of setting up objections to the various points of his arguments and then answering them, in a way very similar to that of the Puritan Thomas Gouge, whose work he republished – although Binney extended the significance of this discipline to stress the *interrelated* benefits to men's religious and business life, which was a central focus for Victorian evangelicals.[32] While evangelicals had always argued for the stewardship of wealth, the concept was highly ambivalent. The very idea of property as held in trust from God could justify *either* the retention of it as divinely ordained *or* the obligation to dispense it to others. The principles of systematic beneficence argued that for a Christian the will of God had to be uppermost in his treatment of all his property, not just that specifically appropriated for religious and charitable purposes. A man should not be able to be satisfied with giving money to the abstract poor while he neglected his responsibility to his family or his workforce.[33] Nor could the conscience of the immoral trader be salved by the donation to religious or charitable causes of funds acquired by dubious means. The Baptist Hugh Stowell Brown set up a vivid opposition between 'lucre' and 'filthy lucre' to make the point that money gained dishonestly could not become clean even if spent liberally; and became filthy when honestly made but wrongly used. Those who generously relieved suffering with one hand had often contributed to it with the other.[34] Detailed illustrations were followed through to confront some of the most obvious forms of self-justification which could be produced to resist sytematization and the setting aside of a tenth. It was emphasized that the injunction to set aside a tenth related to clear income and conflicted neither with capital reinvestment nor with legitimate personal expenditure. The setting aside of regular amounts at a regular time was discussed in close conjunction with the need to set aside sums well before the acts either of giving or of spending.[35] In each case, the practice could conduce to the safeguarding of motivation as well as to thoughtfulness and efficiency. The establishment of a method and a way of thinking needed to come before anything else.

Systematic beneficence had a strongly integrative purpose. The primacy of the obligation to set aside money for religious purposes was put forward as a means of increasing cohesion within the community of church or chapel, a point of particular relevance to Nonconformists at a time of great debate about the criteria of church membership. There were particular concerns about a tendency to turn a blind eye to the moral failings of the prosperous, who might themselves seek out membership as a sanction of respectability. As Robert Spence said, 'The worldling who now professes Christianity because it is fashionable and perhaps profitable, would not be so willing to enter a community where he would be expected to give a 1/10th of his income to God.'[36] At the same time systematic beneficence would help to sustain the sort of character which could withstand the broader dissemination of the ethos of consumption. The very speed at which life was lived threatened the exercise of any of the powers of contemplation and reflectiveness on which self-control and moral independence needed to rest. Work itself was a stewardship, whose status depended on the moral purposes with which it was invested. If we work for the sake of work without any clear idea of our object in life, 'not only is our direct influence for good diminished, but our mind becomes correspondingly contracted and enfeebled'. The emphasis on cheapness and quickness of supply could destroy pride in production, as well as conducing to a more widely corrosive superficiality and lack of commitment.[37]

The emphasis on the need for individuals to build structures to combat such trends was particularly relevant to the specific audience addressed by all this literature. It was not aimed at the flashy speculator who thrived on risk, or at the complacent devotee of conspicuous consumption, but at a middle- and lower middle-class constituency with more moderate ambitions and more complex moral dilemmas. As Thomas Binney put it:

> Our special mission is neither to the very rich nor to the very poor. We have a work to do upon the thinking, active, influential classes – classes which fill neither courts nor cottages, but which, gathered into cities and consisting of several gradations there, are the modern movers and moulders of the world.[38]

In the mid-century the fluctuations and instabilities of the expanding economy were felt particularly by small and medium-sized businesses in sectors such as grocery and drapery, where the largest number of bankruptcies occurred.[39] The function of this literature was both to be challenging and to offer reassurance and support – to indicate that people's frequent sense of being under intolerable pressure was both common and surmountable – and so to help to sustain legitimate commercial life. Hence the emphasis of the exemplary biographies that their subjects were not people of extraordinary talent, but practised extraordinary diligence and pursued a fixed purpose which would be a safeguard in times of commercial reverse.[40] Stress was laid on an individual's responsibility towards his family, his private religious life, his other activities and his own health. There was no heroism in a highly pressured anxious business life which caused him to neglect any of these.[41] The overworking of employees was deplored, as were some of the justifications offered by employers for not providing leisure opportunities for their workforce. In 1858 the *Baptist Magazine* put the point forcefully:

> Those who, by severe self-discipline or natural aptitudes, are able to devote *all* their time and energies directly to spiritual things deserve all honour . . . But to those who take this position and condemn every innocent relaxation, I say be consistent . . . Do not condemn amusements, and devote all your energies to the *business of this life*, and the pursuit of wealth.[42]

Evangelicals took the lead in the early-closing movement, urging employers to take a stand in resisting consumer pressure for late opening hours, and rallying consumers to recognize the implications of their demands.[43] The primary emphasis on employers (and on those who had the aspiration to become employers) was none the less significant. It was here – it was felt – that real change could best be instituted. Although consumers, and indeed shareholders, were urged to recognize their responsibilities, the limitations of their scope to effect change were also acknowledged. Moreover, the plea of satisfying customers was all too easy a way out for businessmen.

A large part of the literature was targeted at the young, and was produced or promoted through evangelical organizations like the YMCA. This was a critical area of concern given the specific pressures to which the young were subject – and the large expansion in employment opportunities in towns and cities for young men (and later in the century women) in the white-collar world of clerks and warehousemen. Romanticism informed an optimism about the potentialities of youth, but youthful energy needed to be directed and supported if it was to withstand the temptations of city life – temptations both to recreational vice and to commercial misdeeds. Organizations like the YMCA offered a community of the like-minded, to which young men could gravitate who might not immediately join or feel part of a chapel.[44] It could then help to develop the right instincts and act as a support group to enable people to resist pressures to do what they felt to be wrong. The creation of communities of trust was one crucial way in which the framework of an ethical economy could be maintained.

The disciplinary practice of the Nonconformist churches provided one very practical way of doing this – and here Nonconformists had a distinctive mechanism for sustaining themselves as communities of trust. Unlike the Anglican Church, Nonconformist churches had very specific conditions of membership, and instituted committees of investigation if it came to their notice that any member had transgressed the rules. The most frequently investigated cases were those of dishonesty, insolvency, adultery, drunkenness and non-attendance. A man who became bankrupt was automatically investigated. The examinations were conducted by committees selected from amongst the congregation; in each case a report was presented to the church as a whole, and after discussion it was decided whether the offence was serious enough to warrant exclusion from membership. It has been suggested that over the nineteenth century, those chapel communities which took a more sympathetic view of the secular world were led to loosen their discipline.[45] But in fact the points seem to be confused. More sympathetic views of the secular world were certainly manifested, but not a less vigorous attempt to keep up the standards of church members acting *in* the world. Although there is evidence that investigators found it difficult to analyse the increasingly complicated facts of cases brought before them, they persisted in their task. The exercise of this sort of discipline was not simply punitive. It was also meant to be a means of helping people who were faced with difficult problems. They were encouraged to share these problems, and the church community would offer support (moral and in some cases financial) and sympathy (if merited) to strengthen their resolve to carry through the morally approved course. The very fact that people thought it worthwhile to submit to investigation is itself a sign of a degree of consensus about the value of such activities. In forty years of records at Carr's Lane Chapel in Birmingham where R. W. Dale was minister, there is only one recorded case of someone refusing to come before the committee.[46] One man even came all the way from Scotland to defend himself against charges of embezzlement. He was unsuccessful, and ended up being separated formally from the church.[47] Disciplinary investigations did not stand apart from the ordinary life of the chapel; they were complementary to the broader moral framework within which the chapel was seen to operate.

The reinforcement of this moral framework of course helped to maintain the usefulness of church membership as a public index of moral and business respectability.[48] At the same time, the interest in belonging to a church on the part of middle-class members was not confined to the easy acquisition of social respectability or economic contacts. Each submitted himself to processes of discipline in which neither social standing nor wealth was respected. One of the most striking examples of this is that of the investigation in 1866–7 of the Baptist builder and contractor Morton Peto by members of Bloomsbury Chapel – the chapel which Peto himself had built and of which he was the most prominent member. A good employer, he had none the less over-reached himself in arranging finance to build the London,

Chatham and Dover Railway, and his firm fell with the celebrated collapse of Overend, Gurney in 1866. He acknowledged insufficient vigilance in relation to the ramifications of responsibility, and although the committee cleared him of dishonesty, they did criticize him for taking on too much liability, and remarked that 'we cannot forget that something more than conventional morality is demanded from the followers of Christ . . . not to assume positions in which the duties are inconsistent one with the other and to avoid the appearance of evil'.[49]

Such inquiries were also intended to serve an exemplary function. This had several facets. The investigation could show that all members of the church community were treated alike. It could also make explicit the integrative role of such discipline by virtue of the fair way in which the cases were treated. Most importantly, the detailed setting out of the case could act as a spur to self-examination on the part of other members of the church, and also prevent garbled rumours developing in close-knit communities where the fact of a member's bankruptcy would in any case be known. All the background circumstances of a case were taken into consideration and, in deciding a verdict, the way in which the business had been run over a period was more important than the immediate fact of exposure. In some cases where a man had not shown sufficient care in ascertaining the real state of his business, confidence was expressed in the man's integrity, but regret at his lack of prudence: discussion of the circumstances and the delivery of a reprimand completed the exemplary purpose.[50] In other cases ignorance was felt to be blameworthy, and more severe penalties were imposed.[51] In Carr's Lane in 1869 a man was expelled for having been bankrupt more than once without having improved the way in which he conducted his business.[52] The behaviour of the person being investigated before the church was taken very seriously. In another case in Carr's Lane in 1858 Mr Dabbie's situation was felt to be very difficult, and sympathy was expressed, but his real crime proved to be his evasiveness in front of the committee.[53] The church meeting could also be used as a forum for discussion and adjudication of a particular business friction which had arisen between members of the same congregation. In Birmingham East Methodist Circuit, a local preachers' meeting in 1853 was used to sort out a festering trade dispute.[54] In such ways the chapel could facilitate business relations, and act as a sanction for good practice.

In the approach adopted to all these cases the disciplinary practice was absolutely in accord with the ethical preaching of the ministers serving the congregations. At Bloomsbury Chapel Peto's minister William Brock was a noted contributor to the debate on commercial morality and its relationship to national life, as was R. W. Dale at Carr's Lane. Thomas Binney, Congregationalist minister of King's Weigh House from 1829 to his death in 1874, took enormous pains over those in his chapel suffering business difficulties. His preaching to businessmen, large and small, who constituted a significant part of his congregation, was held to have been particularly effective because he had been in commerce himself: for nine years he had worked at a bookseller's, apparently never working less than twelve hours a day.[55]

The chapel community offered a framework within which individuals involved in business life could exercise – and be seen to exercise – the self-discipline and moral scrupulousness which was their Christian responsibility. A very obvious incentive was offered to develop principles which would lend force to the association of Protestantism with commercial activity. This particular disciplinary structure constituted a well-established Nonconformist tradition. But the ethical teaching which informed it was part of a wider evangelical mission to rework tradition in a modern idiom – to make it plain that received Protestant values could not automatically be assumed to retain their power. The target was the conscience of the individual Christian, in particular the individual who held a position of sufficient responsibility to be able to make choices and to influence behaviour. It was recognized that the individual conscience was operating in a complex structure of social ethics, but it was felt that an individual *conception* of responsibility would continue to be relevant in a business world of which trust was a fundamental part. Evangelicals had a crucial role in underlining this point and living it out. This process would be as important for the maintenance of their own identity as a religious movement as it was for the integrity of the commercial community of which they constituted such a prominent part.

Notes

[1] See, for example, A. Maclaren, *Fidelity to Conscience: A Lecture delivered at Willis's Rooms, St James's for the Central United Bartholomew Committee* (London, 1862), 53–5; J. C. Ryle, *Baxter and his Times* (London, 1853), a lecture delivered to the YMCA in Exeter Hall, p. 23; W. C. Magee, 'Richard Baxter, his life and times: A lecture', in *Lectures delivered before the Dublin YMCA* (Dublin, 1862), 3–5, 37.

[2] J. Baillie, *Brownlow North Esq.: What He Was; What He Did; and How He Did it. In Memoriam* (London, 1876), 13, 19 (Baillie edited *The Crucifying of the World, by the Cross of Christ, by Richard Baxter,* 1861). Cf. L. L. Doggett, *History of the YMCA,* 2 vols. (New York, 1919, 1922), i. 67.

[3] W. Anderson, *Progress; or The International Exhibition* (London, 1862), 3.

[4] R. Spence Hardy, *Commerce and Christianity. Memorials of Jonas Sugden of Oakworth House* (London and Edinburgh, 1858), 192.

[5] C. M. Birrell, 'The influence of the present times on personal religion', *Papers Read before the Baptist Union of Great Britain and Ireland at its autumnal session in Cannon Street Chapel, and Wycliffe Church, Birmingham, October 12th and 13th 1864* (London, 1865), 84.

[6] H. Stowell, 'The Christian man in the business of life', *Manchester Lectures: Christianity in the Business of Life* (London, 1858), 95.

[7] R. H. Tawney, *The Acquisitive Society* (London, 1921; Brighton, 1982 edn), 181–2.

[8] R. W. Dale, *The Old Evangelicalism and the New* (London, 1889), *passim.*

[9] For a wide-ranging discussion of some of the ways in which this process developed, see R. Samuel, 'The discovery of puritanism, 1820–1914: A preliminary sketch' in J. Garnett and C. Matthew (eds.), *Revival and Religion since 1700: Essays for John Walsh* (London, 1993), 201–23.

[10] S. Martin, *The Church and the Nation* (London, 1862), 23.

[11] S. Martin, *Conformity and Nonconformity in 1862* (London, 1862), 13–14.

[12] See, for example, *This World and the Next: The Impossibility of Making the Best of Both. Some Reply to Mr Binney's Lecture* (London, 1856).

[13] A. Maclaren, ' "So did not I" A word to the young. Nehemiah v. 15', in *Sermons Preached in Union Chapel, Manchester; Communion and Contentment* (London and Manchester, 1859), 90ff.

[14] W. Landels, *'Business is Business'. A Lecture delivered before the YMCA in Exeter Hall, November 23 1875* (London, 1876), 23–5.

[15] W. T. Rosevear, *The Essential Spirit of Puritanism in Relation to the Needs of Today* (Leicester, Glasgow, London, 1869), esp. 4–9.

[16] See, for example, Hardy, *Commerce and Christianity*; P. Lorimer, *Healthy Religion Exemplified in the Life of the late Mr Andrew Jack, of Edinburgh* (London, 1852); W. Arthur, *The Successful Merchant* (London, 1852), discussed below; B. Gregory, *The Thorough Business Man. Memoirs of Walter Powell, Merchant, Melbourne and London* (London, 1871); J. Stacey, *A Prince in Israel; Sketches of the Life of John Ridgway* (London, 1862).

[17] See, for example, H. Stowell, *A Model for Men of Business: Lectures on the Character of Nehemiah* (London, 1854); W. Brock, 'Daniel a Model for Young Men', *Lectures delivered before the YMCA in Exeter Hall, 1852–53* (London, 1853); W. Guest, *The Young Man Setting out in Life* (London, 1867); J. Baillie, *Scenes of Life, Historical and Biographical; chiefly from Old Testament Times; or, Chapters for Solitary Hours, and for the Sunday at Home* (London, 1861).

[18] T. Pennington, 'Spiritual and secular diligence compared', in *Religion in its Relation to Commerce and the Ordinary Avocations of Life* (London, 1852), 221–4.

[19] For a particularly grudging example, see *The Efficacy of Faith in the Atonement of Christ, Exemplified in a Memoir of Mr William Carvosso* (2nd edn., London, 1836), 58.

[20] W. Arthur, *The Successful Merchant: Sketches of the Life of Mr Samuel Budgett, late of Kingswood Hill* (London, 1852), 27.

[21] Ibid., 138, 142, 174, 83, 34.

[22] See, for example, *Life-Studies: or, How to Live, illustrated in the Biographies of Bunyan, Tersteegen, Montgomery, Perthes and Mrs Winslow* (London, 1857).

[23] W. Arthur, *'Heroes', Lectures before the YMCA, 1850–61*, 335.

[24] R. W. Dale, 'The necessity of doing the will of God', *The Evangelical Revival and Other Sermons* (London, 1880), 116–17.

[25] R. W. Dale, 'The use of the understanding in keeping God's law', *Weekday Sermons* (London, 1867), 10–37; 'The education of the conscience', *The Evangelical Revival and Other Sermons* (London, 1880), 95–6, 98–106.

[26] Arthur, *Successful Merchant*, 61.

[27] See, for example, Stacey, *A Prince in Israel*, 67; W. Kirkman, *T. C. Hincksman of Lytham (1799–1883)* (n.d. ?1885); *Heroic Men: The Death-Roll of the Primitive Methodist Ministry* (London, 1889), 49.

[28] See J. Harris, *Mammon; or Covetousness the Sin of the Christian Church* (London, 1836); W. Arnot, *The Race for Riches; and Some of the Pits into which the Runners Fall* (Edinburgh, 1851).

[29] J. W. Reeve, 'The activity of worldliness in the last days', *Present Times and Future Prospects* (London, 1854), 36.

[30] T. Binney, *Is it Possible to Make the Best of Both Worlds?* (London, 1852), 109, 110.

[31] The Systematic Beneficence Society, established in 1860.

[32] T. Gouge, *The Surest and Safest Way of Thriving – or, a Conviction of That Grand Mistake in Many, that What is Given to the Poor is a Loss to their Estate* (1673), republished as *Giving the Surest Way of Thriving* in 1856 by the evangelical Partridge and Co., with a recommendatory preface by Thomas Binney. See also Binney, *Is it Possible . . .?* and *Money* (London, 1865).

[33] *London City Mission Magazine* (Jan. 1852), 6; J. Rattenbury, 'Haste to be rich', *Religion in its relation to Commerce and the Ordinary Avocations of Life* (London, 1852), 142–3, 150–2.

[34] H. S. Brown, 'Lucre and filthy lucre', *'Manliness' and Other Sermons* (London, 1889 edn), 157.

[35] J. Ross, *The Lord's Portion Stored on the Lord's Day* (London, 1861), 36, 84.

[36] R. Spence, 'The Jewish law of tithe, a guide to Christian liberality', *Gold and the Gospel* (London, Edinburgh and Dublin, 1853), 263. See also A Wesleyan Minister (J. Withington), *Temporal Prosperity and Spiritual Decline* (London, 1866), 100–1.

[37] A. M. Pollock, *The Object of Life* (Dublin, London, Edinburgh, 1859), 16; J. B. Brown, *Competition, the Labour Market and Christianity* (London, 1851), 12–16; Stacey, *A Prince in Israel*, 49. See also Spence, 'Jewish law of tithe', 279–80.

[38] T. Binney to the Congregational Union, May 1848, *Congregational Year Book* (1848), 9; cf. J. Kennedy to the Congregational Union, 1872, *Congregational Year Book* (1873), 86: 'Our congregations belong for the most part to the *middle* middle class'. See also P. Seaver, 'The Puritan work ethic revisited', *Journal of British Studies*, 19 No. 2 (1980), 35–53, for a seventeenth-century comparison.

[39] V. M. Lester, *Victorian Insolvency: Bankruptcy, Imprisonment for Debt, and Company Winding-up in Nineteenth-Century England* (Oxford, 1995).

[40] Arthur, *Successful Merchant*, 63; Gregory, *The Thorough Business Man*, 2–3; Stacey, *A Prince in Israel*, 17; P. Lorimer, *Healthy Religion Exemplified*, 101.

[41] S. Martin, *Money; its History and Philosophy and its Use and Abuse* (London, 1850), 16; J. Todd, 'Men of business: their position, influence and duties' and J. F. Stearns, 'Men of business: their intellectual culture', in *The Man of Business Considered in Six Aspects: A Book for Young Men* (Edinburgh, 1864), 51–93, 139–76.

[42] *Baptist Magazine*, 50 (1858), 406.

[43] See, for example, G. Smith, 'The golden rule opposed to the late-hour system', *Sermons by Wesleyan Methodist Ministers* (1852–3); J. Cumming, 'Labour, rest and recreation', *Lectures delivered before the*

YMCA in Exeter Hall 1854–55 (London, 1855), 42. See also A. J. Harvey, *From Suffolk Lad to London Merchant* (Bristol, 1900), 48–50, for a reference to the firm of Bartrum, Harvey and Co., who reduced their weekday hours, despite the fact that not everyone in the same trade and district followed the same course. James Harvey was a regular member of William Brock's Bloomsbury Chapel congregation.

44 F. A. West, 'Young men; their dangers and duties', in *Memorials of the Rev. Francis A. West*, ed. B. Gregory (London, 1873); W. Guest, *Life: What will you do with it?: An Address to Young Men* (London, 1866); J. C. Symons, *The History and Advantage of Young Men's Associations* (London, 1856), 8; C. Binfield, *George Williams and the YMCA* (London, 1973).

45 R. W. Ram, 'The evolution of five Dissenting communities in Birmingham, 1750–1870' (University of Birmingham Ph.D. thesis, 1972), 57, 308, 316.

46 Birmingham Central Library, Carr's Lane Discipline Committee, book 2 (July 1859–July 1894), 93–4.

47 Ibid., 54–8 (Dec. 1865).

48 Compare P. Bolitho, *The Story of Methodism in the Liskeard Circuit 1751–1967* (Truro, 1967), 39. Cf. M. Weber, 'Die Protestantischen Sekten und der Geist des Kapitalismus', *Gesammelte Aufsätze zur Religionssoziologie* (Tübingen, 1922–3), i. 207–36, selected and translated in Hans Gerth and C. Wright Mills (eds.), *From Max Weber: Essays in sociology* (London, 1970), 302–22.

49 B. and F. Bowers, 'Bloomsbury chapel and mercantile morality', *Baptist Quarterly*, 30 (1984), 210–20. It is inferred by Brian and Faith Bowers that chapel members were happy to revel in Peto's success for as long as he was successful; only when he failed did they begin to question the basis of his success. By definition, of course, this kind of disciplinary case only arose when failure had occurred, or dishonesty was revealed. What is significant, however, is the extent to which the disciplinary practice accords with the general pastoral emphasis of the church. Moreover the striking point is that the chapel would not allow its judgement to be coloured by awareness of Peto's generosity and other virtues, virtues which they continued fully to acknowledge. See also Carr's Lane Discipline Committee, Book 2, pp. 219–53 (August 1865): three noted members of the congregation (one of whom had himself been on the Disciplinary Committee appointed for 1865) were investigated in connection with the suspension of the Penny Bank. Two resigned and one was dismissed.

50 Carr's Lane Discipline Committee, book 1, p. 107 (Mar. 1856); book 2, pp. 46–7 (Aug. 1864).

51 Ibid., book 2, pp. 78–9 (Dec. 1872) and p. 39 (Oct. 1862).

[52] Ibid., book 2, pp. 69–70 (Mar.–June 1869).

[53] Ibid., book 1, p. 116 (Oct. 1858).

[54] Birmingham Central Library, Minutes of Local Preachers' Meetings in the Birmingham East Circuit (1851–67), Local Preachers' Meeting, Belmont Row Class Room, 9 and 17 June 1853 (no page nos.). Cf. Carr's Lane Discipline Committee, book 1, pp. 8–9 (Sept. 1840); ibid., book 2, pp. 54–8 (Dec. 1865); Birmingham, Cannon Street Baptist Church, Deacons' Minutes, i (1829–53).

[55] For biographical details, see C. M. Birrell, *The Life of William Brock, D.D., First Minister of Bloomsbury Chapel, London* (London, 1878); A. W. W. Dale, *The Life of R. W. Dale of Birmingham* (London, 1898); E. P. Hood, *Thomas Binney: His Mind, Life and Opinions* (London, 1874); E. Hodder, *Life of Samuel Morley* (London, 1887), 60–4.

7

Dissent and the peculiarities of the English,
c.1870–1914

HUGH McLEOD

Mary Hatch was born into a comfortable middle-class home in Dewsbury in 1886. Her father was a corn factor who had built up his own business. He had educated himself through Mechanics Institutes, and remained an avid self-educator all through his life: he went to science lectures and was reading Gibbon for the third time when he died. He and his wife were Congregationalists who had converted from Anglicanism, apparently because of a mixture of their hostility to the gentry and the fact that they were 'rabid teetotallers'. 'And I mean rabid', added Mary: her parents were very hospitable, but guests were informed at the start that it was a non-drinking, non-smoking household. They were both fervent radicals, and their home acted as a local Liberal headquarters during elections. Mary's father spoke at anti-war meetings during the Boer War and she remembers him returning home dripping wet after being pelted with bad eggs and rotten tomatoes. He was also president of the town's temperance society and she remembers a midnight mission organized by their chapel, when they marched through the streets late at night and sang hymns outside pubs. Her parents were enthusiasts for music, the theatre and cricket – though definitely not on Sundays. Mary had a clear sense of where Nonconformists stood in the local hierarchy of status: the Church of England were 'the moneyed people', while the Catholics were 'absolutely scruffy', and she and her sisters were forbidden to go near Dawes Green, the Catholic area. However, they changed their views of Catholicism a little when one of her sisters fell ill with smallpox – their own minister, who was worried about his family, did not visit her, but the Catholic priest did.[1]

Here we have one of the many faces of late Victorian Dissent, and perhaps one of the most familiar – prosperous, respectable, politically hyperactive and radical, in some respects puritanical, though not in a killjoy sense. There were many other faces, some of them quite different. I will describe three others more briefly, each of which reveals features to which I shall return later.

Vera Frith was born in Edmonton in 1883. Her father was a basket-maker. Her parents held religious meetings in their home, where they would read from the Bible and sing Sankey hymns. They also attended a mission hall, and they never went out except to activities organized by the mission, to which their few friends were all connected. They were Conservative in politics. Vera's most vivid memory from childhood was of a row at their Church of England school. She and her sister had not been christened, because their father did not believe in it: 'And this Vicar was terribly cross because we was at a church school, St Barnabas. And Norah got up and started screaming, and rushed home 'cos he said we wouldn't go to heaven because we weren't christened.'[2]

William Barnes was born in 1900 in Keighley. His father was a steel forger, while his mother had at various times been a spinner, had kept a shop and had taken in washing. His father went to the club every Sunday morning (and twice a year went with his workmates to the York races), and every Sunday evening he went to the Wesleyan chapel. The children all went to Sunday school and chapel. Their mother only went on special occasions, like anniversaries, but she and her husband read the Bible together before going to bed, and all the family sang hymns together on Sundays. At election times factory workers were expected to wear the colours of their employer's party, and the younger members of the family complied for fear of losing their jobs, but their father was presumably less vulnerable: as a supporter of the Independent Labour Party, he 'wore his red'. The Wesleyan chapel was the only place of worship in the neighbourhood and on normal Sundays the mainstay of the congregation were the 'better classes', the clerks and teachers. But on special occasions 'everybody went'. 'And everybody seemed to muck in when they got in the chapel. When they got outside, well, they just split up again.'[3]

Finally, a woman, whose name is not recorded, interviewed by an oral historian in Bristol. She was born in 1895. Her father was a boot checker and later a Co-op manager. The family had much in common with Mary Hatch's. They were teetotallers and pacifists, as well as being great readers. They did not like the children playing in the streets, for fear that they would fall in with 'rougher' playmates. When their daughter once stole as a young girl, she and her mother knelt together and prayed for forgiveness – she never stole again. The family was also religiously on the move. The father began as a Strict Baptist, but left because his chapel was too dogmatic, and joined another Baptist church. Later he became a Unitarian. Finally he got interested in socialism, 'which he felt was a practical form of Christianity with people if they are really true Socialists wanting the good of everybody and well, as people have said, working towards what Christ was trying to teach'. The implication seems to be that socialism replaced the chapel in his life, though this is not explicitly stated.[4]

I

These four families were among the several million in later Victorian and Edwardian England which were attached with varying degrees of commitment and enthusiasm to Protestant Dissenting churches. Within this small group we can see examples of the many different social contexts within which Dissent flourished in this period, and we can see cases of prevailing orthodoxy (for instance, Liberalism, teetotalism and sabbatarianism), of new trends (for instance, growing interest in Labour and socialist politics), and of more heterodox behaviour (such as going to clubs and race meetings – and, indeed, voting Conservative, though by the later part of this period that too was on the increase). I shall be concentrating here on orthodoxies and new trends, though it needs to be remembered that there were always Dissenters who dissented in greater or lesser degree from their own co-religionists. I shall return later to these individual examples in order to illustrate more general points in my argument. This chapter is in two parts. The first, which is factual, attempts to show that by comparison with predominantly Protestant countries in continental Europe the Dissenting denominations were both uniquely strong in England, and in some respects distinctive in their forms and social location. The second part, which is more speculative, explores some of the ways in which the strength of Protestant Dissent shaped English religion, politics and culture in this period, and suggests that some of the distinctive and, in a European context, peculiar features of English society can be explained in terms of this strong Dissenting influence.

It is of course impossible to provide any precise statistics of the proportion of Dissenters in the English population. The British census never provided information on religious affiliation, as happened in, for instance, Ireland, Germany, the Netherlands or Australia. However, the many censuses of church attendance that were undertaken during the later nineteenth and early twentieth centuries provide some indications. The best-known example is the national Religious Census of 1851 which found that 44 per cent of reported attendances in England on census Sunday were at Dissenting chapels, 61 per cent of those in Scotland and 80 per cent of those in Wales. Since, according to most calculations, around 40 per cent of the adult population in England and Scotland and perhaps as many as 55 per cent in Wales, attended some place of worship on the day of the census, it is clear that a very substantial proportion of the population was taking part in Dissenting services. All the indications are that if a similar count had been made in the 1880s and 1890s or the early 1900s the proportion of churchgoers who were Dissenters would have been higher. Robin Gill has compared church attendance in 1851 with that in 1881 in a group of twenty-eight large towns. He found that Nonconformist attendance increased slightly from 55 to 58 per cent of the total. In another group of towns where counts were held both in 1851 and 1902–4 there was a very slight increase in the Nonconformist share of attendances from 52.5 to 53.4 per cent between the two dates.[5] We also know, of course, that there was a substantial increase in the proportion of the total population living in urban areas during the second half of the nineteenth century, which meant that large numbers of people were moving out of an environment where the Church of England was dominant and into one which was more pluralistic, but where the majority of places of worship and the majority of churchgoers were Nonconformist. Clearly these figures overstate the proportion of Nonconformists in the total population. On the other hand it would be going too far to follow Michael Watts, who counts as Nonconformists only those who attended a chapel on the day of the census.[6]

There were many degrees of Nonconformist belonging, and we shall seriously understate the extent of the Free Church constituency if we only count the inner core of those who were church members, and the also highly committed group of these who, without becoming members, attended week by week. Apart from these, of whom there must have been some who normally attended chapel, but were prevented by illness or work from doing so on the day of the census, there were those like Mrs Barnes who regarded themselves as Nonconformists, and whose religious commitment was reflected in their daily life, but who seldom attended services. And how do we count those, like her neighbours in Keighley, who only came to chapel for big occasions like Sunday school anniversaries, but would no doubt have said they were Wesleyans if they had been asked by a census enumerator? It is also known that, especially in the first half of the nineteenth century, there was a big turnover of Nonconformist members.[7] The Methodists in particular recruited on a large scale, only to lose many of the recruits within a few years, whether for individual reasons, or as a result of one of the numerous disputes which embittered the history of nineteenth-century chapels, sometimes dividing whole denominations. The most notorious example was the Fly Sheets controversy of 1849–50 which resulted in the loss to the Wesleyan Methodists of about a quarter of their members. Many of the dissidents became Wesleyan Reformers. But many dropped out of Methodist membership altogether (and indeed Methodist membership as a proportion of total population never returned to the level it reached in the 1840s). What happened to these ex-Methodists? Are we to assume that they ceased to be Nonconformists in any meaningful sense as soon as they stopped taking an active part in chapel life? There are some famous examples of those who loudly proclaimed their Nonconformist identity, although they had left the chapel. A more backhanded tribute to the strength of invisible religious ties was made by an evangelist in 1840s Birmingham, who reported that 'on my visits I find ten backsliders of the Wesleyan denomination to two of all the sects of the Christian church', and clearly hinted that intensive exposure to cheap Methodist emotionalism had inoculated them for life against the pure Calvinist gospel which he was preaching.[8] There were also those whose denominational identity was less clear, since they attended Anglican and Dissenting services with equal readiness, sometimes going to church in the morning and to chapel in the afternoon and evening.[9] On the other hand, the proportion of those in later Victorian and Edwardian England with no denominational identity at all has been greatly exaggerated. Oral history interviews with those born in this period indicate that the great majority remembered their parents as being 'church', 'chapel' or 'Catholic' and, if 'chapel', as belonging to a specific denomination. It seems reasonable to assume that the proportion of the population who regarded themselves as Nonconformists lay somewhere between the 18 per cent calculated by Watts on the basis of actual chapel attendance and the approximately 50 per cent of churchgoers who chose chapel.

Among the countries of continental Europe, the Netherlands came closest to England in terms of the size and importance of the Protestant communities outside the Dutch Reformed Church. Since church and state had been separated in 1796, these communities could not technically be regarded as 'Dissenting', but in terms of social realities there were a good many parallels between the English and Dutch situations. The Dutch Reformed Church, though no longer legally established, was still the church of the well-established social élites and the church which retained at least the nominal adherence of the great majority of Protestants. However, as many as 12 per cent of the population in 1899 (or one-fifth of the Protestant population) identified themselves with other Protestant churches. These fell into two main categories. On the one hand there were the long-established communities of Lutherans, Mennonites and Remonstrants, which were mainly middle-class in their social constituency and tended towards liberalism in politics and theology. On the other hand there was a variety of newer groups which had emerged in the course of the nineteenth century, mostly strongly Calvinist in theology, relatively conservative in politics, socially broadly based, but with a tilt towards the lower middle class.[10] Sweden also had some parallels with Britain, both in terms of overall denominational structure and of the relative strength of Free Churches. In 1900 about 3 per cent of the Swedish population were actually counted as members of a Free Church.[11] If children of members and those more loosely connected with a congregation are counted, the proportion identifying with the Free Churches must have been considerably larger. Indeed in 1911 as many as 23 per cent of the members of the *Riksdag* claimed to belong to the Free Churches. Some of these churches were of British or American origin, such as the Methodists and Baptists, though there were also indigenous organizations such as the Swedish Mission. The main strength of the churches was in rural areas and, as with their British counterparts, they had an important role both in the Liberal Party and in the very powerful temperance movement.[12]

By contrast, Germany, with the largest Protestant community in Europe, was notable for the overwhelming dominance enjoyed by the *Landeskirchen* and the consequent weakness of the Free Churches. According to the census, 'Other Christians' (those who were neither Catholics nor members of the Protestant *Landeskirchen*) comprised 0.2 per cent of the population in 1871, 0.3 per cent in 1890, and 1 per cent in 1925.[13] Earlier in the nineteenth century Dissenting Christians had on two occasions enjoyed considerable temporary importance. First in the quarter century or so after 1817, there were large numbers of Lutherans, mainly in the eastern provinces of Prussia, who objected to the forced Union of Lutherans and Reformed. Some of them seceded from the *Landeskirche*, but the effect of these protests was eventually weakened by the departure of many of the protesters in pursuit of religious freedom in the United States or Australia.[14] Even more important in the short run were the Dissenting movements of the 1840s, such as the Friends of Light and the German Catholics, which fused modernist theology and democratic politics, and which had an important role in the revolutions of 1848 and 1849. However, these movements were repressed in the reactionary 1850s, and even where they survived never recovered their former influence.[15] In the later nineteenth century the various Free Churches had some localized importance – for instance the Methodists were fairly strong among the miners in Saxony, and the Apostolic Churches, with their prophecies, healings and preaching of an imminent Second Coming, attracted quite large congregations in the working-class districts of north and east Berlin. Even so, their overall impact was small and even in their strongholds their strength in no way compared with that which they enjoyed in many parts of Britain.[16]

Most aspects of English Dissent had their parallels somewhere in continental Europe. However, England stood out in several ways. First, there were the sheer numbers involved. Second, the bewildering diversity of Nonconformity – from Unitarians to Primitive Methodists, from Congregationalists to Brethren, from Quakers to Wesleyans, the theological and liturgical range and the variations in church structures were immense. There are echoes of this in the Netherlands, but even the Dutch could not compare in this respect with England, still less with Britain as a whole. Third, there was the social range of English Dissent. All social groups except for the gentry were to some degree involved. Over the last twenty-five years or so numerous local studies have indicated the many different kinds of social milieu in which the various forms of Dissent were deeply rooted in the later part of the nineteenth century: Primitive Methodist farm labourers in Norfolk, Wesleyan and Primitive miners in Co. Durham and nailers in the Black Country, Wesleyan farmers in Lincolnshire, Baptist small businessmen in Coventry, Congregationalist and Unitarian industrialists in Manchester, Congregationalist professional men in the London suburbs.[17] The statistics provided by Michael Watts for the early and middle years of the century provide less vivid but more comprehensive evidence for Nonconformist diversity, and challenge earlier suggestions that Dissenters were unduly concentrated within a few occupational categories.[18]

By comparison with Germany, English Dissent stood out by its highly political character, by the strong elements within it of education and culture, and by its relative social respectability. The first two elements were certainly present in the German Dissenting movements of the 1840s. But by the later part of the century, the German free churches appealed exclusively to a working-class and lower middle-class constituency, and to those within these classes who had little interest in politics.[19] More generally, even those German Protestants whose involvement in their church was minimal retained a strong prejudice against the 'sects', as they were habitually termed.[20] Such prejudices were certainly not entirely absent in nineteenth-century England, and they frequently found expression in works of literature, where the tendency to present Dissenters in a disparaging light is notorious. However, in most social milieux in nineteenth-century England, Nonconformists were a normal and taken-for-granted presence.[21]

By comparison with the Netherlands, there were important political differences. English Dissenters retained their outsider status and their grievances for longer, which was why so many of them kept both their Liberalism and their militancy right into the early years of the twentieth century. In the Netherlands, the older Dissenting groups such as the Lutherans, Mennonites and Remonstrants remained Liberal, but ceased to be militant, as they were drawn into the liberal establishment in the first half of the nineteenth century. The militant element in nineteenth-century Dutch Dissent were the ultra-Calvinists, who came together in the later years of the century under the charismatic leadership of Abraham Kuyper, and who attacked the establishment from a more conservative direction.[22] By comparison with Sweden, where the free churches were a mainly rural and small town phenomenon and where they had little impact on the labour movement, English Nonconformity was more broadly based socially and politically.

II

In the second part of the chapter I am going to discuss four aspects of England in the later nineteenth and early twentieth centuries, which were in my view substantially influenced by the strength of Protestant Dissent. I shall emphasize the importance of this factor by drawing comparisons with the situation in Protestant areas of Germany. The four points are the retardation of secularization in England, the puritan ethos of nineteenth-century English life, the distinctive character of Liberal and socialist politics in England and the character of popular Protestantism.

The retardation of secularization in England by comparison with Protestant areas of Germany is most clearly reflected in churchgoing statistics. Robin Gill's figures for weekly church attendance as a proportion of total population in twenty-eight large English towns in 1881 shows an average of 35 per cent, comprising Anglicans 13 per cent, Nonconformists 20 per cent and Catholics 2 per cent.[23] In Protestant Germany these figures would have seemed high even in the more pious rural areas: in the cities they would have seemed incredible. (They would have seemed more normal in the Catholic regions of southern and western Germany, where churchgoing was much higher than in the Protestant north and east.) Part of the difference lay in the fact that attendance at services of the Protestant *Landeskirchen* in German cities was somewhat lower than attendance at Anglican services in English cities. For instance, around the end of the nineteenth century, the proportion of Protestants attending a service of the *Landeskirche* was 1 per cent in Berlin, 5 per cent in Ulm, 6 per cent in Hanover and and about 7 per cent in Dresden.[24] But the most important factor was the vastly greater strength of the free churches in English cities. English Nonconformity was able to penetrate those milieux where alienation from the church was most frequent in Germany. These included the urban working class[25] and the liberal middle class. Agnosticism was well-established among the educated middle class in Germany by the 1830s and 1840s, but made little headway in England before the 1880s and 1890s. Similarly among the politically militant members of the working class a synthesis of Marxism, Darwinism and anti-clericalism was normal in Germany by 1900, whereas in England this combination, though far from unknown, was a minority option. There were plenty of those who, like William Barnes's father, combined Labour politics with Nonconformist religion, and those uninvolved in the church were far less likely than their counterparts in Germany to be militant secularists.[26]

In the nineteenth century the main precipitants of secularization were political and social. In Germany from at least the 1820s onwards orthodox theology was closely bound up with conservative politics.[27] In Prussia, for instance, the pietists saw obedience to the divinely ordained authorities as a religious duty, and they were bitterly opposed to all liberal and democratic movements. This stance was forcefully expressed in their paper the *Kreuzzeitung,* with its slogan 'Forward with God for King and Fatherland'. As a result, political liberals, including most members of the educated middle class, were very open to religiously heterodox ideas. Their counterparts in England could, however, as Dissenters, combine orthodox religion with political liberalism. So far as the working class was concerned, the Methodists in particular established forms of local religious community, in which working-class people could hold positions of responsibility, and styles of worship were adapted to local cultures. One consequence of this was that the Bible retained a significant place in popular culture and continuing power as a radical text, whereas in Germany by the later nineteenth century conservatives had gained a near-monopoly in the political use of the scriptures. The last radical movement in England whose rhetoric was dominated by biblical language was the agricultural labourers' movement of the 1870s, a large proportion of whose leaders were Methodist preachers.[28] However, the continuing potency of such rhetoric was demonstrated as late as 1924, when the West Yorkshire Labour MP, Ben Turner, told the House of Commons:

> You have either got to scrap the preparations for war or scrap the New Testament. I am going to stand for the New Testament as against this policy of cruisers . . . An hon. member asked whether we believe in the ideal embodied in the New Testament that if a man smites you on one cheek you shall turn the other. That is the finest way to stop violence and war . . . I shall stand by the Sermon on the Mount. It is the great fundamental and moral principle that will save all nations from destruction.[29]

Turner, who was said to always carry a Bible in his pocket, and to make frequent reference to it in his speeches, was by this time unusual in the directness of the link between his political arguments and their religious justifications. However, the difference between the situation in Britain and in Germany had been well illustrated by two surveys carried out shortly before the First World War. British Labour MPs, when questioned about the books or authors that had influenced them, most frequently mentioned the Bible. A survey which questioned members of the Social Democratic trade unions in various parts of Germany about, among other things, their reading habits, indicated the popularity of anti-religious writers and of those German classic writers who were most noted for their critical approach to religion.[30]

My second area of difference is the puritan ethos of nineteenth-century English life. This was most clearly manifested in the different character of Sunday. Other aspects included the strength of the temperance movement and the high degree of reticence governing the public discussion of anything to do with sex. One small, but telling example of the latter is the fact that a historian of sexuality in imperial Germany has used published working-class autobiographies as a principal source.[31] Such a method would be impossible for a British historian. Sunday in such north German cities as Berlin or Dresden had a very different character from that which it had in English cities. The differences were at several levels.[32] Legal restrictions on the opening of places of business and entertainment were more extensive in England, convinced sabbatarians were more numerous in England, and in England sabbatarians had more influence on the prevailing standards of respectable behaviour. For instance, a man born in a Liverpool working-class family in 1904, whose parents were professed agnostics, recalled that their Sundays were very quiet, that they wore Sunday clothes, and that 'ostentatious games and work were frowned upon'. A man born in a London working-class family in 1899, whose mother only went to church for special occasions like the Harvest Festival and whose father never went, recalled that Sundays were 'purgatory', and that they would be limited to going for a walk 'very sedately', or to reading books 'sort of Pilgrim's Progess and something of that sort'. For more fervently religious families Sunday was often the high point of the week and, in particular, the Sunday evening ritual of singing hymns to the accompaniment of the piano or harmonium was the supreme moment of togetherness for the family, as it was in the Barnes family in Keighley:

> Well me father used to try and keep the Sabbath as the Sabbath. And we always finished up at night with this organ at Sunday you know, and everybody singing, and then they had to do an individual turn you know, and you'd always get to tell your dad what you'd learnt at Sunday School and what you'd been talking about you know – and that.

They sang 'hymns and all sorts', his father's favourite being 'The Rugged Cross', and tears ran down his cheeks as they sang it. The 'all sorts' no doubt included more secular songs, such as those from the music halls, and it was this unself-conscious mixing of sacred and profane which indicated that hymns had become a generally accepted part of the popular culture of the day. It was equally reflected in the comment by the Liverpool man, mentioned above, that they included hymns in their Sunday evening singsongs, 'even though we were heathens'.[33]

Teetotalism spread less widely than sabbatarianism in later Victorian England, but its influence ran deeper, as it was so often central to a whole view of the world. Teetotallers were, like Mary Hatch's parents, 'rabid' in their beliefs, because drink seemed to be closely bound up with the things which they abhorred, and it appeared as one of the principal obstacles to the achievement of the things that they hoped for. While the connections are not fully spelled out in Mary Hatch's account, they appear clear enough. The things which her parents most valued, such as education, hard work, independence, gentleness, and healthy forms of amusement, all seemed to be associated with temperance, whereas drink was associated with all the things that they hated, ranging from 'scruffiness' or grovelling before social 'superiors' to the disreputable pleasures of the music hall, and even to violence.[34]

The strength of these various forms of puritanism in nineteenth-century England owed a great deal to the Nonconformist churches because of their success in popularizing and bringing about the internalization of values which in Germany often came from 'above' and lacked popular resonance, or else were the province of much more limited social circles. For instance, attempts by the state in various parts of Germany to promote Sunday observance in the 1850s were widely discredited by the fact that they so often came as part of a package of reactionary measures, designed to turn back the clock after the failure of the revolutions in 1848–9.[35] And while German temperance campaigns were associated with the liberal bourgeoisie, rather than conservative aristocrats, a study of the movement concludes that it was 'elitist and aloof, never departing from the tradition of reform from above', and failed to achieve the levels of popular support attained by its British counterpart.[36]

The importance of Dissent was most obviously decisive in shaping the distinctive character of Liberal and socialist politics in nineteenth- and early twentieth-century Britain. The Liberal Party and later the Labour Party were religiously pluralistic, both in terms of their electorate and of their local and national leadership. They drew strong support from religious minorities of all kinds, including not only Nonconformists, but also Roman Catholics, Jews and Secularists.[37] They retained a significant degree of support from members of the Church of England (and the Church of Scotland), but Protestant Dissenters had a particularly important role. At the national level the Liberal leadership remained heavily Anglican right up to the end of the nineteenth century, in spite of the steady increase in the number of Nonconformist MPs. However, at local level things were quite different – at least in the towns. The first elected borough councils in 1835 were frequently dominated by Nonconformists and, whether as voters, as activists or as leaders, the role of Nonconformists in local Liberal politics remained central throughout the century.[38] Wald argues on the basis of a statistical study of general elections from 1885 to 1910 that the best predictor of the result in any constituency was the proportion of churchgoers worshipping in Nonconformist chapels in 1851.[39] In the early history of the Labour Party Dissenting chapels were important because so many activists and leaders were Nonconformists or came from a Nonconformist background. Over half of the Labour MPs elected in 1906 claimed to be Nonconformists, and at least 37 per cent of the Labour MPs elected in 1929 claimed affiliation to one of the free churches.[40]

There were three areas where the Nonconformist influence on Liberal and Labour politics was especially important. The first was in locally based programmes of urban reform, such as the civic gospel of the mid-Victorian years or the Lib–Lab Progressivism of the late Victorian and Edwardian years. The second was the strong pacifist streak which has been an important aspect of the radical and socialist traditions in British politics. The third influence was of a more general kind and concerns the structure rather than the content of progressive politics.

To begin with the last point first: one of the most important differences between British and German politics in the period between the 1860s and 1930s lay in the fact that in Germany the divide between middle-class and working-class politics, and between Liberals and those further to the left, was more clear-cut. The 1860s and 1870s saw the decisive split between Liberals and Social Democrats in Germany, whereas in Britain most of the former Chartists had moved into the Liberal Party.[41] In spite of the growing strength of British socialism from the 1880s onwards, the Liberal Party continued up to 1914 to receive most of the working-class vote, and most of the Labour MPs elected up to this time entered Parliament with Liberal support. When in the 1920s Labour replaced the Liberals as the main party of the left, they inherited not only most of the fomer Liberal electorate, but many former Liberal activists and even former Liberal MPs. Throughout this period religious Nonconformity was one of the binding forces on the left of British politics, in much the same way as anti-clericalism was in France and Spain, modifying class antagonisms, providing commonalities of language, mentality, and identity, and thus facilitating these transitions.[42]

Moving on to the role of Dissenters in urban politics: in the 1860s and 1870s Nonconformist preachers played a major part in promoting a wider vision of the city and in supporting activist borough councils. The best-known examples were George Dawson and R. W. Dale in Birmingham, whose large congregations included many town councillors, journalists and businessmen, and who were among the most vocal supporters of Joseph Chamberlain's reforming regime in the 1870s. Dale was severely critical of the older forms of evangelicalism, which had, in his view, encouraged excessive individualism and an irresponsible other-worldliness. He was strongly convinced of the need for Christians to be social and political activists, and he was particularly concerned to persuade Christian businessmen to become town councillors, Guardians of the Poor and members of hospital committees.[43] He thus provided a theological basis for Chamberlain's enlightened paternalism.

By the 1890s Nonconformist political rhetoric was more aggressively democratic. If any one institution could be held to embody the distinctive Nonconformist political style during this period, it would be the London County Council during the era of Progressive control between 1889 and 1907.[44] Nonconformists were conspicuous on the Progressive benches generally. They were well represented among the leadership, including most notably Sir John Benn, and also in the Labour section of the party, where Nonconformists such as Will Crooks and Frank Smith sat beside the Secularist John Burns. The combination of municipal socialism and puritanism which characterized Progressive policies faithfully reflected the views of large numbers of Nonconformist voters and especially the views espoused by Nonconformist preachers. The LCC was pro-labour (trying in its direct labour department to act as a model employer); it had a high-profile involvement in questions of health and sanitation, where LCC inspectors aroused the ire of many landlords and restaurant-keepers; it was a big spender on education and on 'healthy' forms of entertainment, such as parks, bands, sport and boats; and it had a very hostile attitude to pubs and music halls, which also felt the weight of LCC inspections – leading critics to label the Progressives 'faddists, pharisees and prowling prudes'.[45] Councillor Richard Roberts, a teetotaller and for many years chairman of the music-halls committee, riposted: 'As a radical Nonconformist, I do not regret a revival of the puritan sentiment, which has always characterised English Liberalism in its best days.'[46] In more pungent terms, a Baptist minister wrote in his church newsletter during the 1907 LCC election that 'The Progressives draw support from all followers of Jesus Christ – the Moderates [Conservatives] from company promoters, slum landlords, drinksellers, bookmakers, and brothelkeepers.'[47]

The pacifist streak of British radicalism and socialism was reflected both in the relative weakness of the revolutionary wing of British socialism and in the relative strength of anti-war movements. Nonconformists or those from a Nonconformist background seem to have played a prominent part in all of these. During the Boer War the Liberal Nonconformist *Daily News* published a Peace Manifesto signed by 5,270 Nonconformist ministers. Local 'Stop the War' committees also seem to have had a high level of Nonconformist involvement.[48] While many commentators have stressed the fact that Nonconformist opinion was divided and that some leading ministers were vocal supporters of the war,[49] this seems to me far less significant than the fact that so many Nonconformists (and socialists) did oppose the war, in spite of the overwhelming social pressures to support the patriotic cause, and the active persecution which opponents of the war faced – as instanced by Mary Hatch's father. During the First World War, opposition was much less than it had been in the Boer War, and some former pro-Boers such as the Primitive Methodist preacher, Arthur Guttery, became outspoken patriots.[50] However, one study of the religious affiliations of a group of conscientious objectors found that 95 per cent of those whose denomination was known were Nonconformists.[51] One of the most prominent anti-war campaigners, Fenner Brockway, whose parents were missionaries and who was himself a former Congregational church worker, but had become an agnostic, is a striking example of the many ex-Nonconformists upon whom the chapel had left a lasting imprint. The probable connections between Nonconformity and pacifism were particularly apparent in a study of the religious outlook of Labour MPs published in 1931. This showed a number of cases of Nonconformist MPs who had been conscientious objectors during the First World War (including several who were imprisoned). Not that they always received the support of their chapels: for instance, the strongly anti-war Baptist, Fred Messer, who became MP for South Tottenham, had resigned his church membership during the period 1914–19, presumably because of lack of support. Nathaniel Micklem, later to be principal of Mansfield College, resigned his pastorate of a church on the outskirts of Manchester because of opposition to his anti-war preaching.[52] The point is not that most Nonconformists were anti-war, but that so many of the relatively few people bold enough to adopt such a radically unpopular stance were Nonconformists.

A final issue is that of the character of popular Protestantism in England. Three important positive features, the centrality of preaching, Bible-reading and hymn-singing, were shared with Protestantism in many other countries. I have already suggested that Nonconformist preachers may have played a major part in popularizing the Bible. Hymn-singing was a central part both of Anglican and Nonconformist worship, and each may have contributed to the extraordinary popularity which hymns enjoyed in the later Victorian period.[53] Preaching was also important both in Anglican and in Nonconformist worship, but it was the Dissenters who laid the greatest stress on preaching and from whom a disproportionate number of the most famous preachers were drawn.[54] Preachers, like hymns, had a popularity which extended far beyond the conventionally religious: the Victorian Sunday was for many people a day for sermon-tasting, in which preaching as an art-form was savoured by those sufficiently detached to travel from church to church, enjoying the performance without being prejudiced by denominational loyalties or theological predilections. Here we have one clue to another distinctive feature of English religion in this period, namely the relatively high proportion of men in church congregations. This point must not be exaggerated: in England, as in more or less every part of the Western world in the nineteenth and early twentieth centuries, the majority of adult churchgoers were women. But the 61 per cent of London churchgoers in 1902–3 who were women (compared with 54 per cent of the general adult population which was female), was somewhat less than the 66 per cent in New York's Manhattan borough, the slightly over two-thirds of Berlin Protestant congregations who were women, and the over 80 per cent of Catholic churchgoers who were women in some parts of France. The difference between London and Berlin or New York is explained by the relative success of London's Nonconformist chapels in attracting male worshippers. 65 per cent of Anglican churchgoers and 64 per cent of Catholics were women, but only 56 per cent of Nonconformists. The reasons for this are complex, but one factor seems to have been that male churchgoers tended to attach more importance to the sermon than did female churchgoers, and tended to be attracted in disproportionate numbers to churches where the emphasis was on preaching and the preacher was believed to be eloquent. This was certainly true of working-class men, usually regarded as the least churchgoing element in the population.[55]

One equally important negative feature also needs to be emphasized – the relatively marginal position of the sacraments. The contrast here with Protestant north Germany is particularly striking. In Germany the rarity of regular churchgoing contrasted with the large proportion of Protestants receiving communion at least once in the year. At the end of the nineteenth century, the number of communicants was dropping, but the ratio of communions to Protestant population was still around 40 per cent.[56] If only the population aged fourteen and over are counted, it is clear that the majority of those eligible to receive communion were doing so at least once in the year. In England most of those who attended Nonconformist services never became church members and so were not eligible for participation in the Lord's Supper. Anglican churchgoers were equally reluctant to participate in communion, although the figures were increasing in the latter part of the nineteeenth century, presumably under Anglo-Catholic influence.[57] Similarly in Germany the overwhelming majority of children were baptized in the later nineteenth and early twentieth century – after a temporary drop in the 1870s at the time when civil registration was introduced.[58] Fewer figures are available in England, though clearly most children were baptized there too. However, there are reasons for thinking that the hold of the baptismal rite on the popular imagination was less in England. In the first place there were a number of denominations which either rejected infant baptism, as the Baptists and Brethren did, or dispensed with the rite altogether, as with the Salvation Army and the Quakers. So that there were considerable numbers of children and young people from devoutly Christian families who, like Norah Frith, had not been christened, and smaller numbers of devoutly Christian adults who because of the principles of their own denomination or for more personal reasons were not baptized. But it would also appear that, at least in the middle decades of the nineteenth century, there were many migrants to the towns who did not have their children christened – if we are to judge by the number of clergy who made special efforts to identify unbaptized children or who offered inducements to neglectful parents.[59] In view of the very high levels of attendance at Sunday school by children of the urban working class in the later nineteenth century, this seems to reflect not so much indifference to religion in general as a relaxed attitude to the sacraments. Perhaps the most telling point about the relatively small part played by the sacraments in English popular religion is James Obelkevich's observation that there were few superstitions associated with them.[60] By contrast, in and around Berlin, an area of mainly Lutheran tradition, baptism in particular was surrounded with superstitious beliefs: sick children, it was believed, could be cured by baptism, and adults too sometimes procured baptismal water to ease their own pains; similarly, the baby had to be held by a man during the sprinkling of the water, or else ill would befall. And the hold of baptism on the popular imagination in Berlin is most vividly conveyed by these comments by a Berlin clergyman in 1880:

> In summer the number of emergency baptisms is large. Death knocks at the door of culpable negligence and causes terror. Post-haste they send for the clergyman. He must come quickly – but immediately – make good what laziness has spoiled. They demand vehemently that in spite of other urgent business the emergency baptism should be carried out at once.[61]

III

The period 1870–1914 was in some ways a golden age of English Dissent. Yet numerical decline was already beginning. The peak of numbers in relation to population probably came in the later 1880s, though decline only became a major issue around 1910, when numbers began to fall absolutely.[62] Some of the ways out of Dissent have already been hinted at. The most obvious example was politics, and especially socialist politics, as in the case of the Bristol man quoted at the beginning of this chapter, whose political convictions grew directly out of his religious convictions, but seem in the end to have supplanted them as his principal concern. In the early years of the twentieth century, and even more so in the 1920s, there were many like him. Another important route was through anti-puritanism, with sabbatarianism being the most widely resented of the Nonconformist shibboleths. Nonconformist identity was also being weakened by the removal of most Nonconformist grievances and by broader cultural currents, including a higher valuation of liturgical worship and of the place of art and music in religious life, which made Nonconformists more open to Anglicanism and even, to some extent, to Roman Catholicism.[63] The Dissent of these years is still so close to us and so familiar that we find it hard to regard it with any degree of detachment. Yet placed in a European context it is both a rather strange and a very remarkable phenomenon – pious and radical, puritanical and widely cultured, militantly sectarian yet with a strong sense of responsibility for society.

Notes

[1] Paul Thompson and Thea Vigne, Interviews on Family Life and Work Experience before 1918, University of Essex Oral History Archive (hereafter, 'Essex Interviews'), no. 143, 11–12, 19, 24, 29, 37, 39, 41–2, 45, 48–9, 52.

[2] Ibid., no. 5, 15.

[3] Ibid., no. 339, 34, 45, 48–51, 70.

[4] Bristol People's Oral History Project, Avon County Reference Library, Bristol, Interview no. 34, pp. 12, 35–6, 44, 47–8.

[5] Robin Gill, *The Myth of the Empty Church* (London 1993), 305–8, 322.

[6] Michael R. Watts, *The Dissenters*, ii. *The Expansion of Evangelical Nonconformity 1791–1859* (Oxford, 1995), 127.

[7] Robert Currie, *Methodism Divided* (London, 1968), chap. 3.

[8] Geoffrey Robson, 'The failures of success: working class evangelists in

early Victorian Birmingham', in Derek Baker (ed.), *Religious Motivation*, Studies in Church History 15 (Oxford, 1978), 388.

9   Frances Knight, *The Nineteenth Century Church and English Society* (Cambridge, 1995), 24–36.

10 Michael Wintle, *Pillars of Piety: Religion in the Netherlands in the Nineteenth Century* (Hull, 1987), 3; Peter van Rooden, 'Secularization, dechristianization and rechristianization in the Netherlands', in Hartmut Lehmann (ed.), *Säkularisierung, Dechristianisierung, Rechristianisierung im neuzeitlichen Europa* (Göttingen, 1997), 141–2; Rob van der Laarse, *Bevoogding en Bevinding: Heren en kerkvolk in een Hollandse provinciestad, Woerden 1780–1930* (The Hague, 1989 includes English summary).

11 Franklin D. Scott, *Sweden: The Nation's History* (Minneapolis, 1977), 411.

12 Ibid., 411–12, 427.

13 Lucian Hölscher, *Weltgericht oder Revolution* (Stuttgart, 1989), 107.

14 Christopher Clark, 'Confessional policy and the limits of state action: Friedrich Wilhelm III and the Prussian Church Union 1817–40', *Historical Journal*, 39, No. 4 (1996), 985–1004.

15 R. M. Bigler, *The Politics of German Protestantism: The Rise of the Protestant Church Elite in Prussia 1815–1848* (Los Angeles, 1972); Friedrich Wilhelm Graf, *Die Politisierung des religiösen Bewusstseins* (Stuttgart, 1978); Sylvia Paletschek, *Frauen und Dissens: Frauen im Deutschkatholizismus und in den freien Gemeinden* (Göttingen, 1990).

16 Rudiger Minor, *Die Bischöfliche Methodistenkirche in Sachsen* (dissertation, Karl-Marx-Universität, Leipzig, n.d.; copy in Queen's College Library, Birmingham); Christoph Ribbat, *Religiöse Erregung: Protestantische Schwärmer im Kaiserreich* (Frankfurt, 1996).

17 Alun Howkins, *Poor Labouring Men* (London, 1985); Robert Moore, *Pit-men, Preachers and Politics* (Cambridge, 1974); Eric Hopkins, 'Religious Dissent in Black Country industrial villages in the first half of the nineteenth century', *Journal of Ecclesiastical History*, 34, No. 3 (1983), 411–24; James Obelkevich, *Religion in Rural Society: South Lindsey 1825–1875* (Oxford, 1976); Clyde Binfield, *Pastors and People* (Coventry, 1984); Simon Gunn, 'The ministry, the middle class and the "civilizing mission" in Manchester, 1850–80', *Social History*, 21, No. 1 (1996), 22–36; Clyde Binfield, 'Hebrews hellenized? English evangelical Nonconformity and culture, 1840–1940', in Sheridan Gilley and W. J. Sheils (eds.), *A History of Religion in Britain* (Oxford, 1994), 322–45.

18 Watts, *Dissenters*, 303–27. See also Mark Smith, *Religion in Industrial Society: Oldham and Saddleworth 1740–1865* (Oxford, 1994). For the older view, see Alan Gilbert, *Religion and Society in Industrial England* (London, 1976), 146–8.

[19] Ribbat, *Religiöse Erregung*, 21; Hölscher, *Weltgericht*, 126–30.

[20] Ribbat, *Religiöse Erregung*, 165–92.

[21] Valentine Cunningham, *Everywhere Spoken Against: Dissent in the Victorian Novel* (Oxford, 1975).

[22] Van Rooden, 'Secularization'; Sjouke Voolstra, ' "The hymn to freedom": the redefinition of Dutch Mennonite identity in the Restoration and Romantic period (*ca* 1810–1850)', in Alastair Hamilton, Sjouke Voolstra and Piet Visser (eds.), *From Martyr to Muppy* (Amsterdam, 1994), 187–202.

[23] Gill, *Empty Church*, 305.

[24] Hugh McLeod, *Piety and Poverty: Working Class Religion in Berlin, London and New York 1870–1914* (New York, 1996), 83; P. Wurster, *Das kirchliche Leben der evangelischen Landeskirche in Württemberg* (Tübingen, 1919), 85; P. Pieper, *Kirchliche Statistik Deutschlands* (Freiburg im Breisgau, 1899), 238–9; P. Drews, *Das kirchliche Leben der Evangelisch-Lutherischen Landeskirche des Königreichs Sachsen* (Tübingen, 1902), 93–5.

[25] It is now clearer that historians in the 1960s and 1970s, such as K. S. Inglis in his *Churches and the Working Classes in Victorian England* (London, 1963), considerably underestimated the extent of working-class involvement in organized religion. For a summary of recent work on the social composition of later Victorian English churches, see Hugh McLeod, *Religion and Society in England 1850–1914* (London, 1996), chap. 1.

[26] For fuller discussion of these issues, see McLeod, *Piety and Poverty*, chaps. 4–5.

[27] Friedrich Wilhelm Graf, 'Die Spaltung des Protestantismus. Zum Verhältnis von evangelischer Kirche, Staat und "Gesellschaft" im frühen 19. Jahrhundert', in W. Schieder (ed.), *Religion und Gesellschaft im 19. Jahrhundert* (Stuttgart, 1993), 170; Hans-Jürgen Gabriel, 'Im Namen des Evangeliums gegen den Fortschritt. Zur Rolle der "Evangelischen Kirchenzeitung" unter E. W. Hengstenberg von 1830 bis 1849', in Günter Wirth (ed.), *Beiträge zur Berliner Kirchengeschichte* (Berlin, 1987), 154–76. See also Bigler, *German Protestantism*.

[28] Nigel Scotland, *Methodism and the Revolt of the Field: A Study of the Methodist Contribution to Agricultural Trade Unionism in East Anglia 1872–96* (Gloucester, 1981).

[29] Franz Linden, *Sozialismus und Religion* (Leipzig, 1932), 139.

[30] A. Levenstein, *Die Arbeiterfrage* (Munich, 1912), 326–34, 383–403; W. T. Stead, 'The Labour Party and the books that helped to make it', *Review of Reviews* (1906), 568–82.

[31] R. P. Neuman, 'Industrialization and sexual behavior: Some aspects of

working-class life in imperial Germany', in Robert J. Bezucha (ed.), *Modern European Social History* (Lexington, 1972), 270–98.

32 Drews, *Das Kirchlich Leben*, 89; Hugh McLeod, 'Introduction', in McLeod (ed.), *European Religion in the Age of Great Cities* (London, 1995), 15. For England, see John Wigley, *The Rise and Fall of the Victorian Sunday* (Manchester, 1980).

33 Essex Interviews, no. 108, 12, 14; no. 236, 15–16; no. 339, 28, 33, 45.

34 The temperance movement is well covered by Brian Harrison, *Drink and the Victorians* (London, 1971) and Lilian Lewis Shiman, *Crusade against Drink in Victorian England* (London, 1988). But the mentality of the individual abstainer remains little explored.

35 Friedrich Gustav Lisco, *Zur Kirchengeschichte Berlins* (Berlin, 1857), 286–7; Thomas Nipperdey, *Deutsche Geschichte 1800–1866* (Munich, 1983), 676.

36 James S. Roberts, *Drink, Temperance and the Working Class in Nineteenth Century Germany* (Boston, MA, 1984), 132.

37 G. I. T. Machin, *Politics and the Churches in Great Britain 1869–1921* (Oxford, 1987); Stephen Koss, *Nonconformity in Modern British Politics* (London, 1975); Steven Fielding, *Class and Ethnicity: Irish Catholics in England 1880–1939* (Buckingham, 1993); Geoffrey Alderman, *The Jewish Community in British Politics* (Oxford, 1983); Edward Royle, *Radicals, Secularists and Republicans: Popular Freethought in Britain 1866–1915* (Manchester, 1980).

38 R. J. Morris, *Class, Sect and Party: The Making of the British Middle Class* (Manchester, 1990); Derek Fraser, *Urban Politics in Victorian England* (London, 1979); D. W. Bebbington, 'Nonconformity and electoral sociology, 1867–1918', *Historical Journal*, 27 (1984), 634–5; Barry M. Doyle, 'Urban Liberalism and the "lost generation": politics and middle class culture in Norwich, 1900–1935', *Historical Journal*, 38 (1995), 626–7.

39 Kenneth D. Wald, *Crosses on the Ballot* (Princeton, 1983), p 150.

40 Ibid.; Linden, *Sozialismus*, 155. See also Leonard Smith, *Religion and the Rise of Labour* (Keele, 1993), which stresses the many connections but also the tensions in the relationship.

41 Breuilly, *Labour and Liberalism in Nineteenth-Century Europe* (Manchester, 1994), 115–16 and *passim*, which includes systematic discussion of differences between the political development of Hamburg and Manchester.

42 See Eugenio F. Biagini, *Liberty, Retrenchment and Reform: Popular Liberalism in the Age of Gladstone 1860–80* (Cambridge, 1992), 1–29, for the importance of Nonconformity as a binding force in the Liberalism of the 1870s and 1880s. Moore, *Pit-men*, provides a vivid account both of the importance of Methodism in pre-1914 Liberalism

in Co. Durham and of the post-1918 movement of former Liberal Nonconformists into the Labour Party.

43 David M. Thompson, 'R. W. Dale and the "Civic Gospel"', in Alan Sell (ed.), *Protestant Nonconformists and the West Midlands of England* (Keele, 1996), 109. See also E. P. Hennock, *Fit and Proper Persons* (London, 1973).

44 For a fairly sympathetic view of the Progressive LCC, see Jeffrey Cox, *English Churches in a Secular Society: Lambeth 1870–1930* (Oxford, 1982); for a hostile view, Susan Pennybacker, ' "The millennium by return of post": reconsidering London Progressivism 1889–1907', in David Feldman and Gareth Stedman Jones (eds.), *Metropolis London: Histories and Representations since 1800* (London 1989), 129–62; for more impartial accounts, two essays in Andrew Saint (ed.), *Politics and the People of London: The London County Council 1889–1965* (London 1989), by John Davis, 'The Progressive Council 1889–1907', 27–48, and by Chris Waters, 'Progressives, puritans and the cultural politics of the Council, 1889–1914', 49–70.

45 Pennybacker, 'Millennium', 147.

46 Waters, 'Progressives, Puritans', 64.

47 Cox, *English Churches*, 173.

48 James Munson, *The Nonconformists* (London, 1991), 235; Hugh McLeod, *Class and Religion in the late Victorian City* (London, 1974), 177–8.

49 Munson, *Nonconformists*, 236–9; David Bebbington, *The Nonconformist Conscience* (London, 1982), 121–4.

50 Alan Wilkinson, *Dissent or Conform? War, Peace and the English Churches 1900–1945* (London, 1986), 29–33.

51 John Rae, *Conscience and Politics* (London, 1970), 250.

52 Linden, *Sozialismus*, 123–5; Wilkinson, *Dissent or Conform?*, 49.

53 Jim Obelkevich, 'Music and religion in the nineteenth century', in J. Obelkevich, L. Roper and R. Samuel (eds.), *Disciplines of Faith* (London, 1987), 550–65; John Wolffe, ' "Praise to the Holiest in the Height": hymns and church music', in Wolffe (ed.), *Religion in Victorian Britain*, v. *Culture and Empire* (Manchester, 1997), 59–98.

54 Munson, *Nonconformists*, 112–14; there is good discussion of the cult of the preacher in Pamela Kruppa, *Charles Haddon Spurgeon: A Preacher's Progress* (New York, 1982).

55 For fuller discussion see McLeod, *Piety and Poverty*, chap. 7.

56 Hölscher, *Weltgericht*, 143. For comprehensive statistics, see Lucian Hölscher (ed.), *Datenatlas zur religiösen Geographie im protestantischen Deutschland* (Bochum, 1996).

57 Knight, *The Nineteenth Century Church*, 35–6; Gilbert, *Religion and Society*, 28.

58 Lucian Hölscher and Ursula Männich-Polenz, 'Die Sozialstruktur der

Kirchengemeinden Hannovers im 19. Jahrhundert: Eine statistische Analyse', *Jahrbuch der Gesellschaft für niedersächsische Kirchengeschichte*, 88 (1990); McLeod, *Piety and Poverty*, 179–80.

[59] Alan Bartlett, 'The churches in Bermondsey 1880–1939' (University of Birmingham Ph.D. thesis, 1987), 182–8.

[60] Obelkevich, *Religion in Rural Society*, 271–2.

[61] McLeod, *Piety and Poverty*, 179–81.

[62] McLeod, *Religion and Society*, 172. There is a good discussion of perceptions of and responses to 'decline' in S. J. D. Green, *Religion in the Age of Decline: Organisation and Experience in Industrial Yorkshire, 1870–1920* (Cambridge, 1996).

[63] For full discussion of these issues see Cox, *English Churches*, chap. 7.

8

Victims of success: twentieth-century Free Church architecture

CLYDE BINFIELD

I

'Culture' and 'tradition' are problematic words for evangelical Nonconformists. In any list of naturally associated words, neither 'culture' nor 'tradition' would be hot on Nonconformity's heels, for it is a well-known fact that Nonconformists are culturally challenged. Only sociologists would want to take issue with that. Tradition implies memory, and continuity comes into it. Culture includes aesthetics and insofar as an aesthetic implies a sense of place, and therefore has a context, continuity comes into that too. So what of my present concern, Nonconformity's aesthetic element?

That must most obviously mean chapels. The aesthetic element comes into play the moment a building committee has been convened with an architect in mind, for they are people of their time and class and their scheme will reflect the fact. It comes more directly into play with the decisions taken to attract worshippers. Here it meets with tradition in the seriousness with which the key question is answered: how will this scheme meet our needs and advance our cause? How will it work for us? Hence that still common, if vulnerable, building type, the chapel, almost certainly still clothed in our mind's eye in some shade of Dissenting Gothic, so obviously churchy yet so obviously not a parish church, a precise, suggestive, often painful convergence of the meeting of culture and tradition.

If it is a well-known fact that Nonconformists are culturally challenged it is an equally well-known fact that, with some possible Edwardian exceptions, they have built little of note in the twentieth century. The meeting houses of their heroic age are now admired, perhaps because so few remain in use; the chapels of their golden age increasingly have their champions, usually from outside the tradition; but their buildings of the present age are resolutely ignored. Since there have been at least eighty years of the present age such ignorance can only be dismissed as nonsense, unless we bring a third well-known fact to our aid. It is a well-known fact that Nonconformity is in decline, and there can be no mileage in the architecture of decline. None the less there has been a great deal of Nonconformist building in the present century. Some of it certainly reflects success, all of it reflects determination, and all of it is prospective. It lays claim to the future.

All buildings, of course, lay claim to a future. Consequently they interest the historian in two ways. How, as they age, have they had an impact on that future? And what references do their fabric and usage make to the past? A building interprets the past and the future as well as the present of its builders. My present concern is with two notable Nonconformist buildings of the mid-twentieth century. They were victims of success in the double sense that they were untimely replacements of loved and famous predecessors and that they have defined the options for a future which changed more rapidly and decisively than most of their rebuilders anticipated. They are certainly notable within the supposedly limited world of Nonconformity. They are the City Temple, London, and Punshon Memorial Church, Bournemouth, the former Congregational, now United Reformed, the latter Methodist, originally Wesleyan. They were completed in 1958, but for both, and especially for the City Temple, there was a long and suggestive prehistory.[1]

II

The Great Ejectment's Bicentenary, 24 August 1862, Black Bartholomew's Day, focused the mind on the minister as martyr, his people as saints. It focused the will on principles to be announced. Here, for mind and will, was a heritage to be conserved. Consequently the eye was focused too, on the chapel as building type. The Bicentenary furnished the occasion, perhaps the excuse, for what would have happened anyway, a builders' bonanza which lasted for at least fifty years. Here too heritage was a pretext. Thus, in Birmingham, a Baptist new building (to continue the heritage metaphor) was 'prodigally ornate' in its Gothic, and when the commandingly evangelical vicar of St Martin's made public his surprise the Congregational R. W. Dale, still quite new at Carr's Lane, rose to the bait:

> It is true that . . . our fathers did not build places of worship with graceful spires, and columns crowned with clustering beauty, and windows rich with purple and gold; they did not feel secure enough in their liberties to invest their money in buildings, of which new political convulsions might deprive them. Even in the trust-deed of my own place of worship, built in the middle of last century, provision is made for the disposal of the edifice should it ever become illegal to employ it for the purposes of Independent worship; so insecure, even then, in the judgement of our fathers was the religious liberty of the country. They erected mean buildings in obscure places for another reason too; if the magistrate did not touch them, the mob might . . . And as men who have been in prison long get to like the very darkness of their cells, and feel ill at ease when their chains are removed, our fathers got to like the plain dull buildings to which necessity had originally driven them. As for ourselves, we were never in the house of bondage, and have pretty well escaped from its influence, and feel quite at liberty to build our places of worship in another style; and if we sometimes make queer blunders; if 'Dissenting Gothic' affords amusement, . . . we can only say that we are . . . improving already . . . and hope to do better still by and by . . .[2]

Such pointed history lessons were repeated throughout the country. In the City of London two famous chapels improved themselves beyond recognition. The King's Weigh House, on Fish Street Hill, celebrated its enforced emancipation after a decade of uncertainty defined by railway and planning pressures combined with changes in pulpit and pew, by moving in 1891 to the neighbourhood of Grosvenor Square where Alfred Waterhouse's splendid boilerette now survives as London's Ukrainian Cathedral with all the trimmings.[3] Poultry Chapel, by contrast, remained (if only just) in the City. In May 1872 it was sold by auction to the London Joint Stock Bank. In May 1874 it reopened on Holborn Viaduct as The City Temple, its stone laid by Thomas Binney, late of the Weigh House.[4]

As its name suggested, the Congregational City Temple was to the north of the Thames what the Baptist Metropolitan

Tabernacle already was south of it. It was heritage in action. It was certainly up-to-date. Having had its stone laid by the author of 'Eternal Light', it was the first chapel to be lit by electric light in 1880. Twenty-four years later, in 1904, its people were electrified in another way when a robed choir – an affectation which quickly caught on in the more stylish Congregational churches – was introduced. Not that the City Temple was unduly stylish. Its architects, Lockwood and Mawson, were sound provincial practitioners known for chapels in Scarborough and Harrogate, colleges in Nottingham and Bradford, and for Saltaire, the model community which they built for Sir Titus Salt at Shipley. They were stylistically eclectic: various stages of Gothic, with supposedly and at times definitely Venetian touches verging on the Renaissance at Saltaire where they had also exploded their Congregational church into a Greco-Italian, drawing-room world of Corinthian columns, scagliola pilasters and ormolu.[5] Historical references teemed in their work as they did in that of any successful Victorian architect. Fashion, Thomas Cook and John Ruskin had much to answer for in this annexation of the past, back to the future indeed, on behalf of clients who had money, time and a mind for it.

The City Temple had money, time and mind. It cost £70,000. It was primarily a great preaching house, said to hold 2,500.[6] It certainly held great preachers. Its greatest, Joseph Parker (1869–1902) and his successor R. J. Campbell (1903–15), were contrasts in all save national news value.[7] Here heritage supervened. What seemed an almost invincible preaching tradition was symbolized by a great, central pulpit, spacious and marble-faced and costing 300 guineas. This pulpit, the gift of the Corporation of London 'in recognition of the public spirit displayed in the determination to perpetuate a long-existing connection with the City', would have been aesthetically and evangelically inconceivable had Ruskin never written *Stones of Venice*.[8]

There was nothing Venetian about the rest of this Temple. Dramatically sited on its new viaduct, planned with an ingenuity which sadly perplexed later generations and with St Paul's Cathedral suggestively distanced in early commemorative prints, it was manifestly a City church: hardly Wren, yet clothed in Wren's spirit, Wrenaissance before its time, such a church as might interpret the years between Charles II and George I as they would have been had right triumphed. The presence in state of the Lord Mayor and Sheriffs turned its opening into the City's first such official Dissenting occasion. In due time these accumulated doings were celebrated with a thick 'Tercentenary Commemoration Volume'. That came in May 1940.[9]

In the 1940s and 1950s the City Temple was as famous as it had ever been. Its Methodist minister, Leslie Weatherhead, occupied what was arguably the world's most famous Protestant pulpit. He had done so since the summer of 1936. In 1952 its membership stood at 663, a solid army of business and professional men and women leavened by the *Who's Who* world – Lords Leathers and Stamp, Frank Salisbury, the fashionable portrait painter, Colonel Crosfield, who had run the British Legion, Alice Head, who had edited popular magazines with large circulations, judges in waiting, doctors by the dozen.[10] But none of them worshipped on Holborn Viaduct. For on the night of 16–17 April 1941 the City Temple was virtually destroyed in the 'blitz'. Its walls and tower survived, but it was quite unusable. It was seventeen years before Leslie Weatherhead could lead his people back to Holborn Viaduct.

The Second World War offered church builders an opportunity rather than a bonanza. Perhaps it was taken. Coventry Cathedral and the Guards' Chapel are its memorials, London's free churches suffered conspicuously. The Baptists lost their Metropolitan Tabernacle and Westbourne Park; the Congregationalists lost Whitefield's Tabernacle, Christ Church Westminster Bridge Road, Highbury Quadrant and Trinity Poplar; the Presbyterians lost Regent's Square. It was, however, the City Temple which provided the representative loss. Here the church retrospective most faithfully met the church prospective. Here was a test case.

That the City Temple would rebuild was never in doubt. Among central London's Congregational churches only Westminster Chapel rivalled it as a going concern. The question marks lay with the when, where and how. The *when* was a political question, a matter of war-damage claims, post-war building priorities and a brave new planning world in which the regulations were ever proliferating and ever in place. The *where* and the *how* were a mix of imponderables: the practical needs of a particular congregation largely formed by a particular minister, balanced by the associations quite consciously gathered round the past (whatever that was) and by the options to which any present decisions would immediately bind the future. There were responsibilities to the free churches at large and to Congregationalism in particular. There were the memories of 'God damn the Sultan' and 300 years of independent witness, latterly unique, in what was still an imperial capital's commercial hub. There were the possibilities of a witness to Christian psychology and spiritual healing by a congregation regularly drawn from a 25-mile radius. Most imponderable of all there was the merged impact of these memories and possibilities as interpreted in brick-covered, stone-faced, concrete and steel by the architect whom church meeting, church council, rebuilding committee and minister together decided was the man for them.

The City Temple's surviving records are tantalizingly patchy, but its rebuilding records are surprisingly full. They show serious City men (and women) almost uniformly at their best, trying to subordinate sentiment to need, consciously trustees of a heritage which has become worldwide, shrewdly assessing a bewildering succession of options. We may not now feel that they chose wisely. Their rebuilt Temple, as interpreted by a solidly establishment architect, is now inevitably a period piece, undoubtedly powerful in parts, even atmospheric, a St Odeon's in Wedgwood blue, the 'gorgeous, up-to-the-minute meeting place of some odd but wealthy American sect' with its 'smooth, sophisticated Cross', its lift and projector room, its synchronous clocks and a conference room 'more befitting to an industrial corporation'.[11] Yet it was almost not at all like this, for the church's most revealing archives concern the four or more years' work by a quite different architect whose scheme was never built. It is with that scheme that this paper is especially concerned.

Between April 1941 and March 1944 the question of rebuilding surged in waves. The first lasted throughout 1941. The second came with the autumn and winter of 1942–3. The third, long-drawn-out rather than receding, came a year later, 1943–4. That was when the question of an architect came seriously onto the agenda. The early waves are important. The first saw the clearing of debris and the clarifying of concepts.

Downwind of Holborn Viaduct, towards the Ludgate Circus end of Farringdon St, was the nerve-centre of organized English Congregationalism, the Memorial Hall. Although it was a more recent building than the City Temple, it was directly commemorative of the Great Ejectment and beyond, for, with a truly romantic business acumen, the Congregationalists had selected for their national headquarters the site of the Fleet Prison where Puritans and Brownists and Separatists had once languished. The City Temple's Rebuilding Committee met there. Its first meeting was on Tuesday 6 May 1941. The minister, Leslie Weatherhead ('Padre' to those close to him, with some of whom he was on the verge of Christian names and with a very few of whom it was a mutual verge), took the chair. He proved to be a good chairman, which cannot always be said of ministers. There was one apology, from Sir Sydney Robinson, Essex builder turned farmer. Of the five who were present, Albert Clare was the church treasurer and its biographer; he could remember Dr Parker. J. B. Leaver was a solicitor whose firm concentrated on Lancashire (Lytham, Blackpool, Nelson) when not in London. Sidney Berry was the Congregational Union's secretary; his presence demonstrated the importance of the enterprise. Alice Head was the statutory woman; she was also one of the country's most successful women journalists, a pioneer in her profession. Consequently she was typecast as 'Minute Secretary and Rapporteuse to the Church Council'.[12]

The business of that first meeting was predictable. There was the question of war-damage claims. There was the site to be cleared, 'to salvage relics and remnants which had not only a sentimental value but, even, as the chairman pointed out, a considerable financial value on account of their historic associations'. And there was the future. This was not entirely new, for back in 1932 an architect, George Vernon, had prepared a 'reconstruction plan' and now he had written again to the church; but his services were not at present required. There was almost euphoria. Perhaps the future might include the site of St Andrew's, next door? But that scheme 'at the present stage, could only be regarded as a visionary one'. Yet now was a time for visions, masterfully suggested by Dr Berry. One was

> that the rebuilt City Temple should also become the Headquarters of
> the Congregational Union of England and Wales, and the Committee
> enthusiastically welcomed the idea of keeping them in mind as a
> possibility . . . Dr Berry knew he could carry the Union with him . . .

and the Chairman felt that there might be definite advantage both to the City Temple and the Union.

That idea was the first of several to which the committee and its chairman were open, genuinely so, even enthusiastically, yet ever judiciously. Openly hedged bets were an attractive characteristic of this group. Thus, from the first there was talk of an appeal. Leaver, the solicitor, feared lest the government might deduct any appeal money from their due compensation. Berry, the ecclesiastic, said he would take the issue up as a matter of general principle with Trustram Eve, the War Damage Commission's chairman. And Weatherhead, the professional, and Clare, the repository of memory, 'felt most earnestly that it would be a mistake to discourage people from expressing their sympathy in a practical form, now, at the psychological moment, when their feelings had been so strongly aroused'. They met again later that month. Trustram Eve had – informally – turned up trumps; the minister cogitated over a 'Friends of the City Temple' who should covenant their gifts; Sir Sydney 'felt sure that friends in every part of the world would be glad to contribute'; and Dr Berry recommended 'the services of a publicity expert'.[13]

There were six more meetings that year: in June, July, two in September, October and December. The site was, in theory, cleared: that took a month and even then half a ton of scrap lead was still there in September. The publicity expert advocated an illustrated brochure, with Clare and Weatherhead ideally bonded in authorship, to 'embody as many human interest stories as possible in connection with the destruction of the City Temple and would also, of course, include its historical background'. *Rebuilding the Temple* would be a good title and 10,000 copies might be needed. There were useful suggestions about contacts in the States and Canada, where two past ministers now lived and where Dean Lynn Harold Hough had offered his best help. And there were exploratory talks with the Congregational Union.[14]

That was turning into a minefield. It had begun when Sidney Berry 'threw out the hint, with or without premeditation' that the Union might sell its Memorial Hall and join the Temple 'in a new and greater edifice' on Holborn Viaduct. Several on the Union's side were enthusiastic; 'the younger generation in particular would regard it as a distinct advantage to be associated with the City

Temple in this manner'. There were reservations. 'Everybody who knew the City Temple at all intimately was aware of the fact that there was much to criticise in its architectural features, except perhaps the great auditorium itself.' One old denominational war-horse, the timber importer, J. C. Meggitt, was sure that the difficulties were insuperable; the future lay westward and the Union should look 'somewhere near Trafalgar Square'. For the Temple, the scheme was 'at least an *interesting* proposition', but there was the fear that it would affect the 'nature and scope of a world-wide appeal'. The idea was by no means shelved, but the October meeting learned that Berry felt it currently impossible 'to make a definite pronouncement', and by then the appeal was getting up steam and so were schemes for the new church's shape as worship centre. It was becoming clear that the likely costs of rebuilding would be over £100,000; £55,750 might be claimed for war damage to the structure and another £30,500 was due for insured fixtures and fittings. All this presupposed an architect.[15]

If no architect were yet in view, two had already proved their moral worth. After enquiries as to whether his 1932 plans 'had ever been paid for', George Vernon had graciously handed them over to Mountford Pigott, who was assessing the surviving structure. Pigott, who knew that he was not in the running for any rebuilding, none the less prepared two schemes for the December meeting. His proposals included a side pulpit.[16]

Now Weatherhead's own ideas were clearly running on similar lines. Late in October he jotted down for John Dewey, soon to be church secretary and an undoubted hero of the unfolding saga,[17] his ideas for the 'New City Temple'. They included a small chapel, which could serve as children's church (a concept then in special vogue among advanced Congregational churches), a central aisle, a side pulpit balanced by a reading desk, choir stalls facing each other behind pulpit and desk, and an organ with pipes quite out of sight, thus revealing 'the rose-window which used to be behind the organ, and a stained-glass window below the rose-window and behind the altar'.[18] That was the word he used: 'altar', not 'table'. The new City Temple, if its minister had his way, was to conform to an Anglican arrangement; as, indeed, its congregation was already doing since from the first Sunday in June they had been worshipping in St Sepulchre's, at Holborn Viaduct's City end. This was an experience which Weatherhead found aesthetically liberating.[19] At this point 'it was suggested that a study of the plans of Dr Fosdick's Church in New York would be of help in this connection'. Dr Fosdick's church was Riverside, the ultimate in ecclesiastical skyscrapers; John D. Rockefeller had paid for it. Weatherhead was to write to Dr Fosdick and the new City Temple was certainly to owe a great deal to Rockefeller generosity.[20] Meanwhile the Rebuilding Fund stood at £3,071 and a prominent layman, Angus Watson, wrote from Newcastle to ask how much the rebuilding would cost. Watson was not Rockefeller but he was Skipper Sardines, so 'Mr Clare was asked to frame a reply which would, if possible, increase the sympathetic interest which Mr Watson had already shown'.[21]

There was no meeting, 'pending a reply from Dr Fosdick', between December 1941 and November 1942 and there were only three meetings in what I have called the second wave. The Rebuilding Fund reached £5,000; the brochures raised £190; and clear-eyed patience, approaching resignation, replaced vision. For, when it came, Dr Fosdick's 'elaborate brochure descriptive of his Church' made it clear that 'as the construction of this Church had been carried out in harmony with the ideas of Mr Rockefeller, who provided the money, it was felt that the plans could not be of much practical assistance to ourselves unless another millionaire were forthcoming to help make our dreams come true'.[22] It also appeared that the Congregational Union was blowing cold: Mountford Pigott's schemes had distinct limitations, the Union had no funds for the purchase of extra land and its sole current interest in joint occupancy was as a tenant rather than as a co-partner or joint owner. Weatherhead expressed himself in some exasperation to the Union's Alec Glassey:

> he would like to feel that the Congregational Union regarded the City Temple as holding a unique position in the denomination. Not only was it the only Free Church in the City of London, but its appeal and influence were inter-denominational and world-wide . . . Did the Congregational Union really regard the City Temple as its representative Church and did it realise that, contrary to popular but uninformed opinion, it was definitely not a wealthy Church?[23]

The third wave came with October 1943. The Rebuilding Fund stood now at £11,000; the brochure had covered its costs and there were still 2,000 in stock. Gifts came in: £5 from the

Secretary of Ilford Rotary Club; £10 from Rhos-on-Sea Congregational Church; £300 promised by Beresford Street Congregational Church, Auckland, New Zealand (that was an eternity in coming: 'we did not wish to appear importunate'). Approaches were made. One was to the City, with the Great White Pulpit's replacement in mind: 'It was felt that this matter was highly important.' Sheriff Gervase Wood 'requested that the matter should be left with him' and the Lord Mayor designate was sympathetic. Another was to the affably elusive Lord Kemsley whose formation had been in Welsh Congregationalism topped by Paddington Chapel on arrival in London. Kemsley had told Alice Head that he 'would do all he could to help', his Colonel Hordern had been 'most sympathetic', and the editor of the *Sunday Graphic* 'promised to talk to Lord Kemsley with a view to increasing his interest'. Others were fertile in good ideas. There were plans for City Temple Commissioners in Canada, South Africa, Australia, New Zealand, Ireland and Scotland. Colonel Crosfield suggested 'a luncheon to one hundred carefully-selected, influential people to enlist their practical sympathy . . . if this idea found favour he had a friend who would be glad to bear the cost of the luncheon'.[24] Best of all was the indefatigable Sir Sydney.

He placed a collecting box at the bombed church's entrance: by December 1943 it had collected over £30. Next he planned to visit the States, where he could plead the Temple's cause. Unfortunately, although he and Weatherhead pulled all possible strings, he could not obtain an exit visa. So he turned to the Albert Hall. It would be splendid to arrange a fundraising concert featuring the Huddersfield Choral Society, conducted by Dr Malcolm Sargent and crowned by a broadcast address by Dr Weatherhead. Robinson had already provisionally booked the Hall (for £105) and, since Sargent took his time to reply, Robinson phoned him in Belgravia: Sargent seemed to be very interested and helpful – he had advised that artistes' fees (including his own) might be £250, advertising would be another £100 and insurance against loss might take £20: £500 for the Albert Hall.[25]

There were two further developments. The first followed a meeting between Weatherhead and a Catholic priest. That priest was Dr Orchard who before his reception into the Church of Rome had been minister of the King's Weigh House. Orchard's conversion had not entirely cut him off from old friends or old haunts and now he asked whether the City Temple had thought of acquiring the Weigh House. That was in October 1943 and more would be heard of it.[26] The second development came five months later:

> The Chairman reported that during his recent visit to Bournemouth he had met an architect of great distinction and wide experience in the building of Free Churches, Mr Frederick [*sic*] Lawrence, F.R.I.B.A. He had been tremendously impressed by Mr Lawrence's personality, ability and accomplishments, and he would like to hear Dr Berry's opinion of him. Dr Berry endorsed the Chairman's opinions in every respect. He said that Mr Lawrence was a unique personality, with a genius for modern, Free Church architecture. He had an unusual feeling for beauty united to a complete understanding of practical requirements and he would like to underline every word of the Church's opinion of Mr Lawrence.[27]

Lawrence, thus interpreted, delighted them all. In a fit of possibly expensive and certainly precipitate enthusiasm Padre had already suggested that Lawrence visit the ruins, be given a schedule of accommodation as well as Mountford Pigott's plans, and draw up his own draft plans. The Rebuilding Committee confirmed Weatherhead's action: they 'felt quite definitely that we were in no sense committed to the use of the present façade and walls, and that Mr Lawrence should not be hampered in ideas by being expected to make use of any part of the ruins'.[28]

Three dramas now unfolded, to play for the next six years. The first, on which this chapter now concentrates, was that of the architect, his vision and the politics of planning. The second was the still unresolved question of the relationship, if any, between the Congregational Union and its representative – certainly its nearest – church. The third, triggered by Dr Orchard's hint about the Weigh House, was about removal and merger. Each explored the historic tension between church prospective and retrospective. The third brought almost into the open the tension between those, probably the majority, who felt that the future lay with their now historic site and those, like the minister, who were increasingly convinced that the future lay westward.

With the architect there could be no tension. Lawrence was an inspired choice. He was in his early sixties, a Midlander whose practice lay chiefly in the south. His spiritual formation was Methodist but he worshipped in a Congregational church. His professional formation was a deft combination of the practical and the artistic. On the whole his output had been homely in scale, a gently modish vernacular reaching out to art deco. For the past fifteen years, however, he had concentrated on churches, chiefly Free Churches. Three of these, Immanuel Southbourne (1930), Church of the Peace of God Oxted (1935) and St Columba's Worthing (1937), the first two for Congregationalists and the third for Presbyterians, had won considerable acclaim. Here was a man after any building committee's heart. He was extraordinarily easy to deal with; his only possible drawbacks were ill health and deafness. The former had meant frequent visits to Switzerland and Italy; the latter could be convenient if a committee turned difficult (which seldom happened with Lawrence), but it might have implications for the acoustics of his buildings: the Word as sermon is not a priority for the deaf.[29] Here was also a man after the hearts of Berry and Weatherhead alike. Berry's first pastorate had been in Oxted and he had been a guest at the Peace of God's opening.[30] Weatherhead had met Lawrence while lecturing in Bournemouth. The town's Punshon Memorial Methodist Church had been destroyed in May 1943 and Lawrence had already prepared a preliminary scheme for it. Lawrence had a particular rapport with A. E. Whitham, Methodism's leading 'catholic' mystic, who had been Punshon Memorial's minister in the 1930s and Weatherhead's predecessor at Brunswick Leeds, whence Weatherhead had moved to the City Temple.[31] The links could not be more suggestive.

The hallmarks of Lawrence's church work were reverence and a masterly exploitation of material, colour and light. He managed to be at once traditional and up-to-date. His churches tended to have chancels, apses, transepts, side pulpits and central aisles: they were churchy. Organs were banished from sight, light was diffused and, if at all possible, golden. They were traditional in another way. In Italy Lawrence had discovered Assisi. This world informed his architecture. A whole cluster of Nonconformist churches in the Midlands and Home Counties breathed the Franciscan spirit of medieval Umbria. This world, indeed, had taken over Lawrence's life because he now believed that he was a reincarnation of Brother Leo, one of St Francis's companions, and under the name of

'Laurence Temple' he wrote about this in a spiritual biography called *The Shining Brother*.[32] Few of Lawrence's clients were aware of these adventures with the paranormal, though he made no secret of them and one leading Methodist minister, C. Drayton Thomas, both knew of them and shared them.[33] The extraordinary thing is that Leslie Weatherhead, the minister whose spirituality came closest to Lawrence's and who himself later developed a strong interest in parapsychology and came to know several of Lawrence's associates in the field, seems to have been quite unaware of this dimension of Lawrence's life and work. The beauty of it was enough; the Franciscan references were a bonus, in welcome counterpoint to Old Dissent and its Pilgrim Fathers, and the inescapably suburban note was comforting for such a congregation as the City Temple's. Provided he could cope with the frustrations of a difficult site and rise to the demands of a larger church than any he had yet been asked to build, his qualities would meet every need.[34]

So it seemed and was. Weatherhead and his rebuilders were entranced. Lawrence met them at St Sepulchre's on 2 May 1944. He had with him some artfully coloured preliminary sketches which he had prepared at Easter. The minister introduced him. Lawrence, he said, 'seemed to be so much in harmony with the spirit of our requirements and recognised our needs so perfectly that he felt Mr Lawrence should be empowered to prepare further draft plans'. For his part, Lawrence 'said he never made a charge for preliminary work. He felt confident of his ability to prepare plans which would meet with approval and if and when the contract was signed, his fees would be on the usual R.I.B.A. scale.' If they were not approved, then

> his charges for work he had already done would be on a very modest scale. The work itself meant much more to him than the remuneration, and he felt himself to be so entirely in harmony with our ideas that it was up to him to produce plans which would meet with general approval.

There was little more to be said, though Padre said it: 'everyone present felt great confidence in his powers.'[35]

Lawrence developed his plans in a winsome midsummer report.[36] The defining problem was 'the smallness of the site for the purposes required of it'. A secondary constraint was 'the general intention . . . to preserve as much of the existing work as possible'. That meant the front and the back: the side walls would be removed and replaced in steel and reinforced concrete, brick-clad and stone-faced. Community needs would be served by a ground floor hall to seat between 620 and 700, a gallery-level hall for 130, the appropriate lavatories and so on. The ground floor accommodation would be 'tanked', that is to say vertical and horizontal asphalt damp proof courses would form a waterproof tank around the new work. There were to be two flats, a two-bedroomed one for the caretaker and a suite of study, bedroom and bathroom for the minister's use. The former would be by the ground floor hall, the latter at the building's top. Character-istically Lawrentian touches broke through at this point. 'If I could be allowed to omit the office . . . I could give the caretaker a very much happier sitting-room'; while, for the minister, two interior leaded-glass windows, one in the study, the other in the bedroom, looked down on the church's apse and table. 'It is the expression of an ancient wish for a similar personal room from which one could look down upon those glooms and lights which hover about the eastern columns of all great churches.'

And so to that church and the chapel which it was to enfold. The old church had side and rear galleries. The new one would have no side galleries and its rear gallery would have just two columns, the only ones in the building, which would be in nobody's way. Since that gallery was to hold 627, only a hundred fewer than the body of the church, it would be an inescapable, even obtrusive feature. Lawrence planned to soften this by incor-porating under it 'a dome . . . floodlit by hidden electric lights, . . . to give interest and height to this ceiling, and illumination for those below'. Lawrence was an enthusiast for the hidden lighting which was a feature of all his churches. Here there would be 'no glare between any member of the congregation and the minister'.

It was with his chapel that Lawrence waxed most lyrical. Leslie Weatherhead particularly wanted a Thorvaldsenesque statue of Christ at the church's Holborn entrance and a charred cross made from wood salvaged from the old Temple. Lawrence warmed to such symbolism. 'The front . . . with its great tower has stood sentinel for over two generations. It would be a dull mind that failed to recognise that this massive stonework not only has great value as material, but has a greater value as a friend and as a stout symbol.' That was why his sole alterations to the time-honoured façade would be to the entrances, to allow for Padre's concept of Christ's statue and 'my interpretation of his idea'. That had set him thinking:

> It is necessary to confess to a complete change of attitude on my own part in regard to the design of this Chapel. Mr Weatherhead's beautiful idea of the charred cross made me suggest – wrongly as I now think – a Franciscan austerity. Such austerity, with the brick and primitive painted beams I spoke of, would have had an especial virtue among the vineyards of Umbria. Holborn however, is stern, and surrounds the pilgrim with no verdure. Surely here – it seems to me now – is the one place where emphasis should be laid on the charm of the spiritual quest. Holborn itself can be trusted to demonstrate the austerities.
>
> My first idea, when I realised this, was to ask if the Chapel might be dedicated to the Seven Angels of the Presence. In that case, I should have made six windows showing the Great Figures about the Throne, and one niche over the Communion Table containing a statue of Saint Michael.
>
> As discussion at this time, however, presents difficulties I have been content to outline on my coloured drawing a design of dark oak and bronze, of stone and green marble. And it is designed in the Italian manner. I thought it might be well also to continue the scheme of green marble shown on my sketch round all the four walls of the Chapel, and place hidden electric lamps on the cornice.

This was Lawrence of purest essence: charm, diplomacy and purpose, honesty artfully deployed. St Michael? In a Congregational church, even if in a side chapel with its dividing wall prosaically cavity-insulated with slag? There were parallels, almost precedents, at places like Penge and Ealing, not to mention the King's Weigh House.[37] But Lawrence knew better than to insist; there can have been few architects of so truly collegial a temper, least of all when their most important commission to date depended on it. So he turned to other points of architecturally spiritual significance:

> Not for one moment, however, would I ignore the idea of the charred Cross made from the burnt woodwork of the old City Temple. In the vestibule, and behind the statue of Christ which faces Holborn, there

is a blank space. There I suggest forming a 'Hall of Memory' with a niche of marble and a pedestal under. The pedestal would hold in a bronze setting 'The Book Of Remembrance' containing perhaps an account of the burning and of the re-building of the Church, and the names of the members, as they pass on, who have striven for it. Such a book would be written across with great drama and would become a history. Here, at the entrance of the Church in the niche over the 'Book of Remembrance' would I place the charred Cross, which could then fittingly face the congregation on leaving the Church; for truly it is a symbol of the Church, of those whose work makes them part of its spiritual fabric, and of the building itself whose tower has looked down on the destruction of two world wars, and yet still stands uplifted.[38]

It cannot quite be left there. Lawrence was faced with nearly four more years of advocacy – with the Ministry of Works, with the City of London's planning officers (behind whom lurked the County Council which was about to take over their powers), with the Royal Fine Art Commission in the persons of Dr Charles Holden, of London Senate House fame, and Professor William Holford, whose Paternoster Square now awaits its quietus and whose doubts about the shape and principle of the Temple's tower were profound.[39] Lawrence persuaded them all.

He began with the Church Council and Rebuilding Committee. From the first there was general concern about seating capacity and a widely held feeling that the chapel should be separated from the church by a grille rather than a wall. Dr Dewar believed that a 'typically Free Church lay out would look just as impressive and conducive of worship' and Jack Dewey wondered about radial seating. Lady Lennard queried this and that with staccato practicality: 'Gallery must not be too big'; pulpit too high ('people near would get crick in neck'); 'if pulpit is on left, what is tall object with cross shown in sketch of Chancel?': none the less 'The Chancel and Chapel I like very much'. The others agreed: 'an exceptionally good interpretation of our needs', said Dewar; 'clearly a skilled, thoughtful and reverend interpretation', echoed Dewey, while John Tann, the safe manufacturer, positively glowed:

I am thrilled with the majestic proportions of the arches of the Chancel and Apse, and am very pleased that the beautiful lines are unbroken by side galleries. The straight gallery covers nearly two-thirds of the seating space in the Nave and I think it is a splendid idea that a sense of spaciousness is given under this gallery by the floodlit dome . . . [T]he lovely little chapel . . . I think is essential. Also I love the idea of the prominence of the Book of Remembrance.[40]

Lawrence was all amiability. He professed to find such remarks of 'a value hard to estimate'; and he dug in about his Chapel and his Hall of Memory:

The idea between my designs for the Chapel was that it should very definitely be an isolated unit; a silent, spiritual fortress shut away from all influences save those pertaining to a small private church dedicated to the Spirit. Indeed, it was to be a place of escape and refuge and security.

That idea, as I see it, is lost when the grille is introduced. The Chapel loses its personality and becomes an annexe merely of the great church.

As for the memorial:

May I plead for the position of this small shrine to be retained? The charred cross, the book, so full of memories will be degraded and deprived of all significance if placed behind the book counter and between the cupboards. The Memorial should, it seems to me, be quite free and occupy the central position alone, for all the congregation to see as they leave.

I am practical enough to understand quite clearly the value of the central position for a book stall. But there are only three points which distinguish this church from a secular hall; that is which give it a spiritual as well as a social significance. The first is its Chancel, the second is the Chapel – which is now an annexe, the third is the Memorial, which you ask me to hide away. Having made my plea, I put myself in your hands.[41]

Lawrence's Temple was never built. He died suddenly on the last Sunday in May 1948, not long after a particularly satisfying encounter with the planning authorities.[42] He had no partner but there was an unusually promising young heir apparent, Ronald Sims. Unfortunately Sims had yet to qualify; he was still a student of the Architectural Association and the Church Council and Rebuilding Committee used this as the reason, or pretext, to turn to fresh solutions.[43] The impression is given that Lawrence died before his plans were sufficiently advanced, hence the disappearance of his scheme. Or was it that the City Temple lacked the courage to take on an untried young man? They turned instead to the undoubtedly proven Lord Mottistone and Paul Paget, of Seely and Paget.[44] Their thumpingly atmospheric (and considerably less 'Anglican') interpretation worked well enough for Weatherhead. It has not worked for his successors.[45] Lawrence's would have served them all; he was more naturally at home in Leslie Weatherhead's private house of prayer and his public interpretation of it for the City Temple would have communicated it more tellingly to later generations.[46]

There are ends to leave as well as tie. The historically elegant solution – emigration to the King's Weigh House – was not taken. Nor was the historic, that is to say prophetic, solution: for there was no merger with the Marylebone Presbyterians, in whose church the City Temple worshipped between 1947 and 1958; the City Temple set no great pace for the union between Congregationalists and Presbyterians which in 1972 issued in the United Reformed Church. Most frustrating of all for those who are intrigued by Lawrence's stated experience of the paranormal is the fact that his work ceased so abruptly with his death, on this of all commissions, for this of all ministers. 'Laurence Temple' and Lawrence's Temple remain quite separate, even as conjecture. On the other hand, Bournemouth's Methodists had the courage which the City's Congregationalists lacked. For Punshon Memorial, which had first brought Lawrence to Weatherhead's notice, put its trust in Ronald Sims.

III

The story of the rebuilding of the City Temple exposes the chemistry, the interpersonal dynamic, of such an enterprise. It illustrates the harnessing of culture and tradition to the evangelical imperative. The story of Punshon Memorial's rebuilding provides an instructive coda.

William Morley Punshon (1824–81) was in the top flight of nationally known Victorian preachers. Among Wesleyan Methodists he had three claims to fame. He galvanized Canadian Methodism, he championed British watering-place Methodism, and he married his deceased wife's sister.[47] Late Victorian Bournemouth was a young queen of watering places and since Punshon's widow had retired there the town's Methodism was ripe for a memorial to him. After 'most serious legal and other difficulties' a church, described as 'a conspicuous success, the building itself being superior to the drawings of it', was erected in 1886 at moderate cost but with maximum display on a prime site in Richmond Hill.[48] Its style was geometrical Gothic, its materials were Swanage and Bath stone, its architect was Robert Curwen, whose Leys School chapel and St John's Methodist Church, Ashbrooke Mount, Sunderland, remain among the most telling celebrations of late Victorian high Wesleyanism.[49] If Richmond Hill's Wesleyans were none the less overshadowed by Richmond Hill's Congregationalists, they remained an influential society served by distinctive ministers. A. E. Witham (1931–8) and T. H. Kirkman (1938–46) were men of the Lawrence and Weatherhead stamp.[50] This phase of Punshon Memorial's life was ended decisively at noon on Sunday 23 May 1943, during Bournemouth's worst air raid.[51]

As has been seen, the architect for Punshon's replacement had been swiftly chosen. F. W. Lawrence was a close friend of Kirkman, as he had been of Witham; he practised locally, where he had perfected his ecclesiastical style (expressed in a parish church, a Congregational church – both of moderate size, although the latter had been awarded a bronze medal – and two small Methodist churches, as well as a large Methodist church hall[52]) in which late Arts and Crafts almost turned into Art Deco. He was a sound choice as well as a safe one and he promptly prepared alternative schemes, one of them in what his successor described as a 'Modern Romanesque'.[53]

A prompt architect and prompt plans could not, however, guarantee a prompt new building in the brave new world of war-damage claims and building licences, and although the new Punshon Memorial could be presented as the crowning work of Lawrence's practice, it was in fact the work of Lawrence's successor – a study, therefore, in contrast as well as continuity.

The continuity augured well. Ronald Sims was the protégé of both Lawrence and a benevolent local Methodist businessman, J. Rolfe Treadgold. Lawrence, who liked to give his pupils biblical names, called Sims 'Lazarus'. Certainly he was on his way up.

From 1939 to 1941 Sims was articled to Lawrence. Then he was awarded a Leverhulme Scholarship to the Architectural Association where he completed his studies, interrupted by war service, between 1947 and 1949. It had always been understood that he would return to work with Lawrence and although Lawrence's sudden death occurred while Sims was in the final stages of his training, Treadgold purchased the practice and made it over to Sims, who took into partnership another local young man, Patrick Coles, who was to marry Sims's sister. Like Sims, Coles was a prizeman, for he had won the Architectural Association's Senior Entrance Scholarship in 1947, its centennial year. The practice of Frederic Lawrence and Partners reopened formally on 18 July 1949, in Lawrence's old office in Southbourne, opposite Immanuel, the Congregational church which had made Lawrence's name as a church architect. As Coles has recalled: 'I had not ever met Frederic Lawrence, but came over the years that I worked in Southbourne, to understand the quality of work for which he was revered and I was conscious of a lingering professional umbrella.'[54] Sims was to find that umbrella, especially when unfurled by J. Rolfe Treadgold, invaluable in what followed and it was the knowledge that the revived practice would be launched by the important commission for Punshon Memorial which confirmed Sims's audacious decision to start as he meant to go on.

The auguries were good, the opportunities were undoubted, but the terrain was rocky. First there was the matter of credibility, inevitably coloured by the personalities of Sims and Coles. Then there were the equally inevitable diplomacies to be negotiated with the War Damage Commission, the local planning authority and the Methodist Department for Chapel Affairs. There was bound to be confrontation, given two principals 'fresh in the game and possessing that peculiar "A.A.sixth year" brand of confidence'.[55]

Memory was the least of their worries. Methodism in Bournemouth was new, little more than a lifetime's work, like Bournemouth itself; services had begun in the traditional upper room in 1859. Nor were Punshon's people wedded to Richmond Hill. A fresh site, in Exeter Road, had been briskly purchased and cleared. It was eligible and it promised to be flexible; 'fortunately peculiar site, mainstreet frontage (no vehicle access permitted by the planners) with a pleasant rear access road 8 ft lower than the main road'.[56] Given the right conditions, it presented Lawrence with a terrain closer to Assisi's than any which had so far come his way; and Sims himself, in a tactful moment, later assured a powerful correspondent that the 'terraced hill cities of Umbria are dear to my heart and are forever an inspiration'.[57] Planning and financial constraints would ensure that the new Punshon Memorial would strike few who approached it as Umbria-in-Bournemouth, but there could be no doubt as to its potential for prominence.

Sims, backed steadily by Treadgold, who marshalled his fellow trustees, and by A. W. Massey, who had succeeded Kirkman as superintendent minister, seems to have had relatively little difficulty in securing the support of Bournemouth's Methodists.[58] Sims's own account of that process was realistic if cynical. 'I torpedoed all existing bases of settlement with the War Damage Commission and started a new claim', which, after two years of 'many worthless exercises', issued in a more generous award than the experienced Lawrence had managed to extract. It was that, he felt, which had been the key to Bournemouth's Methodist support. Perhaps it was, but Sims underestimated the extent to which he had translated their needs into aspirations. What had begun as 'a problem for war damage settlement' now settled into a battle for a building licence. Despite 'what now appears entertaining correspondence with the Minister . . . at monthly intervals for about two years', Sims was not to win that battle, learning 'that in such matters, the orthodox frontal approach is invariably unrewarding'. Meanwhile he prepared plans and models for Punshon's trustees:

> An uncommonly large number . . . were considered. Some drew criticism from my clients, who, in their hearts, probably liked the 'Romanesque' design and did not know what I was trying to do – nonetheless, there was a good understanding between us in other matters. They were delighted with the result of the war damage business, and they considered me sincere in my approach to design, although there was steadily building opposition to everything I produced, particularly in high places.[59]

The Methodist Department for Chapel Affairs was one of those high places. 'Scheme after scheme drew scorn from this department', recalled Sims; none the less it is from an undated report on an earlier, and presumably scorned, scheme that one can identify the elements which would have appealed to Bournemouth: the massing of the buildings, at that stage to be in dark honey-coloured brick with Purbeck stone 'used sparingly to accentuate important elements'; the generous car parking; the 'Invalid Carriage Entry' ('This is a special feature . . . special provision for the accommodation of invalid chairs during service time will be made'); the 'quiet garden of a semi-private character'; the 'casual seating area where visitors may wait, informal meetings and discussion be carried on and where refreshment from the kitchen may be served'; the church itself, where

> an attempt has been made to produce simple unpretentious harmony, outside and within. The effect has been towards robust dignity in massing with occasional refined detail . . . in special features such as the entrance porch and East End . . . Within, a simple interplay of space and light has been the aim . . . No false dramatic effects have been sought, no symbolism has been indulged.[60]

All that was reassuringly Bournemouth, as well as wateringplace Methodist,[61] and these elements remained crucial to the success of the completed church. This was a pre-stressed concrete structure clad in variegated red rather than dark honey brick. Since the currently open site was likely to be jostled by large buildings, Sims decided to treat its principal façade as urban streetscape rather than as 'church-in-the-round'. This meant:

> a rejection of the facade as normally considered. I tried to break the frontage down into fine parallel planes which were recessed in varying degrees and treated in different ways, tones of brick, texture, etc. I used a very dark red brown mortar, so that brick joint pattern would be subdued and the irregularity of the Swanage handmades would give an interesting texture.[62]

The car parking, cloakrooms, lift, invalid chair ramp, caretaker's flat, kitchen, vestries, lesser halls and projection room (large churches which hoped to benefit from the Rank family's benevolence were well advised to cater for religious and uplifting films; the post-war church must be as comfortable as its chief rival which was now the cinema rather than the public house), all marked the adaptation rather than the rejection of Edwardian institutional religion and this was appropriately spiritualized in the church itself, the main roof exposed in midnight blue, with secondary ceilings below the clerestory windows in idigbo wood, gold anodized aluminium and glass, and idigbo wood used again for pews, table, pulpit, and a great triptych on the wall behind the table, while the floor was blocked in muhuhu, with reconstructed stone for the communion end.[63]

Idigbo, muhuhu, gold anodized aluminium, insulation by 'slabs of cementitious wood wool', floor heating 'using water as a vehicle and oil as a primary source of heat', suggest the technical adventurousness characteristic of chapel architects and in Punshon Memorial's case concentrated in its most controversial, yet traditional, element, the tower. This structure in brick and glass was 'developed as a slender spire surmounted by an alloy cross which may be seen from a considerable distance as it reaches up 132 feet above adjacent ground level'.[64] The church was to accommodate between 650 and 700 worshippers; it was to cost £140,000 (which turned out to be nearer £170,000). For all its up-to-dateness it was refining well-tried patterns. Seaside Christianity was a success story, large congregations were normal. They might even get larger. Sims's plans allowed for the church's conversion into a multi-purpose hall should ever a larger worship-space be needed.

All chapel commissions are compromises and Sims was not good at compromises. He was genuinely grateful to Bournemouth's Methodists, but he was less happy with the Chapel Affairs Department and frankly contemptuous of the Bournemouth Planning Committee. The Department for Chapel Affairs suffered from, perhaps traded on, distance.[65] Manchester was a long way from Bournemouth. Its support was as vital as its caution could be taken for granted. When the department's formidable general secretary, E. Benson Perkins, visited Bournemouth in July 1945, to consider alternative schemes produced by Lawrence, he clearly warmed to the commanding possibilities of the more ambitious of the two schemes but he rejected it none the less:

Any proposals in a particular case which seem to suggest privilege or preferential treatment would have very unfortunate reactions within

Methodism as a whole, and in respect of Bournemouth in particular
. . . I think it quite likely that . . . the matter might be raised in
Conference in a way which everyone interested in the well-being of
Bournemouth, and concerned for Methodism as a whole, would
undoubtedly regret.[66]

Sims received similar treatment from Perkins and his successor Albert Hearn.[67] When he forwarded two more schemes to
Perkins, to add to the two which he had already furnished, he
wearily noted that these 'new' schemes had in fact already been
fully considered and hoped that 'contrary second thoughts at a
later date would not involve the question of confidence in myself
as architect'. One of those schemes, he told Perkins, was 'in
principle at least, based upon my understanding of your alternative', and the other reflected the trustees' instructions.[68] That did
not impress Perkins. When Sims, Perkins and two trustees met to
hammer this out in Westminster's Wesley Club, Perkins was firmly
dismissive of the trustees' scheme. He disliked the shape, the view
from the pulpit, and the placing of the choir:

> experience has shown that a rectangle was the best outline for
> Methodist Church purposes, but unfortunately the Architect was not
> willing to accept suggestions of this kind and it was necessary for me
> to point out that the final word did not rest with the Architect but with
> the Trustees and this Department. I made it quite clear that we should
> not pass this plan . . . without serious alteration.[69]

That reference to the trustees indicates where the department
was vulnerable. Perkins was masterful and autocratic, but he was
also experienced. It would have been irresponsible to fly in the
face of his consultant's criticisms and the local authority's
reservations. Hearn, who was less masterful, bowed to local
Methodism. Recognizing that the trustees 'are really set on
carrying it out more or less as envisaged by the Architect', he felt
that the responsibility was now theirs. 'I told them that having
expressed our views we still held to them . . . I felt it important
that in our records there should be an indication that we did
demur at one or two things.' He wondered whether Prestwich, the
department's consultant, should have 'a final look in view of his
earlier comments and radical criticisms of the whole scheme' and
he understood 'that it is not entirely certain that the plans as a

whole have the approval of the local authority', but he anticipated no real difficulty now on that score.[70]

Hearn was wrong. Three months later Sims received this letter from Bournemouth's town clerk:

> I am instructed to inform you that the planning approval in principle granted in 1943 for the erection of a church on this particular site was granted in the expectation that a church of traditional design would be erected. The Council appreciate that the present submission is in accordance with the modern concept for buildings of this nature. The Council however feel that a Church of traditional design should be erected on the site.[71]

It might be possible to read between these lines to discover a difference of opinion between the Council's professional officers, who were inclined to like the scheme, and with whom Sims had been working for a solution, and its elected representatives, who had been free with sound-bites to the local press about the meat market and the jam factory which Bournemouth's Methodists were planning for the new Punshon Memorial. None the less, having fought to an honourable draw with the church's bureaucracy, Sims now found all his frustrations focused on local bureaucracy. Most of the problems hinged on access. From the first it was clear that there could be no vehicular access from the main road, but there were also official worries about the car park at the rear. That was in 1943. In 1946 there had to be fresh provision for road widening and late in 1950 a previously unmentioned building line was sprung upon the church. All these concerns were met. By May 1954 even the height and form of the spire were felt to be 'entirely satisfactory technically', though it was clear that it was the spire which would be the likely sticking point. Early in September there were press reports that the scheme had been referred back.[72] Yet it was early October before the Town Clerk sent his letter of rejection. Sims 'almost gave up and entered the grocery business, anything!'[73] In fact he appealed to the Ministry of Housing. He declared that he would meet the expenses from his own pocket and resign if the Inquiry went against him.

That was fighting talk. According to Sims, the trustees' solicitor was against the idea and the Department for Chapel Affairs was uneasy: 'scores of efforts were made to see that Methodism did not "fly in the face of local opinion and authority" '.[74] But the trustees remained staunch and the department proved surprisingly firm. Sims's determination had been fuelled by his discovery that although permission had been refused on aesthetic grounds, the local planning committee in fact wanted to use the site as a car park. He wrote reassuringly to Albert Hearn about his plan of campaign.[75] He had marshalled an impressive array of support. A barrister friend had agreed to provide legal advice; he had the good offices of the County Planning Officer and his deputy ('who is a good friend of mine'), the Chief Librarian to the Ministry of Housing, the Vice President of the RIBA (Frederick Gibberd, architect of Harlow New Town, future architect of Liverpool Roman Catholic Cathedral, and himself a Methodist), his old Principal at the Architectural Association (R. Furneaux Jordan, The *Observer*'s architectural correspondent), and Nigel Nicolson, the local MP ('I am not unaware of the value of his direct approach to the Minister'). The best were yet to come, for Sims had the covert support of the borough architect and borough engineer and their deputies, one of whom would be presenting the Council's case should it ever come to a public inquiry ('A situation of which he is painfully aware!') and the all-but-promised support of Dr Thomas Sharp: 'if he is called . . . the Methodist Church can feel that they have the most important and impressive professional witness on this subject that can be obtained'.[76]

Sims was as sure of his ground as he was of his supporters. He could quote precedent and ministerial guidelines:

> A building in the modern style should rarely be opposed, and only on the clearest evidence that the building would be completely inharmonious with its neighbours and entirely out of keeping with its surroundings would the Minister consider there were sufficient grounds for refusing planning permission.
>
> Planning Authorities must be prepared to encourage new ideas in design even though they appear to break with local tradition, and . . . an honest design, however unusual, which will employ good and appropriate materials should be disallowed only in the rarest cases where the neighbouring development appears to demand a particular and different form.

Sims was careful to anchor these general principles in the case at hand. He believed that his church was 'an honest expression of contemporary structure using materials of the finest quality. It is superior (in form and finish) to surrounding development and *positively contributes* to local amenity'. In contrast, its neighbours 'illustrate no local tradition save that of a random eclecticism'. And he neatly turned the Town Clerk's arguments: Clegg had accepted that the church was 'in accordance with the modern concept of buildings of this nature'; that is to say, it was truly traditional since it was the merely imitative (and by that fact retrogressive) which stood outside the sequence of *traditional development*. In sum the Council had made 'frivolous use of our sincere wish to cooperate and grave misuse of Planning Authority'.[77]

The Minister accepted the appeal and the Inquiry was held in Bournemouth Town Hall on 5 January 1955. It was an uncomfortable business. Sims's motives were impugned, the Inspector had to stop proceedings on four occasions and the Council shifted tack to concentrate on its plans for car parking. Sims ungraciously wrote of 'a procession of opinionated officials displaying, equally, their prejudice and ignorance'. On the other hand Sharp was on top form and the Department for Chapel Affairs turned up trumps, sending down its one representative 'who could honestly declare that he liked the scheme'.[78] No wonder Sims wrote appreciatively to Hearn about his support in 'a tense and trying series of events': 'Methodism had done a very sound thing in standing against the sort of opposition to which it was exposed.'[79]

The Inspector's report and the Minister's decision entirely vindicated Sims. Sims's grounds were that Bournemouth Town Council was being 'capricious, vague and unreasonable'; the Council's grounds were 'that the building ought to look like a church in which worship was conducted', especially in so busy and central a position. Noting the trustees' desire 'to march with the times' with a building of 'real significance', and Sharp's view that their new church 'would be the one building of any architectural distinction in the whole locality', the minister reached his decision: 'the building has been well and honestly designed in the modern idiom, and he does not consider that this departure from traditional design will affect the amenities of the immediate neighbourhood.'[80] The church could go ahead, and since building licences were abolished later that year the last obstacles had all but crumbled.

Punshon Memorial made and marked Sims. It was the first, as it was the most obsessive, of his commissions, 'the spinal influence of a longish period of my life, indeed all my practice thus far, ten years in which not a week passed without meetings, letters, or drawings for revised schemes'.[81] When it was built Sims could describe the exterior as 'satisfactory' and take pleasure in the fact that the building manifestly worked: 'the church thrives, fills to the brim, and has been accepted at last. In fact it is surprising how things have changed since the building was finished. People who were outraged by the appearance of drawings and models now accept and even enthuse over the finished building.'[82] And he concluded:

I do not love the building for its merit but now it is finished, it has a place in my heart . . . I doubt whether the building deserves the R.I.B.A. bronze medal that has been awarded, but I feel that I most certainly do. It is an interesting record of how gummed up building became after the war.[83]

There was a price to be paid. The partnership with Coles was dissolved, amid some acrimony, in 1957, and Sims's practice remained more promising than large. There was his first completed church, Wallisdown Methodist (1954); its streamlined façade was the most F. W. Lawrentian of Sims's designs, and its interior 'pleases me still (apart from some fashionable detailing)'.[84] There were his designs for a Methodist church at Offington Park, Worthing, but these were considered 'too modern' and he resigned as its architect.[85] There were three utilitarian buildings for Southampton University and town centre gardens for Nuneaton.[86] He submitted designs to the Royal Academy's Summer Exhibition on six occasions, and was accepted on five;[87] and he entered architectural competitions. Lawrence had competed for Guildford Cathedral in 1932; Sims competed for Coventry in 1951. His design for that, as for St Luke's Liverpool, showed the fascination for the hexagon which had so worried Benson Perkins.[88] But all this was more practice than Practice. Sims was philosophical about it. Competitions were best seen as 'exercises where one might explore one's uncertain thinking': 'I intend to win a competition one day. But the failures are not things I worry about – they are good student-type exercises with sufficient money available, a client out of sight and of constant mind.'[89]

Indeed the ballast of Sims's work in the 1950s was educational. From 1951 to 1954 he was teaching three days a week at the Architectural Association; in 1955 he became an external examiner there; in 1957 he became a lecturer in design at the Southern College of Art; and he had been at pains to tell Hearn that the president of the RIBA had appointed him an adviser on elevation and aesthetic considerations to Hampshire County Planning Authority.[90] Sims, in short, was displaying all the traits of the architects' architect.[91]

The most interesting appreciation of Sims came from his former teacher, R. Furneaux Jordan, whose profile prefaced *The Architect*'s survey of Sims's work as it stood in 1960. It is Jordan's assessment which explains the continuities, despite everything, with F. W. Lawrence, and which identifies the continuing significance of Punshon Memorial now that it has become a period piece, almost a time capsule. For Jordan, Sims was an *interesting* young architect, one of that first post-war generation which had fallen into two unequal, yet related, camps.[92] The larger camp contained:

able young men who, taking the full social and technical implications of the modern movement for granted, immediately climbed on the bandwagon of the day – Herts County Council, the L.C.C. and all that. In one sweep they took the modern movement from its immediate post-war phase, with its delayed action memories of Pavilion Suisse, Impington and left-wing politics, into its prefabrication and Welfare State phase. That was the climate of the earlier fifties.

Sims, however, belonged to a much smaller band

who accepted the full implications of what was going on round them, with complete technical comprehension but also with a fairly big grain of salt. They deliberately . . . remained outside the ideological climate . . . They regarded the new technology as a servant to be used in fulfilling their own plastic or aesthetic intentions – not as a master dictating the intentions. In other words they admired Wright more than Mies . . .

Jordan marvelled at such audacity among such young professionals. It was politically incorrect, almost reactionary. Besides, could it be done, short of genius? In Sims's case, who was, though interesting, no genius, such a stance explained the brash experiments with hexagons, even the 'rather curious echoes of Wright's *art nouveau* days'. But it also explained why this modernist claimed to be a traditionalist, and why he might strike outsiders as an arrogant fellow. For Frank Lloyd Wright's architectural philosophy depended 'on the fact that in the end architecture stands upon the earth', and Sims's work too, 'masculine, uncompromising and sound', strove to be organic. As yet his reach fell short of his grasp, but at least he

> does have that sort of rugged honesty that rejects current solutions and seeks more radical ones – arrived at by hard thinking. It is this dependence upon one's own radical thinking that produces, as in Wright, a certain arrogance of a kind that no one would confuse for a moment with conceit.

Jordan had the measure of his old pupil. As he wrote, Sims was lecturing in America, firing back home 'some very downright statements . . . to some extent – since they tell the story of his relationships with his clients – unpublishable'. Yet that too was like Wright,

> the same self-confidence (arrogance if you will) and the same drastic self-criticism, the same anger with philistinism and bureaucracy, the same faculty for keeping a difficult client's loyalty through a long series of set-backs and trouble – including defiance of the client for the client's own good.

Benson Perkins, Albert Hearn, A. W. Massey and J. Rolfe Treadgold could all say 'Amen' to that.

Ronald Sims's future, like that of Patrick Coles, though their professional paths were not again to cross, lay in Canada. Jordan's association of Sims's work with that of Wright, the quintessentially *American* genius, remains the more persuasive. Two of Wright's most speaking buildings, Unity Temple, Oak Park, Illinois (1905–08), and The Meeting House, Madison, Wisconsin (1946–51), both for Unitarian congregations, are admirably suited for the needs of what, in English terms, would be Protestant Nonconformity. Their strengths lie in colour, texture, technical audacity, and a sense of how worshippers like to sit, and move, and look. In that respect they are as 'traditional' as any meeting house. These are Sims's strengths – the midnight blue roof, the lights like great pearls or tear-drops, the idigbo and muhuhu, the pre-stressed concrete, the excitement still felt by worshippers for whom anything built to house 700 must now reek of triumphalism. They were also Frederic Lawrence's strengths, for all his determination to express them in Umbrian Romanesque. Theirs are buildings in the mainstream, as well as in the stream of Nonconformity's cultural tradition. They deserve to be recognized and celebrated as such.[93]

We may regret that Ronald Sims was not invited to follow Frederic Lawrence at the City Temple as well as at Punshon Memorial. It was clearly out of the question. Yet though both churches so far survive as remarkably complete creations of the 1950s, Sims's Punshon Memorial has arguably survived better than Seely and Paget's City Temple. In 1970, the year after Leslie Weatherhead last assisted at a service in the City Temple, the great gallery was closed off, save for special occasions, the lectern was replaced by a small pedestal pulpit, thus giving the great cantilevered peppermint drum its quietus, and the glass screens at the back of the church were brought forward, all to reduce the seating capacity, as Weatherhead had known would happen.[94] And victims of success? Punshon Memorial was dedicated by Leslie Weatherhead on 17 December 1958, seven weeks after the City Temple's rededication in the presence of the Queen Mother. Heritage, if not tradition, had been justified, by majesty if not grace.[95]

Notes

[1] In the preparation of this chapter I have been particularly indebted to the Revd Dr John Travell, who is preparing a biographical study of Leslie Weatherhead and to the Revd Mia Kyte-Hilborn and the Revd Dr David Hilborn for access to the archives of the City Temple. I am also greatly indebted to Mr James Bettley (formerly of the Royal Institute of British Architects, Head Office), Mr Patrick J. Coles FRIBA, the Revd Brian J. N. Galliers, the Rt Revd John Gladwin, the Revd David Haworth, the late Donald Kirkby (Property Division, the Methodist Church), Dr Peter Nockles, the late Paul Paget FRIBA, Mr

P. E. Robinson and Mr M. Stead (Bournemouth Planning Services Division), Mrs Katharine Spackman (Dorset County Library Services), Mr Robin Street (Property Committee, the Methodist Church).

[2] A. W. W. Dale, *The Life of R. W. Dale of Birmingham* (London, 1898), 170. The church in question was James Cranstoun's Wycliffe Church, Bristol Road, opened in 1861. Birmingham's townscape owes much to Wycliffe's benefactors, the Middlemores. A. S. Langley, *Birmingham Baptists Past and Present* (London, n.d. [c.1939]), 85–7.

[3] Elaine Kaye, *The History of the King's Weigh House Church* (London, 1968), 96–104.

[4] *The Pulpit Jubilee of the Rev. Joseph Parker, D.D. June 19th 1898* (London, 1898), 11. For Thomas Binney (1798–1874) see *DNB*.

[5] B. Hammond, J. Dewey and L. D. Weatherhead, *The City Temple in the City of London; Past, Present and Future* (London, 1958), 16, 27. For Henry Francis Lockwood (1811–78), William Mawson (1828–89) and Richard Mawson (1834–1904) see Alison Felstead, J. Franklin and L. Pinfield, *Directory of British Architects 1834–1900* (London, 1993), 568, 609.

[6] Such was the legend. In 1945 it led to correspondence between the City Temple's architect (F. W. Lawrence) and church secretary (J. H. Dewey). 'I can't help thinking that whoever settled the theoretical accommodation of the old City Temple shut his eyes and thought of a number', wrote the former (15 Nov. 1945). Dewey replied (21 Nov. 1945): 'The exaggerated figures giving up to 2,500 were applicable I believe to Dr Parker's day when the L.C.C. were not so stringent in their requirements, and when every available space including all the gangways was filled up with camp seats to increase the capacity'. Even when that figure was whittled down to 1,871 Lawrence was perplexed: 'it is not by any means clear to me how this number was fitted into the building' (28 Nov. 1945). An important moral is to be drawn: trust not estimates of capacity. For a start Anglicans and Dissenters worked from different scales. The Church of England Incorporated Building Society allowed 720 square inches per sitting; Lawrence allowed 627. City Temple Archives (CTA).

[7] For Joseph Parker (1830–1902) see *DNB*. For Reginald John Campbell (1867–1956) see *Who Was Who*, 1951–60.

[8] A. Clare, *The City Temple, 1640–1940: The Tercentenary Volume* (London, 1940), 111–23, esp. 122.

[9] Ibid.

[10] CTA, The City Temple Members Roll 1952. For 1st Viscount Leathers (1883–1965), Minister of War Transport 1941–5 and Secretary of State for Transport, Fuel and Power 1951–3, and Frank Salisbury (1874–1962)

see *DNB*; for 3rd Baron Stamp (1907–87) see *Who's Who*, 1987; for Col. George R. Crosfield (1877–1962) see *Who Was Who*, 1961–70; and for Alice Maud Head (1886–1981) see *Who's Who*, 1981. Stamp's parents and elder brother were killed in the air raid which destroyed the City Temple. For Leslie Weatherhead (1893–1976) see *DNB*.

11 *Baptist Times* (21 Aug. 1958); *The Times* (12 Aug. 1958); *The City Temple in the City of London*, 38–41.

12 CTA, Minutes of the City Temple Rebuilding Committee 1941–51 (Minutes CTRC), 6 May 1941. Sir Sydney Robinson (1876–1950), Liberal MP Chelmsford 1923–4 and an unsuccessful Liberal parliamentary candidate on six other occasions between 1918 and 1945, Alderman of Essex County Council and breeder of pedigree shorthorns (*Who Was Who*, 1941–50); Sidney Berry (1881–1961), Secretary Congregational Union of England and Wales 1923–48 (*DNB*). Alice Head edited *Woman at Home*, 1909–17, and *Good Housekeeping*, 1924–39. She was a director of Country Life Ltd. and of George Newnes Ltd.

13 CTA, Minutes CTRC, 6 May, 20 May 1941.

14 CTA, Minutes CTRC, 26 June, 28 July, 2 Sept., 30 Sept., 30 Oct., 11 Dec. 1941. Hough, formerly dean of Drew Theological Seminary, New Jersey, 'has, since World War I. filled the City Temple pulpit for a total of a year of Sundays'. *The City Temple in the City of London*, 43.

15 CTA, Minutes CTRC, 28 July, 30 Sept., 30 Oct. 1941; James Claxton Meggitt (b. 1858), Chairman of Congregational Union 1927–8 and Alderman of Glamorgan County Council.

16 CTA, Minutes CTRC, 2 Sept., 30 Sept., 30 Oct., 11 Dec. 1941. R. Mountford Pigott, architect of Congregational Churches at Mitcham and Morden, was a member of Sutton Congregational Church, Surrey. Although he was not in the running for the Congregational City Temple, he secured a complementary prize: the rebuilding of the Baptist Metropolitan Tabernacle, 1957–9 (*Baptist Handbook*, 1959, 'Architectural Supplement', p. xi).

17 J. H. Dewey, of Messrs. J. H. Dewey and Co., Wrestler's Chambers, Camomile St, insurance brokers, recalled as 'rather too consciously a Haileyburian'.

18 CTA, L. D. Weatherhead to J. H. J. Dewey, 22 Oct. 1941. For children's church see C. Binfield, 'The Purley Way for children', in Diana Wood (ed.), *The Church and Childhood*, Studies in Church History, 31 (Oxford, 1994), 461–76; and 'Freedom through discipline: the concept of Little Church', in W. J. Sheils (ed.), *Monks, Hermits and the Ascetic Tradition*, Studies in Church History, 22 (Oxford, 1985), 405–50.

19 The City Temple worshipped at St Sepulchre's from 1941 to 1946: *The City Temple in the City of London*, 35–7; when its rebuilding plans

were first presented they were described as 'not unlike St. Sepulchre's, but without any pillars and with more extensive accommodation'. *The City Temple Tidings* (1945), 38.

[20] CTA, Minutes CTRC, 11 Dec. 1941. Allen and Collens's Riverside Church, particularly attractive to liberal Baptists and Congregationalists under Harry Emerson Fosdick (1878–1969), was opened in 1930, the gift of John D. Rockefeller Jr. (1874–1960), reputedly the world's wealthiest Protestant layman. In 1954 Weatherhead returned from the States with promises of £188,888 18s. 8d.; the church archives retain the cheque (second donation) for $25,000 from Mrs John D. Rockefeller Jr. Her husband gave $250,000. *The City Temple in the City of London*, 45; CTA, letter from Revd Wayland Zwayer, 22 Sept. 1954; *City Temple Tidings*, 40/470 (Jan. 1962), 12.

[21] CTA, Minutes CTRC, 11 Dec. 1941. For Sir Angus Watson (1874–1961), Chairman Congregational Union 1935–6, see *DNB*.

[22] CTA, Minutes CTRC, 3 Nov. 1942.

[23] CTA, Minutes CTRC, 3 Dec. 1942, 12 Feb. 1943. For A. E. Glassey (1887–1970), Liberal MP for East Dorset 1929–31, chief commissioner of the Congregational Union's Reconstruction Fund, chairman of the Congregational Union 1941–2, and the Sir Makepeace Watermaster of his nephew, John Le Carré's, *A Perfect Spy* (1986) see *Who Was Who*, 1961–70.

[24] CTA, Minutes CTRC, 20 Oct., 2 Dec. 1943, 2 Feb., 1 Mar., 30 Mar. 1944. James Gomer Berry, 1st Viscount Kemsley (1883–1968), became a member of Paddington Chapel in 1903; with his brother, the future Lord Camrose, he designed, produced and edited the chapel's *Monthly*, first issued 15 Oct. 1903. Gomer also taught in its Sunday school, was on the committee of its Mutual Improvement Society and married into its leading family; *Manual for the Church and Congregation Worshipping in Paddington Chapel* (1903), 39; (1904), 20, 46, 87–8. Sir Frank Alexander Bt. (b. 1881), Lord Mayor 1944–5, was secretary of Bromley Congregational Church.

[25] CTA, Minutes CTRC, 20 Oct., 2 Dec. 1943; 30 Mar., 2 May 1944.

[26] CTA, Minutes CTRC, 20 Oct. 1943. For William Edwin Orchard (1877–1955), Presbyterian, Congregationalist, and (from 1935) Roman Catholic, see Elaine Kaye and R. Mackenzie, *W. E. Orchard: A Study in Christian Exploration* (Oxford, 1990).

[27] CTA, Minutes CTRC, 30 Mar. 1944.

[28] Ibid.

[29] For Frederic William Lawrence (1882–1948) see C. Binfield, 'Art and spirituality in chapel architecture: F. W. Lawrence (1882– 1948) and his churches', in D. Loades (ed.), *The End of Strife* (Edinburgh, 1984), 200–26.

[30] Ibid, 208. Berry was at Oxted, 1906–9.

[31] CTA, undated cutting, *Evening Standard; Punshon Memorial Methodist Church Bournemouth Centenary 1886–1986* (Bournemouth, 1986). For A. E. Whitham (1879–1938) see Fiona Mary Whitham, 'My Father', in A. E. Whitham, *The Discipline and Culture of the Spiritual Life: A Memorial Volume* (London, 1938).

[32] L. Temple, *The Shining Brother* (London n.d., *c.* 1940–1).

[33] C. Drayton Thomas (1867–1953) ministered in six circuits and wrote and lectured on psychical research. *Who's Who in Methodism* (1933), 226. *Minutes of Conference* (1954), 115.

[34] In 1932 he was one of the 183 competitors for Guildford Cathedral but he was not one of the five shortlisted for the final competition.

[35] CTA, Minutes CTRC, 2 May 1944.

[36] CTA, 'Report on the draft plans for the rebuilding of the City Temple', Midsummer 1944.

[37] Thus Ealing Green Congregational Church's Little Church, designed by P. Morley Horder and opened in 1926 and the chapel of youth, in the north transept of Penge Congregational Church, by H. G. Ibberson and opened in 1934.

[38] CTA, 'Report on the draft plans'.

[39] For Charles Holden (1875–1960) and William, Baron Holford (1907–75) see *DNB*. CTA, Minutes CTRC, 3 Jan. 1947; F. W. Lawrence, 'Plans for the New City Temple, report on two interviews of Jan. 2nd and 3rd 1947'; F.W. Lawrence to Alice M. Head, 24 Jan. 1947; Memorandum re City of London Re-planning, 30 July 1947.

[40] CTA: Comments forwarded to F. W. Lawrence, 23 Feb. 1945. Lady Lennard (Medland Manor, Cheriton Bishop) was the widow of Sir Thomas Lennard (1861–1935), founder of Lennards Ltd.; she ran a wartime hostel for service-women. John L. Tann was governing director of John Tann Ltd., Safe and Strong Room Engineers, established 1795, of 117 Newgate Street.

[41] CTA: F.W. Lawrence to J. H. Dewey, 21 Mar. 1945.

[42] CTA: 'The City Temple Plans: Report of Interview with the City Planning Officer April 5th, 1948'.

[43] CTA: Memorandum L. D. Weatherhead to J. H. Dewey, 15 June 1948; Alice M. Head to J. H. Dewey, 30 June 1948; Minutes CTRC, 22 Aug. 1949.

[44] For the 2nd Baron Mottistone (1899–1963), surveyor of the fabric of St Paul's Cathedral and architect to St George's Chapel, Windsor, see *Who Was Who*, 1961–70; for Paul Paget (1901–84) see *Who's Who* (1984).

[45] Seely and Paget were appointed in July 1952. Ronald Sims claimed the copyright of Lawrence's plans so they presented their own, quite unrelated, plans in Jan. 1953; the cost was then estimated at £250,000

but it proved to be nearer £450,000. Their most thumping elements, the aggressively swooping gallery and the peppermint drum of a great white pulpit are to be attributed to the church council's decision, taken while Weatherhead was president of Methodist Conference, to enlarge the gallery to accommodate likely crowds. That meant that the pulpit had to be much higher than intended – hence its transformation from a pedestal design to a great drum cantilevered from the side wall, 12 feet above contradiction. I am indebted to Dr Travell for this information.

46 This is the title of Weatherhead's most popular work of devotion, *A Private House of Prayer* (London, 1958).

47 He married her while in Toronto, where such marriages were legal. She died within two years and he married for a third time in 1873, the year of his return to England. For Punshon see *DNB*.

48 Wesleyan Chapel Committee Report (1885–6), 151–2. The cost was estimated at £7,500.

49 Robert Curwen, architect of Leys School from 1877 (chapel 1905–6), fl. 1865–1909. See Alison Felstead, J. Franklin and L. Pinfield, *Directory of British Architects 1834–1900* (London, 1993), 230.

50 For Whitham see above, n. 31. For Thomas Horrabin Kirkman (1880–1972) see *Who's Who in Methodism* (1933), 133; *Minutes of Conference* (1973), 145.

51 Punshon Memorial Methodist Church Bournemouth, *Centenary 1886–1986* (Bournemouth, 1986), unpaginated; a cinema, two large hotels and a department store were also destroyed, seventy-seven people were killed and 196 were injured.

52 Ilford Parish Church; Immanuel Congregational (now United Reformed) Church, Southbourne; Barton-on-Sea Methodist Church (now demolished and replaced); Sway Methodist Church (now converted into a dwelling house); St George's Church Hall, Boscombe.

53 'The work of Ronald Sims', *The Architect and Building News* (24 Feb. 1960), 248. The following account is drawn from this; from correspondence and papers lodged with the Property Division, the Methodist Church, and Bournemouth Planning Services Division; and from personal information.

54 P. J. Coles to author, 29 Mar. 1995. J. Rolfe Treadgold (1903–72) was chairman of a large local firm, with a string of shops and restaurants.

55 *Architect and Building News* (24 Feb. 1960), 248.

56 Ibid., 252.

57 Ronald H. Sims to Revd E. Benson Perkins, 15 Mar. 1951. Methodist Church Property Division Archives (MCDPA).

58 For the earlier career of Albert Wesley Massey (b. 1888) see *Who's Who in Methodism* (1933), 152.

59 *Architect and Building News* (24 Feb. 1960), 248.

60 MCPDA, undated extracts from 'Report on design drawings for the rebuilding of Punshon Memorial Methodist Church' by Frederic Lawrence and Partners, A/ARIBA, 93, Southbourne Road, Bournemouth.

61 Thus, that important commonwealth, the choir, was positioned to sing *with* the congregation while yet fulfilling the acoustical recommendations of the Archbishop of Canterbury's Committee, 'which considered this matter exhaustively'. Extracts from ibid.

62 *Architect and Building News* (24 Feb. 1960), 254.

63 *New Methodist Churches – Report of the Department for Chapel Affairs 1961* (unpaginated).

64 Ibid.

65 In 1933, at the time of Methodist union, it was responsible for 'the supervision of the erection and renovation of Methodist Church premises throughout the connexion, authority to issue Grants and Loans to Trusts which contribute annually to the General Chapel Fund, and reviews all Trust Deeds and Renewals affecting Methodist premises in draft before being engrossed'. *Who's Who in Methodism* (1933), 23.

66 For Ernest Benson Perkins (1881–1974) see *Who's Who in Methodism* (1933), 175; *Minutes of Conference* (1974), 185. He wrote: 'Experience suggests that a more prominent position does not necessarily mean the attraction of more people, but this scheme would have the advantage of providing Methodism with a more prominent building as the central church in Bournemouth'. E. B. P., 'Memorandum of visit to Bournemouth at the invitation of the Superintendent Minister and Circuit Stewards to consider new suggestions respecting the site for the Punshon Memorial Church', undated (describing visit of 13 July 1945).

67 For Albert Hearn (1888–1982) see *Who's Who in Methodism* (1933), 103.

68 MCPDA, Ronald H. Sims to Revd E. Benson Perkins, 21 May 1951.

69 MCPDA, E. B. P., 'Memorandum of interview between the Rev. A. J. Cull, Dr Duncan Coomer and another trustee, the architect, Mr Sims and the Rev E. Benson Perkins on Tuesday, 19th June, 1951 in the Wesley Club, Westminster'. The reference to the plan's shape might reflect Sims's fascination with the hexagon. Duncan Coomer (b. 1882) was a retired bank manager, Old Leysian, and historian, active in the Methodist Sacramental Fellowship.

70 MCPDA, Revd Albert Hearn to W. Shaw, 9 July 1954. Hearn also came from another Methodist tradition: Perkins had been Wesleyan, but Hearn came from the less centralized United Methodist Churches.

71 MCPDA, A. L. Clegg, Town Clerk, Town Clerk's Office, Town Hall,

Bournemouth, to Messrs. Frederic Lawrence and Partners, 7 Oct. 1954.

[72] MCPDA, 'Punshon Memorial Methodist Church Bournemouth: Chronological Diary of Town Planning Interviews, Submissions and Decisions', 30 June 1943–13 Sept. 1954.

[73] *Architect and Building News* (24 Feb. 1960), 250.

[74] Ibid.

[75] MCPDA, R. H. Sims to Revd A. Hearn, 28 Oct. 1954.

[76] For Sir Frederic Gibberd (1908–84) and Thomas Wilfred Sharp (1901–78) see *DNB*. For Nigel Nicolson (b. 1917) see *Who's Who* (1997).

[77] MCPDA, R. H. Sims to Revd A. Hearn, 28 Oct. 1954.

[78] *Architect and Building News* (24 Feb. 1960), 250–2. The well-disposed Methodist was W. Oliver Phillipson (1904–88), who became general secretary of the department in 1958. See *Minutes of Conference* (1989), 46.

[79] The letter was handwritten. MCPDA, R. H. Sims to Revd A. Hearn, 10 Jan. 1955.

[80] MCPDA, W. B. Vince, Ministry of Housing and Local Government, London SW1, to the Trustees, Punshon Memorial Church, 7 Mar. 1955: endorsed '*IMPORTANT*, not to be destroyed'. Sharp was unfair; or, rather, later generations will recognize that Bournemouth possesses a remarkably good collection of late Victorian, therefore Gothic, therefore 'churchy', churches.

[81] *Architect and Building News* (24 Feb. 1960), 252.

[82] Ibid., 254. Sims's old principal, Furneaux Jordan, felt that the building 'had too many parts, too many bits and pieces'. Ibid., 247.

[83] Ibid., 252.

[84] Ibid., 250, 254. It cost £9,200 and seated 230.

[85] Ibid., 253.

[86] For Southampton he designed a sports pavilion, a computer building (about whose site he was especially enthusiastic), and a hydraulics laboratory. The Nuneaton gardens were the result of a competition entered with Mary Braendle in his final year at the Architectural Association and in the course of working for Geoffrey Jellicoe: 'We won the thing. The job went very well, but I have not seen the gardens for some time . . . Vandalism was the only serious concern. Even the contractor's bulldozer lost all its holding nuts, I remember'. Ibid., 254, 258.

[87] He refused to rubbish the Royal Academy; its Summer Exhibitions were significantly representative of the field, and if they were poor affairs, they were only 'as bad as architects make it'. Ibid., 258.

[88] Ibid., 251, 252.

[89] Ibid., 258. He received an honourable mention for Poole Technical College.

[90] Ibid., 247; MCPDA, R. H. Sims to Revd A. Hearn, 28 Oct. 1954.

[91] In this light one might see his relationship, which developed during the building of Punshon Memorial, with E. W. H. Gifford of the Gifford Udall Prestressing System. He found Gifford to have 'a lively mind and great stamina', quite different from the 'normal provincial engineer'. *Architect and Building News* (24 Feb. 1960), 254.

[92] R. Furneaux Jordan, 'The work of Ronald Sims', *Architect and Building News* (24 Feb. 1960), 246–7. This section is based on Jordan's profile.

[93] It is suggestive that Punshon Memorial's centenary brochure makes no reference to its architects, Robert Curwen or Ronald Sims.

[94] I am indebted to Dr Travell for this information.

[95] *The City Temple in the City of London*, 42–3; Punshon Memorial Methodist Church Bournemouth, *Centenary 1886–1984*, unpaginated.

Index